A CONCISE ENCYCLOPEDIA OF THE OZARKS

Compiled by

LARRY WOOD

Hickory Press
Joplin, Missouri

Published by

Hickory Press
Joplin, MO

ISBN: 9780970282965
Library of Congress Control Number: 2015900141

Table of Contents

List of Illustrations

Preface

One of the first tasks I faced in undertaking the compilation of an encyclopedia of the Ozarks was to define in my own mind the general boundaries of the Ozarks. I had to revisit my definition of those boundaries each time I considered individual entries dealing with people, places, or events associated with the border areas of the Ozarks. *Did this event actually take place in the Ozarks?* is typical of the questions I found myself repeatedly asking.

Even geographers and geologists do not always agree on the limits of the Ozarks. Some say the Ozarks extend north of the Missouri River, and some even say they extend east of the Mississippi River to include the so-called Illinois Ozarks, while others use those rivers as natural boundaries that help define the Ozarks. I have largely accepted the scientific definition of the Ozarks as outlined by Milton Rafferty, former professor of geography and geology at Missouri State University, in his book *Ozarks: Land and Life.* According to Rafferty, the boundaries of the Ozarks are marked in a general way by important rivers: the Mississippi River on the east; the Missouri River, including a narrow band of hills north of the river, on the north; the Grand River on the southwest; the Arkansas River on the south; and the Black River on the southeast.

Science, however, does not tell the whole story. There exists what might be called a cultural or popular conception of the Ozarks that corresponds only in a very general way with the geographic boundaries. There are people in certain areas that are geographically well within the limits of the Ozarks who do not usually consider themselves part of the Ozarks. At the same time, there are people in certain areas that lie somewhat outside the geographic limits of the Ozarks who nonetheless identify themselves as Ozarkians (or Ozarkers, as some residents prefer to be called). For example, a couple of years ago I heard Dr. Brooks Blevins of Missouri State University's Department of Ozarks Studies tell a story on Ozarks Public Television of the time he was driving south from Jefferson City on Highway 63, stopped in the German-settled community of Vienna, Missouri, and was told by locals that he was not yet in the Ozarks, despite the fact that Vienna, by all geographic definitions, is well within the Ozarks. Conversely, the people who live around Clarksville, Arkansas, obviously consider themselves to be on the edge of the Ozarks, since the institution of higher learning there is called the University of the Ozarks, even though Clarksville is, by most geographic definitions, not in the Ozarks but instead part of the Arkansas River Valley.

So, while I accept the scientifically established boundaries of the Ozarks, as delineated by geographic formations like the Mississippi River, I have, for the purpose of considering entries in this book, narrowed those boundaries somewhat by incorporating a good dash of culture and popular opinion into my judgment as to whether a certain person, place, or event was associated with the Ozarks. Generally speaking, the farther on the fringes of the Ozarks that a place is located or an event happened, the less likely it is to be included in the book. This principle has been applied especially to locations where even many of the residents themselves do not consider their areas to be in the Ozarks, such as the Mississippi River and Missouri River border counties. In other words, some of the border areas of the Ozarks, by design, have received less attention than the interior areas.

At the same time, I have tried to err on the side of caution in deciding whether an entry was to be included in the book. If there was doubt in my mind as to whether a person, place, or event was associated with the Ozarks, I tried to include at least a mention of it. In the case of towns, for example, the general rule of thumb I tried to follow was this: the less populous the community and the farther on the fringes of the Ozarks it is located, the less likely it was to be included. No doubt, however, I have made omissions that some readers might question.

I also realize that, as a lifelong resident of the Springfield and Joplin areas, I am more familiar with southwest Missouri than other parts of the Ozarks, and it is therefore likely that I might have included more entries or more detailed information about certain entries dealing with southwest Missouri than other parts of the Ozarks simply because of my greater familiarity with the region. If such a disparity exists, I can only say that it is not the result of a deliberate intent to slight other areas of the Ozarks.

Finally I should emphasize that this is a *concise* encyclopedia. It contains only entries that I deemed relatively important. For example, in compiling geographic entries, I considered countless small communities that I might have included, but I decided to omit many of them that never had a significant population and never played a major role in the local area nor had anything particularly remarkable in their history. Also, the entries that I did include purposely contain only a minimal or introductory amount of information.

A

Adair County, Oklahoma Located in the Oklahoma Ozarks bordering Arkansas, Adair County was founded in 1906 from the Goingsnake and Flint districts of the Cherokee Nation. Westville was initially the county seat, but Stilwell became the county seat in 1910.

Afton, Oklahoma—Afton is a town of slightly over 1,000 people situated on old Route 66 in Ottawa County at the western edge of the Ozarks. For many years, especially during the heyday of Route 66, Afton was widely known for its Buffalo Ranch. Today Afton is home to the Afton Public Schools, and one of the town's biggest attractions is the 1930s DX station along old Route 66 that has been restored as a vintage automobile museum.

Akins, Zoe Byrd—Zoe Byrd Akins was an American playwright, poet, and author born in Humansville, Missouri. In 1935, she won a Pulitzer Prize for her dramatization of Edith Wharton's *The Old Maid*.

Alamo, Tony—Tony Alamo is an evangelist and founder of Tony Alamo Christian Ministries based partly in the Alma, Arkansas, area. Usually considered a cult, the organization condemns the Catholic Church and the U. S. government. In 2009, Alamo was convicted of transporting underage girls across state lines for sexual purposes and sent to prison.

Alba, Missouri—Alba is a town of about 550 people in Jasper County. It was the hometown of the baseball-playing Boyer brothers. Seven brothers signed professional contracts, and three; Cloyd, Ken, and Clete; played in the big leagues. They attended high school at Alba in the 1940s and 1950s, but the town no longer has a high school.

Albatross, Missouri—Albatross is a small village that sprang up along old Route 66 in Lawrence County after the highway was established in the 1920s. Today, it barely survives as a crossroads village located at the junction of Highway 96 and Highway 39

Alexander, Henry McMillan—Henry McMillan Alexander was the founding chairman of the University of Arkansas's Department of Government, later renamed the Department of Political Science. Alexander was an advocate of the city manager form of government, and several towns in Arkansas adopted his model.

Alicia, Arkansas—Founded in 1873 as a railroad stop, Alicia is a town of about 125 in southern Lawrence County.

All American Redheads—The All-American Redheads was a touring women's professional basketball team from 1936 to 1986. The team got its start at Cassville, Missouri, and was headquartered there for the first twenty years of its existence, before moving to Carraway, Arkansas, in the mid-1950s. Sometimes called the female Harlem Globetrotters, the Redheads often competed against and beat men's teams, and they also put on ball handling and shooting exhibitions.

Allenville, Missouri—Laid out in 1869, Allenville is a village of about 115 people in southern Cape Girardeau County.

Alley Spring, Missouri—Alley Spring is an unincorporated community in Shannon County that grew up around Missouri's seventh largest spring. A mill was built on the spring in the mid-1800s, and the community acquired its name when John Alley established a post office at the site some years later. The current mill was built about 1894. Today, the historic mill and other structures at the site such as a one-room schoolhouse, as well as the immediately surrounding grounds, are maintained by the National Park Service as part of the Ozarks National Scenic Riverways, while the larger Alley Spring Natural Area, including the spring itself, is maintained by the Missouri Department of Conversation as a state park.

Allison, Arkansas—See Sylamore, Arkansas.

Alma, Arkansas—Alma is a town of about 5,000 people in Crawford County at the southern edge of the Ozarks. Formerly home to an Allens, Inc. canning factory, Alma used to bill itself as the "Spinach Capital of the World," and its water tower, painted to resemble a can of spinach, was known as the largest spinach can in the world. Although the spinach plant has closed, Alma still holds an annual Spinach Festival. Alma is home to the Alma Public Schools, which shares a performing arts center with the Alma Educations and Arts Foundation. The performing arts center draws audiences from miles around to its varied lineup of musical and theatrical performances staged throughout the year.

Alpena, Arkansas—Alpena is a small town located along Highway 62, mostly in Boone County on the Boone-Carroll county line. It was established as Alpena Pass in the early 1900s as a point along the

Missouri-North Arkansas Railroad, but the word "pass" was later dropped from the name. At the time Alpena was formed, nearby Carrollton was in decline, and some of the buildings from Carrolton were torn down, brought to Alpena, and reassembled at the new town. Today, Alpena has a population of about 400 people and is home to the Alpena School District.

Alsups of Douglas County—The Alsups were a politically influential family during the Civil War era in Douglas County, Missouri. They were known throughout the region for raising fine race horses, and they drew widespread notoriety for a legendary feud with the Fleetwood family prior to the war. Most of the male members of the

Monument to the Alsups and their superior race horses near Ava, Mo. *Photo by the author.*

family joined the Union army during the war, and after the war, several Alsups held political office in Douglas County. As Radical Republicans, they opposed former Confederates and lukewarm Unionists alike, and their iron-fisted rule sometimes spawned violence, such as the killing of John Hatfield by Alsup allies in 1871. The influence of the Alsups faded after Shelt Alsup lost his bid for reelection as sheriff of the county in 1878 and he and the new sheriff, Hardin Vickery, killed each other in a gun battle the following March.

Altenburg, Missouri—Founded in 1839 by German Lutherans, Altenburg is a town of about 350 people in southeastern Perry County.

Alton, Missouri—Founded prior to the Civil War, Alton is the seat of Oregon County, located in the south central part of the state on the Arkansas border. Alton was the birthplace of George Washington "Jumbo" McGinnis, a famous Major League Baseball player during the 1880s. The town has a population of about 700, and it is home to the Alton R-4 School District.

Altus, Arkansas—Altus is a town of about 800 people in Franklin County at the southern limits of the Ozarks. It was the setting for the first season of the *Simple Life*, starring Paris Hilton and Nicole Richie. Altus attracted an influx of Germans and German-speaking Swiss in the late 1800s. It is home to several wineries. It is also home to Our Lady of Perpetual Help Church (St. Mary's Catholic Church) and Ozark Middle School, and it is the former home of Hendrix College.

Alum Cove Natural Bridge Recreation Area—Alum Cove Natural Bridge Recreation Area is a recreation area in the Ozark National Forest in southern Newton County, Arkansas. The main feature of the area is the Alum Cove Natural Bridge, a huge stone arch that forms a natural bridge, and the site also offers hiking and picnicking.

Ameren Corporation—Created in 1997 with the merger of Missouri's Union Electric Company and the neighboring Central Illinois Public Service Company, Ameren Corporation is a power company based in St. Louis that serves 2.4 million electric customers and 900,000 natural gas customers, many of them in the northern and eastern Missouri Ozarks. The company's origins date to the early nineteenth century. The Union Electric Company built Bagnell Dam on the Osage River to form the Lake of the Ozarks.

Annapolis, Missouri—Annapolis is a town in southern Iron County that was established about 1870 under a different name, but when the St. Louis, Iron Mountain and Southern Railroad reached the town a few years later, it was renamed for Anna Allen, wife of the railroad president. Annapolis was nearly wiped out by the Great Tri-State Tornado of 1925. Today, Annapolis is home to the South Iron School District, hosts an annual event called the Freedom Fest each October, and has a population of about 500 people.

Anderson, Missouri—Anderson is a town of about 2,000 people in McDonald County. A picnic grounds and church resort called Beaver

Springs was located near the present site of Anderson during the Civil War era. In the late 1880s, Robert Anderson opened a store at the location, and a post office called Anderson was established. The town of Anderson was laid out and sprang into importance after the Kansas City, Pittsburg, and Gulf Railroad built a station there in the early 1890s. McDonald County High School and the administrative offices of McDonald County R-1 Schools are located at Anderson.

Anderson, William T. "Bloody Bill"—Bill Anderson was a Missouri guerrilla during the Civil War. He was allied with William Quantrill during 1863, but he and his followers broke with Quantrill in Texas in the spring of 1864 and returned to Missouri. Although most of Anderson's activities were confined to the Missouri River counties, the guerrillas captured a man in Greene County and killed him in Polk County on their way north. Anderson's heinous deeds in northern Missouri during the summer of 1864 earned him the posthumous nickname "Bloody Bill."

Andrews, Glen—Glen Andrews was a professional bass fisherman who won two World Series of Sport Fishing championships in the 1960s. Born and raised near Lead Hill, Arkansas, he was a successful guide on Table Rock, Bull Shoals, and Beaver lakes, and he started a lure company at Lampe, Missouri, before moving the business to Rogers, Arkansas, in 1965. Andrews also promoted fishing tournaments and wrote a syndicated outdoor column for the *Springdale News* called "Anglers World."

Andrews, Lloyd "Arkansas Slim"—Born in 1906 near Gravette in Benton County, Arkansas, Lloyd "Arkansas Slim" Andrews was an entertainer and a film actor, best known as a comedic sidekick to cowboy stars like Tex Ritter during the 1940s. Later he went into children's television, and he hosted the "Fun Club" for KOAM TV in Pittsburg, Kansas, for many years.

Apple Industry—The Ozarks has a history of growing apples that dates almost to the time the first white settlers arrived. Apple production as a commercial industry reached its peak in the late 1800s and early 1900s. In 1890, Missouri, with the Ozarks counties in the southwest and south central parts of the state leading the way, was the biggest apple-producing state in the Union with 25,000,000 bushels. Arkansas, especially the northwest corner, was also a leading producer of apples. In the early 1900s, over four million apple trees were growing in Benton and Washington counties alone, but production steadily waned after the peak year of 1919. The Ben Davis was the most commonly cultivated variety during northwest Arkansas's heyday of apple production.

Appleby, John Tate "Jack"—Born in Fayetteville in 1907, John Tate "Jack" Appleby was a biographer of English kings and a longtime associate editor of the *American Historical Review*. He is also remembered for *Suffolk Summer*, a memoir of his time traveling in southeastern England at the end of World War II.

Arcadia, Missouri—Arcadia is a town of about 600 people in Iron County less than a mile south of the county seat of Ironton. It was laid out about 1849 and was one of only two communities within the boundaries of Iron County when the county was organized in 1857.

Arcadia Valley—The Arcadia Valley is an area of southeast Missouri in the St. Francois Mountains that includes the towns of Arcadia, Ironton and Pilot Knob. It was a popular resort area during the late 1800s.

Arcola, Missouri—Arcola is a small village on state Highway 39 in northern Dade County. A community called Sun's Creek or Son's Creek was established in the vicinity prior to the Civil War, but the name was changed to Arcola during the 1870s. During the early nineteenth century, Arcola had both an elementary school and a high school, but they consolidated with Greenfield many years ago.

Argyle, Missouri—Argyle is a village of about 160 people in southern Osage County.

Arkansas & Missouri Railroad—Established in 1986, the Arkansas & Missouri Railroad operates a 150-mile route between Monett, Missouri and Fort Smith, Arkansas. Its home office is in Springdale.

Arkansas and Oklahoma Railroad—The Arkansas and Oklahoma Railroad was a railroad that operated very briefly around the turn of the twentieth century between Rogers, Arkansas, and Grove, Oklahoma.

Arkansas Apple Festival—The Arkansas Apple Festival is an annual festival held each fall in Lincoln, Washington County. Originally a celebration of the apple-growing heritage of northwest Arkansas, the festival today is mainly an arts and crafts fair.

Arkansas Black Apple—The Arkansas Black is an apple that was first cultivated in northwest Arkansas near Bentonville about 1870. A variety of the Winesap apple, the Arkansas Black is round and medium sized, and its dark red skin gives the variety its name. Arkansas Blacks are still grown today but make up only a small percentage of the apple crop in Arkansas.

Arkansas Blue Bird of Happiness—see Leo Ward

Arkansas County Doctor Museum—The Arkansas Country Doctor Museum is located in Lincoln in northwest Arkansas in an eleven-room building that served three successive physicians from 1936 to 1973 as a combined home, office, and clinic. The museum features vintage medical equipment and a hall of honor for area physicians of bygone days.

Arkansas Democrat-Gazette—Tracing its roots to the *Arkansas Gazette* founded in 1819, the *Arkansas Democrat-Gazette* lays claim to being the oldest continuously published newspaper west of the Mississippi River. Headquartered at Little Rock, it also publishes a northwest Arkansas edition at Lowell.

Arkansas Mounted Rifles—The First and Second Arkansas Mounted Rifles were two Confederate regiments of Arkansas troops organized shortly after the beginning of the Civil War near Bentonville by Brigadier General Ben McCulloch. Intended as a unique battalion that could not only ride as cavalry but also dismount and fight as infantry, the two regiments first saw significant action at the Battle of Wilson's Creek, and they continued to serve throughout the war.

Arkansas-Missouri League—The Arkansas-Missouri League (originally called the Arkansas State League) was a Class D baseball minor league from 1934 to 1940 that operated in northwest Arkansas and southwest Missouri. Towns represented in the league included Bentonville, Carthage, Cassville, Fayetteville, Monett, Neosho, Rogers, and Siloam Springs. The league produced several future major leaguers, including Walker Cooper, Ralph Houk, Sherm Lollar, and Mickey Owen.

Arkansas, Oklahoma and Western Railroad—The Arkansas, Oklahoma and Western Railroad served northwest Arkansas between Rogers and Siloam Springs between 1908 and 1911.

Arkansas State University-Mountain Home—Arkansas State University-Mountain Home is a campus of the Arkansas State University System, which is headquartered at Jonesboro. Associate degrees are offered at Mountain Home, and more advanced degrees are available through the university system.

Arkansas Traveler—"Arkansas Traveler" may refer to a tune, a dialogue, or a painting, all of which date from the mid-nineteenth century. The tune and the dialogue or skit had their origins around 1840 when Colonel Sanford Faulkner got lost in rural Arkansas, stopped to ask directions at a local squatter's home, and subsequently started performing a dialogue and fiddle tune called "The Arkansas Traveler" based on the experience. In 1856, Arkansas artist Edward Payson Washbourne painted a picture based on the meeting between the Traveler and the Squatter. The image of the Arkansas Traveler also spawned a humorous newspaper by that name, founded in 1882. The Traveler, in print and in humorous performance, came to perpetuate a negative, "hillbilly" image of Arkansas and, by extension, the Ozarks. In recent years, however, the negative connotation of the name has lessened, as suggested by the fact that the student newspaper at the University of Arkansas is called the *Arkansas Traveler*.

Arlington, Missouri—Arlington is an unincorporated community on I-44 in western Phelps County. When what is now the BNSF Railroad was being built, Arlington was briefly its terminus, and it was thought the place would become an important town. Its population in 1874 was about 150, but it never got much beyond that figure.

Armstrong, O.K.—Orland "O.K." Armstrong was a politician and journalist who was born in Willow Springs, Missouri, in 1893 and grew up in the Ozarks. He served several terms in the Missouri Legislature and one term during the early 1950s as a U. S. congressman from southwest Missouri. He pursued a career in journalism before, during, and after his life in politics. He was a frequent contributor to the *Reader's Digest* and was especially known as a crusader against pornography. He died in 1987 and is buried at Springfield.

Arno, Missouri—Arno is a small community in western Douglas County. It was a place of some importance during the early days of the county and even served as the county seat from 1869 to 1870, but today little remains to suggest its former prominence.

Arts Center of the Ozarks—Founded in 1967, the Arts Center of the Ozarks is a combined gallery for the visual arts and theater for the performing arts in Springdale, Arkansas. Community theater

productions, art exhibits, and classes for both the visual and
performing arts are among the center's offerings.

Asbury, Missouri—Asbury is a town of about 205 people in Jasper
County near the Kansas border at the western edge of the Ozarks. It
was laid out in 1896 on the line of the proposed Kansas City, Pittsburg
and Gulf Railroad and grew very rapidly after the railroad was opened
the following year, but it soon declined.

Ash Grove, Missouri—A town in Greene County, Missouri, about
fifteen miles west of Springfield, Ash Grove was established as an
unincorporated village in 1853. It was incorporated in 1870 and
enjoyed a growth spurt later in the 1870s after a railroad was built
between it and Springfield. Ma Barker (nee Arizona Clark) was born
at Ash Grove in 1873. Ash Grove's current population is
approximately 1,500. It is home to the Ash Grove R-4 Schools.

Ashcroft, John—John Ashcroft, who grew up in Springfield, served
as governor of Missouri from 1985 to 1993. Later he was elected as a
U. S. senator from Missouri, and he served as U. S. Attorney General
during President George W. Bush's first term.

Ashley, Hubert Carl "Hugh"—Born in 1915 in Searcy County,
Arkansas, Hubert Carl "Hugh" Ashley wrote and recorded some of
the earliest known recordings of Ozarks folk music. As a teenager, he
played on early radio stations in the Ozarks as a member of his
father's band, The Ashley Melody Men. In 1929, he became an
original cast member of the Beverly Hillbillies radio program, and
during the 1930s he wrote and recorded music in Los Angeles and Las
Vegas. After World War II, he settled in Harrison, Arkansas, where he
ran Ashley's Music Store for many years and wrote songs for famous
country music stars like Red Foley and Brenda Lee.

Ashmore Station, Missouri—Ashmore Station was a stop along the
line of the Butterfield Stage. It was located about four and a half miles
northwest of present-day Clever. A historic marker is at the site.

Assemblies of God—The Assemblies of God is the world's largest
Pentecostal denomination. Founded in 1914 in Hot Springs, Arkansas,
the church now has its headquarters in Springfield, Missouri.

Atlantic and Pacific Railroad—The Atlantic and Pacific Railroad
grew out of the Pacific Railroad and was a predecessor of the Frisco
Railroad. It helped build the first road to Springfield, Missouri,

although it had become the South Pacific Railroad by the time the tracks reached Springfield in 1870.

Attica, Arkansas—Attica is a small community in Randolph County north of Pocahontas. It was an important settlement in the early nineteenth century along the old military road and prospered briefly after it got a post office in 1890, but today it is a virtual ghost town.

Aurora, Missouri—Aurora is a town of about 7,000 people in Lawrence County. Laid out in 1870 as a station along the railroad, the town enjoyed a growth spurt after lead was discovered in the area in 1885. In 1917, an infantry company from Aurora that was waiting to be shipped out to World War I befriended a hound dog and ended up taking the dog overseas with them. When the war ended, the dog returned safely to Aurora with the soldiers. The "Houn Dawg" became the town's mascot and still serves as the mascot of the Aurora R-8 Schools. During the 1900s, the MFA Milling Company operated one of the largest feed mills in the world at Aurora, and the huge grain elevators still stand as landmarks at the north edge of town.

Aurora Springs, Missouri—Aurora Springs is a small village in northern Miller County. As a booming mineral water resort town during the early 1880s, it was at one time the largest town in Miller County, with a population of about 700.

Austin, Moses—Moses Austin was instrumental in developing the lead mining industry in eastern Missouri during the very early 1800s. Called the "Lead King," he was the father of Stephen F. Austin and is considered the founder of the town of Potosi, where he is entombed.

Ava, Missouri—The county seat of Douglas County, Ava was established in 1870 near Militia Springs, a settlement in central Douglas County that had grown out of a Civil War military encampment, and the new town became the county seat in 1871. Today, it is home to the Missouri Fox Trotting Horse Breed Association, and the town hosts the annual Missouri Fox Trotter Fall Show and Celebration. It is also home to the Ava R-1 School District. The only incorporated town in Douglas County, Ava has a population of about 3,000.

Avilla, Missouri—Avilla is a village of about 125 people in eastern Jasper County. The fourth oldest community in Jasper County, it was laid out in 1858. It is home to the Avilla R-13 Schools, a K-8 district.

Avoca, Arkansas—Founded in the early 1880s, Avoca is a town of about 500 people located east of Rogers in Benton County.

B

Babbtown, Missouri Babbtown is a small community in southwest Osage County. Settled during the 1860s by German Lutherans, it was a prominent village for several decades, but it faded in importance after the railroad bypassed it in the early 1900s and another town, Meta, grew up along the railroad.

Back Yonder, An Ozark Chronicle—Published in 1932, *Back Yonder, An Ozark Chronicle* is the autobiography of Charles Wayman Hogue. The book chronicles his growing up years in Van Buren County, Arkansas, during the late 1800s, and it has been praised for its honest and unvarnished depiction of life in the Ozarks during the nineteenth century.

Bagnell, Missouri—Bagnell is a town in western Miller County on the Osage River. Platted by and named for William Bagnell, it grew up in the early 1880s around the terminus of a branch of the Missouri Pacific Railroad that was supposed to connect Jefferson City and Lebanon but got only as far as the future site of Bagnell. The town enjoyed a spurt of business and prosperity during the late 1920s and early 1930s during construction of Bagnell Dam but has since dwindled in significance.

Bagnell Dam—Located on the Camden-Miller county line, Bagnell Dam impounds the Osage River to form the Lake of the Ozarks. Completed in 1931 by the Union Electric Company, the dam measures 148 feet tall and 2,543 feet long. Construction of the dam, which began just months before the stock market crash of 1929, provided jobs for thousands and provided a boost to the rural economy during the Depression.

Bailey, Wendell—Wendell Bailey is a politician from Willow Springs, Missouri. He served one term in the U.S. House of Representatives from 1981 to 1983 and later served two terms as the Missouri State Treasurer.

Baker, Samuel Aaron—Samuel Aaron Baker was an educator and Republican politician who was born in Patterson, Missouri, in 1874. He served as Missouri's Superintendent of Schools from 1919 to 1923 and as governor of the state from 1925 to 1929.

Baker, Norman G.—Norman Baker was a quack doctor who turned the Crescent Hotel in Eureka Springs into a "hospital" and health resort during the late 1930s before federal charges for mail fraud were filed against him.

Bakersfield, Missouri—Bakersfield is a village in southeast Ozark County near the Arkansas border. A community named Waterville was a pre-Civil War forerunner to Bakersfield. In 1873, the community acquired its first federal post office, and the name was changed to Bakersfield in honor of James Baker, the town's principal landowner. Today, Bakersfield has a population of about 300, and it is home to the Bakersfield R-4 School District.

Bald Knobbers—The Bald Knobbers were a vigilante group that arose in Taney County, Missouri, during the mid-1880s in response to the perceived unwillingness or inability of county officials to punish lawbreakers. The Bald Knobber movement had political overtones, as many of the county office holders were ex-Confederates, while most

Nat Kinney, leader of the Bald Knobbers. *Courtesy Christian County Library.*

of the Bald Knobbers were former Union soldiers or sympathizers. The Bald Knobbers, or Citizens' Committee as the group was officially known, first drew widespread notoriety when they broke Frank and Tubal Taylor out of the county jail at Forsyth and hanged the brothers from a tree just outside town in the spring of 1885. After the Taylor lynchings, a group called the Anti-Bald Knobbers was formed to oppose the Bald Knobbers, and people throughout the region came under pressure to choose sides. The vigilante movement quickly spread to neighboring Christian County, where, in March of 1887, the Bald Knobbers killed two men who dared to oppose them. Later the same year, a number of the Christian County Bald Knobbers were arrested, four of them were convicted of murder, and three of them were hanged on the Ozark square. By 1888, Bald Knobberism had already started to wane, and in August of that year, the final death knell of the group sounded when Nat Kinney, leader of the Taney County faction, was killed in Forsyth by an Anti-Bald Knobber. See Hartman, Mary and Elmo Ingenthron. *Vigilantes on the Ozarks Frontier*. Gretna, La.: Pelican Publishing Co., 1988.

Baldknobbers—The Baldknobbers is the name of a musical group that has been performing regularly in Branson, Missouri, since 1959, making the group Branson's first regular country music show.

Ballard, Oklahoma—Ballard is a small community in northeast Adair County a mile or so south of Watts. It is administered by the Watts city government.

Bandini, Pietro—Father Pietro Bandini was a Jesuit priest and missionary who established Tontitown in northwest Arkansas in 1898 as a colony for Italian immigrants.

Banta, Parke M.—Parke M. Banta was a politician from the area of Iron and Washington counties, Missouri. He served one term in the U.S. House of Representatives from 1947 to 1949.

Baptist Bible College—Located in Springfield, Missouri, and founded in 1950, Baptist Bible College is a conservative Bible college affiliated with the Baptist Bible Fellowship International. It offers degrees related primarily to ministerial and religious studies. Notable alumni include Jerry Falwell.

Barber, Oklahoma—Barber is an unincorporated community in southeastern Cherokee County.

Barker-Karpis Gang—The Barker-Karpis gang was a notorious band of outlaws during the gangster era of the Depression years that operated at times in the Ozarks. Members of the gang included Alvin Karpis and brothers Fred and Arthur "Doc" Barker. According to legend, the Barker brothers' mother, Arrie "Ma" Barker, was the leader of the gang, but her actual involvement was minimal. One of the gang's more infamous activities in the Ozarks was the involvement of two members of the gang, thought to be Karpis and Fred Barker, in the killing of Howell County sheriff C. Roy Kelly in December of 1931 at West Plains, Missouri.

Barnett, Missouri—Barnett (aka Barnettsville) is a town of about 205 people in eastern Morgan County. Settled about 1870, it was virtually destroyed by a tornado in April of 1880.

Barnhill, John Henry "Barnie"—John Henry "Barnie" Barnhill was a football coach at the University of Arkansas in the late 1940s, later the school's athletic director, and the man after whom Barnhill Arena, formerly home to the school's basketball teams, is named.

Baron, Oklahoma—Baron is an unincorporated community in Adair County on U.S. Highway 59 between Stillwell and Westville.

Barrens—The Barrens is an extensive upland area in Perry County, Missouri, containing numerous large sinkholes.

Basin Park Hotel—Built into a hillside, Basin Park Hotel is a historic hotel in Eureka Springs, Arkansas, which features all seven of its floors as ground floors.

Basketry—Basketry or basket making is the process of interlacing short, flexible fibers to form containers. Although basketry is not unique to the Ozarks, the craft has a long tradition in the region, and it is kept alive today by craftsmen whose products are prized as much for their artistic appeal as for their utilitarian value. The Gibson family of Washington County, Arkansas, and Leon Niehues of Madison County, Arkansas, are among the basket makers of distinction in the Ozarks today.

Basketville, Missouri—See Clementine.

Bass Pro Shops—One of the world's leading retailers of hunting, fishing, and other outdoor recreation merchandise, Bass Pro Shops had its beginnings in Springfield when founder John L. Morris started selling bait and tackle from a Brown Derby liquor store owned by his father. Bass Pro Shops was incorporated in 1971, and its headquarters

is still located in Springfield on South Campbell. The Wonders of
Wildlife Museum, which Morris helped finance, is located next door.
Bates, James Woodson—James Woodson Bates was lawyer and
statesman who served as a nonvoting delegate from Arkansas
Territory to the U.S. House of Representatives from 1819 to 1823.
During his service in Congress, he moved from Sebastian County to
the settlement that would become Batesville, and when the town was
platted in 1821, it was named in his honor.
Batesville, Arkansas—Batesville is a town of about 10,250 people
and the seat of Independence County. Settled prior to 1820, it is the
oldest city in Arkansas. During its very early days, it was called Poke
Creek or Poke Bayou after the stream that empties into the White
River at the site and was also sometimes called Napoleon. It was
platted in 1821, made the county seat about the same time, and shortly
afterwards named Batesville in honor of James Woodson Bates,
Arkansas Territory's representative to Congress. Located on the
White River, it was an important river port during pre-Civil War days.
During the war, it was the site of two minor skirmishes, on May 3,
1862 and February 4, 1863. There was also skirmishing around
Batesville during the Batesville Expedition in the spring of 1864.
Notable people born in Batesville include former NASCAR driver
Mark Martin and former Major League Baseball player Rick Monday.
Batesville was home to the Soulesbury Institute for several years prior
to the Civil War and briefly after the war. Today, the town is home to
Lyon College, the University of Arkansas Community College at
Batesville, the Batesville Public Schools, and the Old Independence
Regional Museum.
Battlefield, Missouri—Battlefield is a town of about 6,000 people in
Greene County at the southwest edge of Springfield. Named for the
nearby Wilson's Creek Battlefield, the town was a small village for
many years but has grown rapidly in recent years as a suburb of
Springfield.
Battle of Carthage State Park—See Carthage, Battle of.
Baxter County, Arkansas—Located in north central Arkansas
bordering Missouri, Baxter County was formed in 1873 from territory
taken from Izard, Marion, Fulton, and Searcy counties. Governor
Elisha Baxter, acting while legislators whose counties would be
affected by the proposal were home and unable to vote on the issue,

created the new county almost unilaterally, and it was named for him. Mountain Home became the county seat when the county was formed.

Baxter Springs, Kansas—Baxter Springs, in the extreme southeast corner of Kansas, was a Union military outpost during the Civil War, and it was founded as a cow town immediately after the war because of its status as a layover point along the Shawnee Trail. Although lesser known than rough-and-tumble cow towns like Dodge City that came later, Baxter Springs roared just as loudly for a few years. Baxter Springs was also noted as a mining town during the lead and zinc mining boom of the early 1900s in southeast Kansas and northeast Oklahoma. The population of Baxter Springs today is about 4,200. It is home to the USD 508 Baxter Springs Public Schools and to the Baxter Springs Heritage Center and Museum.

Main Street of Baxter Springs, circa 1880. *Courtesy Baxter Springs Heritage Center & Museum.*

Baxter Springs, Battle and Massacre at—The Battle and Massacre at Baxter Springs, Kansas, was a Civil War action that occurred on October 6, 1863, when Confederate guerrillas under William Quantrill attacked the fort there and, after being repelled, attacked and virtually annihilated a Union wagon train and its escort under command of General James G. Blunt that were on their way to the fort.

Baxter, Annie White—Elected to the office of county clerk in Jasper County, Missouri, in 1890, thirty years before women were granted the right to vote, Annie White Baxter was the first female elected to a county-wide office in the state of Missouri and one of the first in the United States. A street in Joplin is named for Annie Baxter.

Baxter, Elisha—Elisha Baxter was a politician from Batesville, Arkansas. At the outset of the Civil War, he opposed secession and was arrested and indicted for treason by the Confederate government. He escaped, fled north, and was commissioned a colonel in the Union Army. He began raising a regiment around Batesville but resigned before it was fully organized. After the war, Baxter was chosen by Governor Isaac Murphy as a U.S. Senator from Arkansas, but opposition arose and he was never seated. In 1872, Baxter's election as governor sparked the Brooks-Baxter War, during which Baxter's gubernatorial opponent, Joseph Brooks, and his allies physically removed Baxter from office. He was soon restored to office by President Grant, and he served until 1874. He died at Batesville in 1899. Baxter County is named after him.

Bear Creek Springs, Arkansas—Bear Creek Springs is an unincorporated community on U.S. Highway 65 in northern Boone County. A post office named Francis existed at the site before the community became known as Bear Creek Springs. The community was once an incorporated town, but little remains there today except the historic Bear Creek Motel, listed on the National Register of Historic Places.

Beatles, Stopover of—The only time the Beatles ever came to the Ozarks was a brief stopover in September of 1964 near the end of the group's first full-fledged American tour. On their way from Dallas to New York, the Fab Four flew into Walnut Ridge, Arkansas, and then took a smaller airplane to a ranch near Alton, Missouri, for a weekend getaway. The occasion is still commemorated at both Walnut Ridge and the Alton ranch.

Beaver, Arkansas—Beaver is a town of about 100 people in northern Carroll County. It is the site of a historic swinging bridge sometimes called the "Golden Gate of the Ozarks."

Beaver Creek—Beaver Creek is a tributary of the White River that flows through Douglas and Taney counties, Missouri. It is popular with fishermen and paddlers.

Beaver Lake—Beaver Lake is a reservoir in northwest Arkansas that was created by the building of Beaver Dam on the White River during the 1960s. The lake, covering almost 32,000 acres, is popular for fishing, boating, and other outdoor recreation. The dam is located a few miles west of Eureka Springs.

Beaver Station—During the Civil War, Beaver Station was the site of a Union outpost called Fort Lawrence located in the southwestern corner of present-day Douglas County, Missouri. Confederate troops under Colonel Emmett McDonald skirmished with Enrolled Missouri Militia at Fort Lawrence in early January of 1863 as McDonald was on his way to join General John S. Marmaduke at the Battle of Springfield.

Beck, Helen Gould—Helen Gould Beck, whose stage name was Sally Rand, was a burlesque dancer and actress who was famous for her ostrich feather fan dance and her balloon bubble dance. Her most famous appearance was at the 1933 Chicago World's Fair where she was arrested for indecent exposure several times in the same day. She was born at Elkton in Hickory County, Missouri, in 1904, and returned to the Ozarks on several occasions, including at least one appearance at the Ozark Empire Fair in the early 1940s and an appearance at Elkton for a community celebration in 1976. She died in 1979.

Bee Bluff—Bee Bluff is a scenic bluff that rises precipitously to a height of about 550 feet on the Current River about eight miles northeast of Eminence, Missouri.

Bee Branch, Arkansas—Bee Branch is an unincorporated community located on U.S. Highway 65 in southern Van Buren County. It is home to the South Side Bee Branch School District.

Beeler, Joe—Joe Beeler was a well-known western artist and cofounder of the Cowboy Artists of America. Born in Joplin, Missouri, in 1931, he grew up in northeast Oklahoma.

Bell, Oklahoma—Bell is a community of about 545 people in southeastern Adair County near the Arkansas border.

Bella Vista, Arkansas—Bella Vista is a town of about 25,000 people on U. S. Highway 71 in Benton County just south of the Missouri state line. Originally begun in the 1910s as a summer resort, it became an affluent retirement community in 1965. It grew rapidly but did not incorporate as a municipality until 2006. The popular Bella Vista Arts and Crafts Fair is held each October.

Belle, Missouri—Belle is a town of about 1,400 people on the border of Maries and Osage counties. It grew up along the Chicago, Rock Island, and Pacific Railroad after the road was built through a small portion of northern Maries County in 1904. Belle is home to the Maries County R-2 School District.

Bellefonte, Arkansas—Bellefonte is a town of about 530 people on U. S. Highway 65 in northern Boone County. It was founded about the time of the Civil War and got its name from some nearby springs or "beautiful fountains." When Boone County was formed in 1869, Bellefonte was the largest community in the county, but the new town of Harrison was named the county seat. Bellefonte prospered during the late 1800s, when it was home to North Arkansas College (similar to a modern high school and not to be confused with the present-day junior college by the same name). The prosperity continued into the twentieth century, but the town declined during the Depression and has never fully recovered.

Belleview, Missouri—Belleview is an unincorporated community in northern Iron County named for the valley in which it is located. "Belleview" is an anglicized version of "Bellevue," which is the name the French gave the area in the late 1700s.

Bendavis, Missouri—Bendavis is an unincorporated community on State Highway 38 in west Texas County. James J. Burns, who hoped to build a town on the site, gave the place its name during the early twentieth century to advertise his orchard of Ben Davis apples. His plat for the town was recorded in the county court, but Bendavis never amounted to much more than a post office and general store. Today it is a mere wide place in the road.

Bennett, Marion T.—Marion T. Bennett was an attorney and politician from Buffalo, Missouri. When U.S. Congressman Phillip Allen Bennett died in office in late 1942 after being re-elected, Marion T. Bennett was chosen in a special election to complete his father's term. He was then re-elected for two additional terms.

Bennett, Phillip Allen—Phillip Allen Bennett was a politician from Buffalo, Missouri. He served one term as Missouri's lieutenant governor and was a U.S. congressman from January 1941 until his death in December of 1942.

Bennett Spring State Park—Bennett Spring State Park is a state park located about ten miles northwest of Lebanon, Missouri, on State Highway 64. Known especially for trout fishing, it is a popular spot for a variety of outdoor activities. The location appeared on maps during the early 1800s as Big Spring. It became known as Brice Spring after James Brice built a mill there in 1837. Later a larger mill was constructed by Peter Bennett, and the place was called Bennett Springs. When the state park was established in 1923, it took the name of the nearby community, minus the final "s."

Bennetts River—Bennetts River is a tributary of the North Fork River that forms in Howell County, Missouri, and flows south-southwest through Fulton County, Arkansas, and into Baxter County, Arkansas.

Benton County, Arkansas—Benton County, located in the northwest corner of the state, was formed in 1836 from territory taken from Washington County and named after Missouri senator Thomas Hart Benton, who had played a key role in Arkansas's admission to the Union. Bentonville, also named after Senator Benton, was named the county seat in 1837.

Benton, Maecenas E.—Maecenas E. Benton was a U. S. congressman representing southwest Missouri during the late 1800s and early 1900s and was the father of artist Thomas Hart Benton. He lived at Neosho and is buried there.

Benton, Thomas Hart—Thomas Hart Benton was a famous American painter and muralist who was a leader of the Regionalist art movement during the 1920s and 1930s. Among Benton's many noted works are a mural at the state capitol in Jefferson City entitled *Social History of Missouri* and a mural at the Joplin city hall entitled *Turn of the Century, Joplin*. The namesake of his great uncle, Missouri senator Thomas Hart Benton, the younger Benton was born and grew up at Neosho.

Benton, Thomas Hart, homecoming of—Thomas Hart Benton Day was a homecoming celebration held at Neosho for famous artist and native son Thomas Hart Benton on May 12, 1962. The event was attended by dignitaries and newsmen from across the country as well as thousands of local people.

Bentonville, Arkansas—Bentonville is a city of about 36,500 people and the seat of Benton County. A post office was established at the site in 1836 and named Osage after the Osage Indians that had formerly inhabited the area. Benton County was established in the same year, and Bentonville was laid out in 1837 as the seat of the new county. Both the county and its seat were named after Missouri senator Thomas Hart Benton. The Osage post office was renamed Bentonville in 1843. Bentonville is home to Wal-Mart and to the Bentonville Public Schools

Bentonville College—Bentonville College was an institution of higher learning that operated in Bentonville, Arkansas, from 1895 to 1901, when it became Bentonville Ouachita Academy. About ten years later, the buildings were taken over by Bentonville High School.

Bentonville, Action at—The Action at Bentonville on February 18, 1862, was a raid on the town by a Union detachment under Brigadier General Alexander S. Asboth that resulted in the capture of over thirty Rebel soldiers, a similar number of horses, and a quantity of supplies. It was part of the maneuvering leading up to the Battle of Pea Ridge in early March of 1862.

Berger, Missouri—Berger is a town of about 220 people in northwest Franklin County.

Bergman, Arkansas—Bergman is a town of about 450 people in eastern Boone County. It was preceded by two or three settlements in the general area, including Keener, which was a fairly substantial town during the 1880s about a mile south of present-day Bergman. Bergman itself was laid out as a railroad town in the early 1900s and incorporated in 1905. It was named after Edith Bergman, whose father provided the land for the town and requested it be named after her. She became the town's first postmistress. Bergman is home to the Bergman Public Schools.

Bernice, Oklahoma—Bernice is a town of about 565 people in northwest Delaware County on the banks of Grand Lake. It was laid out along the railroad in 1912 by partners Rose Mode and Charles Lee and named after Mode's daughter. The town prospered early on but declined during the 1920s and 1930s. It was moved to higher ground in 1939 and 1940 during construction of Pensacola Dam, and the old town site was flooded by Grand Lake. Bernice has revived in recent years as a vacation and retirement community and sometimes bills itself as the "crappie fishing capital of the world."

Bernice State Park—Bernice State Park is an 88-acre Oklahoma State Park near Bernice that offers fishing and boating access to Grand Lake.

Berry, James Henderson—James Henderson Berry was soldier, lawyer, and politician from Carroll County, Arkansas. He served in the Confederate army as a lieutenant and had a leg amputated after being wounded at the Battle of Corinth in October 1862. After the war, he turned to politics and was elected governor of Arkansas in 1882. He served in the U.S. Senate from 1885 to 1907. He is buried at Berryville, which was named after his uncle.

Berryville, Arkansas—Berryville is a town of about 5,400 people and one of two seats of Carroll County. It was established in the early 1850s and named for Blackburn Henderson Berry, one of the town's founders. Berryville became the county seat in 1875, but in 1883 a second judicial division of the county was established at Eureka Springs. On October 27, 1942, a tornado struck Berryville that killed 29 people and seriously wounded 68. During the mid to late twentieth century, Berryville was sometimes known as the Turkey Capital of Arkansas because of the many turkeys grown and processed there. Berryville was home to Clarke's Academy, a noted private school, from 1867 to 1905, and today it is home to the Berryville Public Schools. It is also home to the Saunders Museum and the Carroll County Heritage Center Museum.

Bethune, Ed—Born and reared in Pocahontas, Arkansas, Ed Bethune is a lawyer and politician who represented Arkansas's Second District, the upper reaches of which extend into the Ozarks, in the U.S. House of Representatives from 1979 to 1985.

Beveridge, Thomas R.—Thomas R. Beveridge was a Missouri state geologist during the mid-1900s, a professor of geology at the University of Missouri-Rolla, and an Ozarks enthusiast. His book *Tom Beveridge's Ozarks* was published posthumously in 1979.

Biehle, Missouri—Biehle is a village of about 50 people in southern Perry County.

Big Flat, Arkansas—Big Flat is a town of about 105 people located primarily in southern Baxter County but slightly straddling the Searcy County line.

Biggers, Arkansas—Biggers is a town of about 350 people at the southeastern edge of the Ozarks in eastern Randolph County. It is the former home of Biggers-Reyno High School, but the Biggers-Reyno School District consolidated with Corning about 2006.

Big Indian Creek, Skirmish at—The Skirmish at Big Indian Creek was a minor action of the Civil War on May 27, 1862, near Letona, Arkansas, in northern White County, involving a detachment of Major General Samuel R. Curtis's Army of the Southwest and a Confederate scouting party.

Big Piney River—The Big Piney River is a tributary of the Gasconade River that flows through Texas, Pulaski, and Phelps counties, Missouri. It is popular with fishermen, canoeists, and other outdoor enthusiasts.

Big River, Missouri—Big River or Big River Mills, as it is sometimes called, is an unincorporated community in northern St. Francois County in the eastern part of the Ozarks. It was established in the early 1800s and is said to have been the first settlement in the county. However, little remains of the community today.

Big River—Approximately 145 miles long, the Big River is a tributary of the Meramec River that winds through the eastern Missouri Ozarks. Rising in western Iron County, it flows through Washington County, St. Francois County, and Jefferson County and empties into the Meramec near Eureka where the Meramec forms the boundary between Jefferson and St. Louis counties.

Big Spring—Big Spring, located near Van Buren, Missouri, is the largest spring in Missouri and one of the three largest in the United States. It was a state park from 1924 to 1969 and is now part of the Ozark National Scenic Riverways.

Big Sugar Creek—Big Sugar Creek is a forty-seven-mile stream that forms in southwest Barry County, Missouri, and flows generally west into McDonald County, where it meanders past Big Sugar Creek State Park, a 2,000-acre wilderness state park, and then converges with Little Sugar Creek to form the Elk River at Pineville.

Big Sugar Creek State Park—See Big Sugar Creek.

Birch Tree, Missouri—Birch Tree is a town of about 700 people located on Highway 60 in Shannon County. A post office was established a mile or two from present-day Birch Tree in 1865 and named for a birch tree near the office. The nearby town grew up in the late 1800s as a logging community. It is the birthplace of former Missouri governor Mel Carnahan and the hometown of former Missouri governor Bob Holden. It once had a high school but consolidated with Mountain View-Liberty in the early 1970s and now has only an elementary school.

Billings, Missouri—Billings is a town of about 1,100 people in western Christian County and the home of Billings R-4 School District. It is also the hometown of Leon Rauch (aka Rausch), lead singer of the Texas Playboys.

Birds—There are an estimated 300-plus species of birds that either inhabit the Ozarks year-round, nest in the region during the winter only, nest here during the summer only, or stay in the region temporarily during migration. Those here only for the summer include many songbirds like thrushes and warblers. Dark-eyed juncos and American tree sparrows, on the other hand, nest in the Ozarks during the winter only. Transients like Canada geese merely pass through in spring and autumn. However, some of the region's most familiar birds, like cardinals and woodpeckers, remain year-round. In addition, there are a number of extinct birds, like the passenger pigeon and Carolina parakeet, that formerly inhabited the area. Bird watching is a popular pastime in certain parts of the Ozarks.

Bismarck, Missouri—Bismarck is a town of about 1,550 people in western St. Francois County. It was founded in 1868 as a railroad town and named after German chancellor Von Bismarck. It is the home of the Bismarck R-5 School District.

Black Bear—Black bears were so common in the early days of white settlement in the Ozarks that Arkansas was even called "The Bear State." However, over-hunting and a reduction in habitat led to their near extinction in the region by the 1930s. Arkansas began reintroducing black bears into the state in the late 1950s. Although many of them live in the eastern and southern parts of the state, a goodly number have roamed into the Ozarks region of Arkansas, Missouri, and Oklahoma. Both Arkansas and Oklahoma now allow hunting of black bears on a very limited basis.

Blackburn, Sylvanus—Sylvanus Blackburn is known for building the first mill in Benton County, Arkansas, on War Eagle Creek about 1838, when he also built a two story home. The home is still standing, and a 1973 reproduction of the mill also stands at the original location, which is the site of the annual War Eagle Arts and Crafts Fair. The mill is the only working mill in Arkansas and is thought to be the only undershot waterwheel mill in operation in the U.S.

Black Mountain—Located west of Fredericktown in Madison County, Black Mountain has the largest change in elevation from base to summit (almost 1,000 feet) of any mountain in Missouri

Black River—A tributary of the White River, the Black River forms from three streams in the Iron and Reynolds County region of southern Missouri and then flows south into Arkansas through Clay, Lawrence, and Randolph counties, at the eastern edge of the Ozarks.

Black River Technical College—Located in Pocahontas, Arkansas, the Black River Technical College is a public community college serving northeast Arkansas and offering two-year degrees. Called the Black River Vocational Technical School when it opened in 1972, it is named for the Black River that runs through the town. It adopted its current name in 1993.

Black Rock, Arkansas—Black Rock is a town of about 660 people in northern Lawrence County. It arose as a timber industry boom town after construction of a railroad to the area in 1882, and the population of the town reached approximately 1,500 by the turn of the twentieth century. Black Rock is home to the Black Rock Public Schools, which are part of the Lawrence County School District.

Blair, Emily Newell—Emily Newell Blair was a writer, feminist, suffragist, national leader in the Democratic Party, and founder of the League of Women Voters. She was born at Joplin, Missouri, in 1877 and graduated from high school at Carthage, where she spent her young adulthood, before becoming a powerful figure in Washington, D.C. circles.

Blanchard Springs Caverns—Blanchard Springs Caverns is a commercial cave system located in Stone County, Arkansas, north of Mountain View. The first systematic exploration of the caverns occurred in the 1950s, although their existence was known at least twenty years earlier. The caverns were opened to the public in 1973.

Bland, Missouri—Bland is a town of about 550 people in western Gasconade County. The post office was established in 1877, and the town was named for U. S. congressman Richard P. Bland, although a store and perhaps one or two other businesses predated the post office.

Bland formerly had a high school but now has only a middle school as part of the Maries County R-2 School District.

Bland, Richard Parks—Richard Parks Bland was a U. S. congressman representing south central Missouri for approximately twenty-five years during the late nineteenth century. He was known as "The Great Commoner" because of his efforts to help the common man and also as "Silver Dick" because of his work on behalf of the silver mines. He is buried at Lebanon, where he lived for many years. The town of Bland, Missouri, was named for him.

Blevins, Brooks—Brooks Blevins is a professor of Ozarks Studies at Missouri State University and the author of several books about the Ozarks.

Bloodland, Missouri—Bloodland was a small town in Pulaski County that was wiped off the face of the map when Fort Leonard Wood was built in the early 1940s. Located on Highway 17, Bloodland at one time was a thriving community with several businesses, churches, and a high school.

Bloodland High School, about 1940. *Author's collection.*

Bloomsdale, Missouri—Settled around 1840, Bloomsdale is a town of about 520 people in northern Ste. Genevieve County. It is the home of Bloomsdale Elementary School.

Blount, Bud—Allen "Bud" Blount (often spelled Blunt) was one of several notorious outlaws to come out of Granby, Missouri, in the years after the Civil War. He blazed a trail of crimes that took him to Arizona and Colorado, among other western states, but he is probably most infamous in the Ozarks for the "Blunt Raid" on Webb City in 1877 and for his murder of a railroad brakeman near Granby in 1890

Blue Eye, Missouri—Blue Eye is a village in southern Stone County bordering Arkansas. It was established a few years after the Civil War and was reportedly named Blue Eye in honor of its blue-eyed first postmaster. Blue Eye, Missouri, has a population of about 130, and it is home to the Blue Eye R-5 School District. The community straddles the state line, and an additional 30 or 40 people live in Blue Eye, Arkansas.

Blue Norther of 1911—The Great Blue Norther of November 11, 1911 (often identified numerically as 11-11-11) was a sudden cold snap that hit the Ozarks on that date and dropped temperatures in Springfield from a record high of 80 degrees in the early afternoon to a record low of 13 shortly before midnight. The occasion marks the only time both a record high and a record low for a particular date have been achieved in the Ozarks on the same day, and the two extremes stood for many years as the record high and the record low for November 11.

Blue Spring—Located in Shannon County, Blue Spring is the sixth-largest spring in Missouri. There is also a Blue Spring in Oregon County.

Bluff Dwellers Cave—Bluff Dwellers Cave is a show cave two miles south of Noel, Missouri. It was discovered in 1925 and opened as a commercial cave in 1927.

Blunt, James G.—James G. Blunt was a Union general during the Civil War. A detachment under his command was the victim of William Quantrill's Massacre at Baxter Springs in 1863, but his forces played key roles in the Union victories at Prairie Grove in 1862 and at Second Newtonia in 1864.

Blunt, Matt—Matt Blunt was governor of Missouri from 2005 to 2009. At the age of 33, he became the second youngest person ever elected to the office. Blunt was born in Strafford, Missouri, and he represented Greene County in the state legislature before running for statewide office.

Blunt, Roy—The father of former governor Matt Blunt, Roy Blunt was elected to the U. S. Senate from Missouri in 2010. Prior to becoming a senator, he was a U. S. congressman representing southwest Missouri from 1997-2011. A native of Niangua, Missouri, Blunt also served over ten years as the Greene County clerk and two terms as Missouri's secretary of state.

Senator Roy Blunt when he was a congressman. *Courtesy Wikipedia.*

Bly, Missouri—Bly is a historic place in Howell County about fifteen miles southwest of West Plains. A post office was established at the site about 1880, and the community grew into a prosperous village of about 200 people. However, the town burned in 1924 and never recovered.

Bobby Hopper Tunnel—The Bobby Hopper Tunnel is a highway tunnel on Interstate 540 in Washington County, Arkansas, just north of the Crawford County line. The only highway tunnel in the state, it was named for the director of the Arkansas Highway Commission during its construction, and it was opened in 1998.

Bobby Hopper Tunnel south of Fayetteville. *Courtesy Wikimedia.*

Bois D'Arc, Missouri—Bois D'Arc is a community in western Greene County named for the bois d'arc or Osage orange tree. It had a predecessor by the same name located about two miles east of the present town. The current town, called New Bois D'Arc at first, was established after the Kansas City, Springfield and Memphis Railroad was built through the area in 1881. Bois D'Arc was a thriving little village for many years, but it has declined since it lost its high school through consolidation in the 1950s.

Boise City, Missouri—Also known as Spring City, Boise City was a community that was established in Oregon County, just across the state line from Mammoth Spring, Arkansas, about 1883 when a railroad was being built to the latter town. Boise City reportedly arose mainly in response to Arkansas's restrictive liquor laws, and it became a lively little town with several saloons and stores where workers from Arkansas could purchase liquor. Now a part of Mammoth Spring, Boise City long ago ceased to exist as a separate town.

Bolduc House Museum—The Bolduc House Museum preserves the home that Louis Bolduc built in Ste. Genevieve, Missouri, in 1792. It is one of the oldest houses in Missouri and a prime example of the French Colonial architecture of the eighteenth century.

Bolin, Alf—Alfred Bolin was a noted Confederate bushwhacker in the Taney County, Missouri, area during the Civil War. His murderous deeds are legendary but, in many cases, hard to document. After Bolin was killed about February 1, 1863, his head was chopped off, and Federal soldiers carried it to Springfield to collect a bounty.

Bolivar, Missouri—Bolivar is the county seat of Polk County. Established in 1840, it was named after the town of Bolivar, Tennessee, which was the home of a portion of the Polk family. The Tennessee town, in turn, was named for Simon Bolivar, the famous South American liberator. On July 5, 1948, a statue of Simon Bolivar in Neuhart Park in Bolivar was dedicated by President Harry S Truman. President Romulo Callegos of Venezuela also took part in the ceremony, and thousands of people attended. The occasion has sometimes been called "Bolivar's greatest day." June 16, 1933, when Charles "Pretty Boy" Floyd kidnapped Polk County sheriff Jack Killingsworth, was also an exciting time in Bolivar. Bolivar has a population of about 10,000 and is home to the Bolivar R-1 Schools. The schools' mascot is the liberator.

Bollinger County, Missouri—Located in the southeast corner of the state, Bollinger County was formed in 1851 from territory taken from Cape Girardeau, Stoddard, and Wayne counties. Dallas (now Marble Hill) was laid out as the county seat the same year. The county was named after George Frederick Bollinger, an early settler in the area.

Bollinger Mill State Historic Site—Bollinger Mill State Historic Site preserves a historic mill in Burfordville, Missouri, in western Cape Girardeau County. The first mill on the site was built in 1800. It was replaced in 1825 by another mill that burned during the Civil War. The current mill was built in 1867 on the foundation of the 1825 mill. The Burfordville Covered Bridge, adjacent to the mill, is also part of the historic site. Both the mill and the bridge are listed on the National Register of Historic Places.

Covered bridge at Bollinger Mill State Park. *Courtesy Wikipedia.*

Bonne Terre, Missouri—Bonne Terre is a town in St. Francois County with a population of about 7,000. It was founded by the French in the 1700s as a lead mining camp. The name "Bonne Terre" was given to the mine by the early French miners because the site was considered "good earth" for producing lead, and the name was eventually applied to the town that sprung up nearby. Bonne Terre is home to the North Francois County R-1 Schools and to the Eastern Reception, Diagnosis and Correctional Center, where Missouri's executions are carried out.

Bonnie and Clyde—The desperate duo of Bonnie Parker and Clyde Barrow crisscrossed the country during the gangster era of the early 1930s, robbing banks and committing other crimes. They engaged in several notorious shootouts with law officers, including one in Joplin, Missouri, in April 1933, in which two lawmen were killed. Although they were originally from Texas, the pair spent considerable time in the Ozarks, laying low or otherwise trying to elude law enforcement. In addition to the shootout at Joplin, Bonnie and Clyde robbed a bank at Oronogo in November 1932, kidnapped a policeman in Springfield in January 1933, killed a police officer near Alma, Arkansas, in June 1933, had a shootout with officers near Reeds Spring, Missouri, in February 1934, and killed another officer at Commerce, Oklahoma, in April of 1934. Bonnie and Clyde themselves were killed by a police ambush in Louisiana later in 1934.

Bonnie and Clyde strike a playful pose. *Courtesy Jasper County Records Center.*

Boone County, Arkansas—Located in the north central part of the state bordering Missouri, Boone County was established in 1869 from territory taken from Carroll and Marion counties, and the new town of Harrison was named the county seat. It has often been reported that the county was named after Daniel Boone, although another story holds that it acquired its name because residents thought that creation of the county would be a boon to the area.

Boone, Nathan—Nathan Boone, the youngest son of Daniel Boone, was an American explorer, fur trader, surveyor, and military officer during the early 1800s. His last home was located near present-day Ash Grove, Missouri, and he died there in 1856.

Boonville, Missouri—Boonville is a town of about 8,320 people and the seat of Cooper County. It was named for Daniel Boone and his sons, who had a salt business in the general area during the very early 1800s. The town was laid out in 1817. It was the site of a Civil War skirmish, the so-called Battle of Boonville, during June of 1861, when Union forces put to flight a body of Missouri State Guard troops under Governor Claiborne Jackson.

Boozman, John—John Boozman represented northwest Arkansas in the U.S. House of Representatives from 2001 to 2011 and has served as a U.S. senator from Arkansas since 2011. He attended the University of Arkansas and played football there and then later became an optometrist in Rogers before turning to politics.

Boston Mountains—The Boston Mountains, extending across northern Arkansas into east central Oklahoma, constitute the southern portion of the Ozarks plateau. The highest and most rugged portion of the Ozarks, the Boston Mountains are often thought of as a separate range, and the Oklahoma portion of the range is usually called the Cookson Hills. Scientifically speaking, the Boston Mountains also comprise one of the four major geographic regions of the Ozarks. The other three are the St. Francois Mountains, the Salem Plateau, and the Springfield Plateau.

Boswell, Arkansas—Boswell is an unincorporated community in the White River Valley of western Izard County. The original settlement that grew up at the site in the 1800s was called Wideman, and it became an important river port community. A railroad was built in the early 1900s, and the train station was called Boswell after the first station agent. In 1906, a post office was established and called Cook, while the town was still known as Wideman. In 1915, the community and the post office changed their name to Boswell. Boswell boomed during the first half of the 1900s but began to decline about 1950, and the population of the place has now dwindled to a very few.

Boudinot, Elias—Elias Boudinot was a leader of the Cherokee Indians who was assassinated by opposing tribal members on June 22, 1839, at Park Hill in what is now Oklahoma for supporting the 1835 Treaty of New Ochota, which ceded Cherokee lands in the East and led to the tribe's removal to western reservations.

Boudinot, Elias Cornelius—The son of Elias Boudinot, Elias Cornelius Boudinot was active in Democratic party politics in Arkansas during the Civil War era and a leader of Confederate Cherokee forces. Rising to the rank of lieutenant colonel, he fought in the Battle of Pea Ridge.

Bourbeuse River—Approximately 150 miles long, the Bourbeuse River is a tributary of the Meramec River. Rising in Phelps County, Missouri, it flows in a generally northeast direction through Maries, Gasconade, Crawford, and Franklin counties and empties into the Meramec near Moselle. The 100-plus miles of this very crooked river that are located in Franklin County cover only 27 airline miles.

Bourbon, Missouri—Bourbon is a town of about 1,630 people in northeast Crawford County along Interstate 44. It began prior to the Civil War when a railroad was being constructed from St. Louis to Rolla. A storeowner near the site of the present-day town imported barrels of bourbon whiskey and sat them on the porch of his store to sell to the railroad workers. His store was called the bourbon store, and the settlement that grew up around it came to be known as Bourbon. Bourbon is home to the Crawford County R-1 School District.

Bower's Mill, Missouri—Bower's Mill is a community in western Lawrence County at the Jasper County line. An important village at one time, it was the site of a Union post during the Civil War, but little remains of the place today.

Boyd, Sempronius H.—Sempronius H. "Pony" Boyd was a soldier and politician from Springfield, Missouri. At the outbreak of the Civil War, he raised the 24th Missouri Infantry for the Union army and served as its colonel during the first half of the war. He served as a member of the United States House of Representatives from 1863 to 1865 and again from 1869 to 1871.

Boyer, Cloyd, Ken, and Clete—Cloyd, Ken, and Clete Boyer were famous baseball-playing brothers from Alba, Missouri. They came from a family of fourteen siblings, including seven brothers. All the brothers signed professional baseball contracts. Perhaps the most accomplished of the brothers, third baseman Ken played fifteen years in the big leagues, primarily for the St. Louis Cardinals, and was the National League MVP in 1964. Older brother Cloyd pitched for the Cardinals and the Kansas City Athletics, and younger brother Clete, also a third baseman, played Major League Baseball for sixteen years, most notably for the New York Yankees.

Bradleyville, Missouri—Bradleyville is a small town in northeast Taney County perhaps best known for its school's outstanding basketball teams during the 1960s, when they won three state championships. Today the town has a population of less than 100, but it is still home to the Bradleyville School District.

Brandsville, Missouri—Brandsville is a town of about 175 people in eastern Howell County. It was laid out in 1883 by the St. Louis and San Francisco Railroad and named for Michael Brand, a large landowner in the area who donated the town site. It was settled largely by German immigrants.

Branscum, Robbie Tilley—Robbie Tilley Branscum was an award-winning children's author who published twenty books between 1971 and 1991. Her childhood in Baxter County, Arkansas, provided the background for many of her books.

Branson, Missouri—Branson is a town of about 10,520 people in Taney County. It was named after Reuben Branson, who ran a general store and post office in the area during the 1880s. Because of the proximity of Lake Taneycomo, Branson has been a popular destination for vacationers since the first half of the twentieth century. During the latter half of the century, the proliferation of theaters and other attractions in the town also made it popular as a live entertainment center. Many nationally known entertainers, such as Moe Bandy, Glen Campbell, Roy Clark, Mickey Gilley, Tony Orlando, Charley Pride, Yakov Smirnoff, Jim Stafford, Shoji Tabuchi, Mel Tillis, and Andy Williams, have performed in or even had their own theaters in Branson. Plumb Nellie Days and Veterans Homecoming are among Branson's popular annual festivals. The town is home to the Branson Landing shopping mall, the Tanger Outlet mall, and the Branson R-4 School District.

Branson Scenic Railway—Branson Scenic Railway is a short-run railroad operating out of downtown Branson and catering to tourists.

Branson Scenic Railway train. *Courtesy Wikimedia.*

Briarcliff, Arkansas—Briarcliff is a resort town of about 235 people in Baxter County near Norfork Lake. The retirement community of Briarcliff-by-the-Lake was established in the 1970s. It was incorporated in 1997 as the town of Briarcliff and upgraded to a second-class city in 2000.

Bridal Cave—Bridal Cave is located about two miles north of Camdenton, Missouri, on Highway 5. Although explored during the 1800s, it was first opened as a tourist attraction in 1948. It gets its name from the fact that one of its rooms, called the Bridal Chapel, is often used for weddings, having hosted more than 2,100 over the years.

Briggs, Oklahoma—Briggs is a community of about 360 people in eastern Cherokee County on U.S. Highway 62. It was reportedly named for John Briggs, a local merchant. Briggs is home to the Briggs Elementary School.

Britt, Elton (aka James Elton Baker)—Elton Britt, whose birth name was James Elton Baker, was a country singer and song writer born at Zack in Searcy County, Arkansas. He was most famous for the World War II era hit "There's a Star-Spangled Banner Waving Somewhere."

Britton, Lane—Lane Britton was a notorious character who killed a man at a Neosho, Missouri, bawdy house in 1875 when he was just seventeen years old and was acquitted of murder. He later killed two lawmen north of Joplin and was never brought to justice.

Britton, Wiley—The older brother of Lane Britton, Wiley Britton was a well-known author, noted for *Pioneer Life in Southwest Missouri, The Civil War on the Border*, and other books.

Broadfoot, Lennis—Born in Shannon County, Missouri, Lennis Broadfoot was an artist known principally for his collection of portraits entitled *Pioneers of the Ozarks*, which were drawn during the late 1930s and early 1940s.

Brockwell, Arkansas—Brockwell is an unincorporated community in Izard County. It is home to the Izard County Consolidated Schools and to the Brockwell Gospel Music School, which offers summer instruction for those seeking to improve their church music.

Brookline, Missouri—Brookline is a small village in western Greene County that grew up along the line of the Atlantic & Pacific Railroad (later the Frisco) after the tracks were laid in the early 1870s. The village consolidated with Republic in 2005.

Brough, Charles H.—Charles H. Brough was an educator and politician who taught at the University of Arkansas at Fayetteville for a number of years during the early 1900s and then served as governor of Arkansas from 1917 to 1921.

Brown, Charlie—Charles H. "Charlie" Brown was a member of the U.S. House of Representatives representing southwest Missouri from 1957-1961. Born in Oklahoma, he attended public schools in southwest Missouri and later Drury College.

Brown, Dee—Author of national bestseller *Bury My Heart at Wounded Knee*, Dee Brown had an interesting connection to the Ozarks. After high school graduation in 1927, he got a job as a printer and fledgling journalist with the *Harrison Times*. During his time at Harrison, he was accused of bank robbery at Jasper, Arkansas, and spent a night in the Newton County jail before the accusation was proved false.

Brown, Egbert B.—Egbert B. Brown was a brigadier general during the Civil War. As commander of the Union's Southwest Division during 1862 and early 1863, he had charge of the forces at Springfield during the Battle of Springfield in January 1863, until he was injured late in the battle. Later in the war, he commanded the District of Central Missouri headquartered at Warrensburg.

Brown, Helen Marie Gurley—Helen Gurley Brown was an author and publisher best known for her book *Sex and the Single Girl* and as the editor-in-chief of *Cosmopolitan Magazine* from 1965 to 1997. She was born in Green Forest, Arkansas, grew up mostly in Little Rock, and, as a young woman, occasionally visited her family in Carroll County.

Helen Gurley Brown, 1964. *Courtesy Wikimedia.*

Brown, J. L.—James Lafayette "J.L." Brown was a leader in the Landmark Baptist movement in Arkansas during the late 1800s and early 1900s. He also served a term in the Arkansas state legislature. Born in Randolph County, he lived mostly in Independence County. Landmark Baptists emphasized the exclusive validity of the Baptist denomination and the authority of the local church. The movement was a reaction to religious progressivism.

Brown, John Elward—John Elward Brown was a prominent evangelist, publisher, radio broadcaster, and educator in northwest Arkansas during the first half of the twentieth century. He established John Brown University at Siloam Springs.

Brownbranch, Missouri—Brownbranch, sometimes spelled Brown Branch, is an unincorporated community on State Highway 76 in northeast Taney County.

Browns Spring, Missouri—Browns Spring, or Brown's Spring, is an unincorporated community in northern Stone County. It dates from pre-Civil War days, when Burton Brown settled there and gave the place its name. It became a resort town for a few years during the early 1900s.

Broyles, Frank—Frank Broyles was a football coach best known for his tenure as head coach at the University of Arkansas from 1958 to 1976. His Arkansas teams compiled an overall record of 144 wins, 58 losses, and 5 ties, and the undefeated 1964 team was named national champions by the Football Writers Association of America.

Brumley, Albert Edward—Albert E. Brumley was a famous gospel music composer and publisher who lived most of his adult life near Powell in McDonald County, Missouri, and died there in 1977. "I'll Fly Away" and "Turn Your Radio On" are among the famous songs he wrote.

Brumley, Missouri—Brumley is a village of about 90 people in southern Miller County. The first post office was established in 1863, a store was opened in 1868, and the town was laid out in 1877. Brumley was a small but thriving community until about the mid-1900s, when it began to decline.

Bruno, Arkansas—Bruno is an unincorporated community in Marion County. See Pyatt, Arkansas.

Bryant Creek—Bryant Creek forms in northern Douglas County, Missouri, and flows generally south for about forty miles into southeast Ozark County, where it joins the North Fork of the White River.

BNSF Railroad—The BNSF Railroad, formerly known as the Burlington Northern Santa Fe, is the principal railway operating in the Ozarks. The previously dominant railway, the St. Louis-San Francisco (aka. Frisco), merged with the Burlington Northern in 1980.

Buckhorn, Skirmish at—The Skirmish at Buckhorn was a Civil War action that occurred on May 25, 1864, near present-day St. James in eastern Stone County, Arkansas, involving Confederate general Jo Shelby's advance under Captain David A. Williams and a band of Union irregulars under bushwhacker Bill Williams. Forty-seven of Bill Williams's men were reportedly killed with no Confederate casualties. A historic marker is located at the site.

Buckskull, Arkansas—Buckskull was a settlement in northern Randolph County across the Current River from present-day Current View, Ripley County, Missouri. Buckskull and nearby Pitman's Ferry were the site of several skirmishes during the Civil War. Although relatively insignificant, they were characteristic of the small-scale actions that typified the Civil War in Randolph County.

Buffalo, Missouri—Buffalo is a town of about 3,100 people and the county seat of Dallas County. Established about 1840, the town got its name from the Buffalo Head Prairie where it was located. It became the county seat of Niangua County (later Dallas County) after the county was formed in 1841. Buffalo is home to the Dallas County R-1 School District.

Buffalo National River—In 1972, the Buffalo River in northwest Arkansas became the first river in the U.S. to be designated a national river. A tributary of the White River, the Buffalo travels about 150 miles, the lower 135 of which flow through an area managed by the National Park Service, where the river is designated the Buffalo National River. This area features several natural wonders, such as Eden Falls, Eden Falls Cave, and the Balance Rock. The upper part of the river is managed by the U. S. Forest Service and is designated a National Scenic River. The river flows from west to east through Newton, Searcy, and Marion counties to its confluence with the White River on the Marion-Baxter county line.

Buford Mountain Conservation Area—Buford Mountain Conservation area preserves almost 4,000 acres at the site of Buford Mountain in northeast Iron County, Missouri.

Bull Shoals, Arkansas—Bull Shoals is a town of about 1,950 people in eastern Marion County on Bull Shoals Lake. It grew up alongside construction of the dam and lake and was incorporated in 1954. It is primarily a retirement and vacation center.

Bull Shoals Caverns—Opened in the 1960s, Bull Shoals Caverns is a commercial cave located at Bull Shoals, Arkansas. Another tourist attraction, an 1890s mountain village, is also located at the site.

Bull Shoals Lake and Dam---Bull Shoals Lake is a manmade reservoir located in northern Arkansas and southern Missouri. Impounding the White River, the dam is located in Marion County, Arkansas, and was constructed between 1947 and 1951. It was dedicated in 1952 by President Harry S Truman. The lake covers about 45,150 acres in Marion, Baxter, and Boone counties, Arkansas, and Ozark and Taney counties, Missouri.

Bull Shoals-White River State Park—Established in 1955, Bull Shoals-White River State Park is a 732-acre Arkansas state park along the banks of Bull Shoals Lake and the White River in Marion and Baxter counties. It features camping and other outdoor activities.

Bunceton, Missouri—Founded in 1868, Bunceton is a town of about 355 people in central Cooper County. It is home to the Bunceton R-4 Schools.

Bunch, Oklahoma—Bunch is an unincorporated community in southwestern Adair County. It was named for Cherokee vice-chief Rabbit Bunch, who lived in the area in the 1880s.

Bunch, Bradley—Bradley Bunch was an Arkansas state legislator from Carroll County and a county judge during the latter half of the nineteenth century, and he wrote the first history of the county. He was also the fourth great uncle of President Barack Obama.

Bunker, Missouri—Bunker is a town of about 450 people located on the Dent-Reynolds county line. It was founded in the early 1900s as a logging and lead mining community. Although lead mining in the immediate area has ceased, a number of sawmills still operate in the vicinity. Bunker is home to the Bunker R-3 School District.

Burch, Milton—Milton Burch was a Missouri State Militia captain during the Civil War who was well-known as a guerrilla fighter in the southwest part of the state. He led a noted expedition into southern Missouri and northern Arkansas in November of 1862.

Burdett, Samuel S.—Samuel S. Burdett was a U. S. congressman from St. Clair County, Missouri, from 1869 to 1873.

Burlington, Arkansas—Burlington is a community on U.S. Highway 65 in northern Boone County. It was once a thriving village but is now scarcely more than a wide place in the road.

Burnett, Crawford and Lavinia—Crawford and Lavinia Burnett were hanged on November 8, 1845, on Gallows Hill (later the site of the National Cemetery) in Fayetteville, Arkansas, for conspiring with their son John to kill Jonathan Sibley for his money. Lavinia was the first woman legally executed in Arkansas. John, who had carried out the murder, fled to Missouri but was captured, brought back to Arkansas; and hanged from the same gallows about a month and half after his parents' double execution.

Burns, Bob—Bob Burns was a nationally known radio and film personality during the 1930s and 1940s who was known by various titles like the Arkansas Traveler that referenced his hillbilly origins, and his performances tended to perpetuate the hillbilly image of Arkansas. Burns grew up in Van Buren, Arkansas.

Burris, Jack, murder of—See Salina, Oklahoma.

Busiek State Forest and Wildlife Area—Busiek State Forest and Wildlife Area is a Missouri state forest about eighteen miles south of Springfield on U.S. Highway 65. It encompasses about 2,500 acres and offers hiking, picnicking, and other outdoor activities.

Butcher, Sam—See Precious Moments Chapel.

Butler County, Missouri—Butler County is located in southeast Missouri at the eastern edge of the Ozarks. It was organized in 1849 from territory taken from Wayne County and named for William O. Butler, a Mexican War general and an 1848 vice presidential candidate. Poplar Bluff is the county seat.

Butterfield, Missouri—Butterfield is a village of about 400 people in central Barry County. It was established in the early 1880s when the Frisco Railroad branched into Arkansas and Butterfield became a station along the line.

Butterfield Overland Express—The Butterfield Overland Express was a stagecoach company that carried the U.S. mail across the country from Tipton, Missouri, and Memphis, Tennessee, to San Francisco from 1858 to 1861. The westbound trail from Tipton passed through southwest Missouri and northwest Arkansas to Fort Smith, where it and the Memphis route converged and continued west as a single route.

C

Cabin Creek, First Battle of—The First Battle of Cabin Creek was a Civil War action that occurred on July 1 and July 2, 1863, in present-day Mayes County, Oklahoma, at the western edge of the Ozarks. Confederate forces under Colonel Stand Watie lay in ambush where the old Texas Road crossed Cabin Creek for a Union convoy under Colonel James M. Williams. Williams learned of the Confederates' entrenched position on July 1 and launched an attack the next day, forcing the Southern forces to flee. In this action, the First Kansas Colored Infantry, which formed part of Williams's force, had the distinction of being the first black troops to fight alongside white troops during the Civil War.

Cabin Creek, Second Battle of—At the Second Battle of Cabin Creek, fought on September 19, 1864, Confederate troops under Brigadier General Richard M. Gano and Brigadier General Stand Watie captured a Union supply train of 300 wagons under Major Henry Hopkins near the same site where the First Battle of Cabin Creek was fought. The action is considered the last significant battle of the Civil War in Indian Territory.

Cabool, Missouri—Cabool is a town of about 2,150 people in southwest Texas County. It was laid out as a railroad town in 1882 and named by the land developers after Kabul, Afghanistan, using an anglicized spelling, although a local legend holds that it was named after an Indian chief with the name Cabool. A post office named Cedar Bluff was a predecessor to Cabool, having been established in the immediate vicinity prior to the Civil War. Cabool is home to the Cabool R-4 Schools.

Cache River—The Cache River is a 213-mile tributary of the White River. It forms in Butler County, Missouri, almost immediately enters Arkansas, and travels in a generally south-southwest direction along the edge of the Ozarks until it angles farther south to join the White at Clarendon, Arkansas.

Calamine, Arkansas—Calamine is an unincorporated community in southeast Sharp County. The state's first commercial zinc mining operation was established at the site in 1856, and the town boomed until the Civil War halted mining. The town was presumably named for the pink mineral calamine, a derivative of zinc, although a local legend holds that it was named after a female miner named Callie. Mining operations briefly resumed during the early 1870s, and the town once again flourished for a while. Today, however, only a few houses remain at Calamine.

Caledonia, Missouri—Caledonia is a village in Washington County about twelve miles south of Potosi. It was founded in 1819 and given the Latin name that the Romans gave to Scotland. It had a population of about 300 during the late 1800s but now has an estimated 135 residents. It is home to the Valley R-6 Schools.

Calico Rock, Arkansas—Calico Rock is a town of about 1,500 people in northwest Izard County. It was developed as a steamboat landing on the White River prior to the Civil War. It is located where Calico Creek flows into the White River, and both the creek and the town supposedly got their names from the river's white bluffs at the site, which early explorers said resembled calico fabric. The town is home to the Calico Rock Public Schools.

California, Missouri—California is the county seat of Moniteau County. Originally called Boonsborough, the town was located about a mile east of the present-day downtown area. When Moniteau County was formed in 1845, Boonsborough was moved to the town's current location, and the name was changed to California shortly thereafter. California has a population of slightly over 4,000, and it is home to the California R-1 School District. Many people in the California area do not think of themselves as living in the Ozarks, but at least the southern portion of Moniteau County is considered part of the Ozarks by most geographical definitions.

Call, Cora Elizabeth Pinkley—A lifetime resident of Carroll County, Arkansas, Cora Elizabeth Pinkley Call was an Ozarks writer, naturalist, folklorist, and historian of Eureka Springs. She founded the Ozark Writers-Artists Guild in 1935 and was its longtime president. The group, which disbanded in the 1960s shortly after Call curtailed her involvement because of failing health, was a forerunner of the present Ozark Creative Writers Group.

Camden, Robbie—Robert "Robbie" Camden was a criminal from Reynolds County, Missouri, who achieved widespread notoriety throughout the eastern Ozarks during the 1930s and became variously known as the Robin Hood of the Ozarks and the Ridge Runnin' Romeo because of his supposed benevolent deeds and romantic appeal. His most infamous crime was the hired-murder of a preacher in Reynolds County in 1933.

Camden County, Missouri—Camden County was established in 1841 as Kinderhook County, and the tiny settlement of Oregon was the county seat. In 1843, Kinderhook County became Camden County, and Oregon's name was changed to Erie. In 1855, Linn Creek became the county seat, and it remained so until the early 1930s when it was moved to make way for Lake of the Ozarks and Camdenton was named the new county seat.

Camdenton, Missouri—Camdenton is the county seat of Camden County. With a population of about 3,800 people, it is also the largest town in the county. Camdenton was laid out as the new county seat after work began on construction of the Lake of the Ozarks in 1929 and the old county seat of Linn Creek was slated to be submerged under water. Located near the lake, Camdenton is a popular resort area. It is home to the Camdenton R-3 School District.

Camp, Arkansas—Camp is an unincorporated community in Fulton County. Some of the earliest settlers in the county settled in the area, which was originally called Indian Camp, but the town did not develop until the 1870s. During the early 1900s, Camp had its own school, but the school consolidated with Salem during the 1930s, and the town continued to decline afterwards until today it has only a few residences.

Camp Crowder—Fort Crowder, or Camp Crowder as it was usually called, was a U.S. Army post during the World War II era that was located just south of Neosho in Newton County, Missouri. Among the notable individuals stationed there was cartoonist Mort Walker, who drew inspiration from Camp Crowder for Camp Swampy of his Beetle Bailey comic strip. The grounds of Camp Crowder were given over to various uses after the war, and some of the buildings formed the core of Crowder College when it was established in the early 1960s.

Camp Joyzelle—For over thirty years, Camp Joyzelle was a summer camp for girls at Monte Ne in Benton County, Arkansas. It closed when Beaver Lake was being built in the early 1960s, and most of the land that had been Camp Joyzelle was ultimately submerged by the lake's water.

Campbell, John Polk—John Polk Campbell was the founder of Springfield, Missouri. Arriving in southwest Missouri from Tennessee in 1830, he settled near the present-day intersection of Jefferson and Water streets. Five years later he laid out Springfield and donated fifty acres to the new town.

Cane Hill, Arkansas—Cane Hill is an unincorporated area in Washington County, about twenty miles southwest of Fayetteville. It is one of the oldest communities in northwest Arkansas, having been settled about 1827. It was also home to one of the first institutions of higher learning in the state, Cane Hill College, which was established in 1850 as Cane Hill Collegiate Institute. The area known as Cane Hill today was originally three rural communities: Cane Hill (later known as White Church), Boonsboro (the current site of the Canehill post office), and Clyde (aka Russellville). None of the communities was ever incorporated.

Cane Hill Murders of 1839—On the night of June 15, 1839, several men came to the cabin of William Wright near Cane Hill, Arkansas, and killed Wright when he came to the door. Wright's wife and a few of the couple's children fled, but the men killed four of the remaining children and robbed the premises. Four men suspected of the heinous crimes were later apprehended and hanged by a "Regulating Company" formed in the wake of the tragedy. The incident still stands as one of the worst mass murders in Ozarks history.

Cane Hill, Engagement at—The Engagement at Cane Hill, often called the Battle of Cane Hill, occurred on November 28, 1862, when Brigadier General James G. Blunt, commanding the 5,000-man Army of the Frontier, surprised Brigadier General John S. Marmaduke and a cavalry force of about 2,000 men while they were gathering winter supplies near Cane Hill, Arkansas. Although casualties were relatively light on both sides, the action was a Union victory, as Marmaduke was forced to abandon the area. Blunt's decision to remain in the area led to the Battle of Prairie Grove nine days later.

Cape Fair, Missouri—Cape Fair is an unincorporated community on Table Rock Lake in Stone County. It was platted in 1892. Jamestown, a forerunner to Cape Fair, was settled in the 1830s at the confluence of the Flat River and the James River. The settlement was largely destroyed by flood in 1844. A new community was later rebuilt on nearby higher ground and named Cape Fair based on an Indian legend that pronounced the confluence of the two rivers a "fair cape," which became "Cape Fair."

Cape Girardeau, Missouri—Established in 1806, Cape Girardeau is a city of about 38,000 people in southeast Cape Girardeau County along the Mississippi River. It is home to Southeast Missouri State University and to the Cape Girardeau Public Schools.

Cape Girardeau County, Missouri—Organized in 1812, several years before statehood, Cape Girardeau County is located in the southeast part of the state along the Mississippi River. Although the boundaries of the Ozarks, as established by geographers, often extend eastward at least to the Mississippi River, people who live in Cape Girardeau County tend not to think of themselves as living in the Ozarks, and the people, places, and events of the county have accordingly been given less attention in this book than counties in the heart of the region.

Caplinger Mills, Missouri—Caplinger Mills is an unincorporated community on the Sac River in northern Cedar County. It was named after Samuel Caplinger, who moved to the site in the 1840s and bought the mill there.

Capps Creek—Capps Creek is a 13.4 mile-long tributary of Shoal Creek that forms in western Barry County, Missouri, and flows into Newton County, where it joins Shoal Creek. It is known for trout fishing and especially for Jolly Mill (listed on the National Register of Historic Places) at the old town site of Jollification in eastern Newton County.

Cardin, Oklahoma—Cardin is a ghost town in northern Ottawa County. It began in 1913 as a boisterous lead mining camp called Tar River. In 1918, the town was officially platted on the land of Quapaw Indian William Oscar Cardin, and in 1920, when the population stood at 2,640, the named was changed to Cardin. After mining was exhausted about 1930, the town faded quickly, and it became a ghost town about 2010 after the last residents accepted federal buyouts of their lead-contaminated land.

Carey, Hobbs—Hobbs Carey was one of several notorious characters to come out of Granby, Missouri, during the post-Civil War years. He rode briefly with the James-Younger gang and participated in the Otterville, Missouri, train robbery.

Carl Junction, Missouri—Carl Junction is a town of about 7,500 people in western Jasper County. It was platted in 1877 by Charles L. Skinner, who gave the town his original German name of Carl and added the word "Junction" because the proposed town was located at the junction of an existing railroad and a proposed railroad spur about nine miles northwest of Joplin. Carl Junction made headlines in 1892 when the fossil remains of two adult and two infant mastodon elephants were found in a mine at the edge of town. They were later displayed at the 1893 Chicago World's Fair. Carl Junction is home to the Carl Junction R-1 Schools.

Carnahan, A.S.J.--A.S.J. Carnahan was a U.S. congressman from southeastern Missouri, serving seven terms during the 1940s and 1950s. Named for Confederate general Albert Sidney Johnston, he was born in Elsinore and was the superintendent of schools there before becoming a congressman. He was the father of Mel Carnahan.

Carnahan, Mel—Mel Carnahan was the 51st governor of Missouri, serving from 1993 to 2000. He was killed in an airplane crash in 2000 while still in office and was subsequently elected posthumously to the U.S. Senate. His wife, Jean, was appointed to fill his office temporarily, and the couple's daughter, Robin, and son Russ also became Missouri politicians. Mel Carnahan was born in Birch Tree, Missouri, and grew up near Elsinore.

Carney Murders—The killing of Jackson Carney and his wife, Cordelia, was an infamous double murder that occurred in Barry County, Missouri, on December 4, 1869. Carney's cousin George Moore was subsequently lynched by vigilantes on the square at Cassville for having committed the murders.

Carroll County, Arkansas—Carroll County was created in 1833 from territory taken from Izard County. Both the new county and its first county seat, Carrolton, were named after Declaration of Independence signer Charles Carroll, who signed his name on the document "Charles Carroll of Carrollton." The continued formation of new counties caused the boundaries of Carroll County to change several times before the current boundaries were defined in 1869. Berryville became the county seat in 1875, and in 1883 the judicial seat was divided into two districts, one at Berryville and one at Eureka Springs.

Carrollton, Arkansas—The first store in what would become Carroll County was established in 1833, and when the county was formed later that year, storeowner Henderson Lafferty persuaded the commissioners to purchase land near his store. The town of Carrollton was laid out on the site, and it became the county seat after a courthouse was built in 1836-37. (County business was conducted at a private residence several miles away for the first few years.) Carrollton prospered for the next twenty-plus years, and although it was devastated by the Civil War, it began to recover until the county seat was moved to Berryville in 1875. The town declined further after a railroad that was built through the area near the turn of the twentieth century bypassed Carrollton. Today, very little is left of the once-thriving town.

Carter County, Missouri—Located in the southeastern part of the state, Carter County was founded in 1859 from parts of Ripley, Shannon, and Wayne counties. Van Buren, which had previously been the seat of Ripley County, became the Carter County seat, and Doniphan was named the new county seat of Ripley.

Carthage, Missouri—Carthage is a town of about 14,400 people and the county seat of Jasper County. The county was formed in 1841, and Carthage was laid out as the seat the following year. It was the site of an infamous double-lynching in 1853, when two slaves were burned at the stake. Today, the town is known for its Maple Leaf Festival held each October and for Marian Days, a reunion of Vietnamese Catholics from across the United States that is held each August. Among the famous people born at Carthage were Hall of Fame baseball pitcher Carl Hubbell, astronaut Janet Kavandi, and zoologist Marlin Perkins, who was host of Mutual of Omaha's *Wild Kingdom.* Carthage is home to the Carthage R-9 Schools.

Carthage, Battle of—The Battle of Carthage was a Civil War battle fought at Carthage, Missouri, on July 5, 1861, between Union forces under Colonel Franz Sigel and Missouri State Guard forces under Governor Claiborne F. Jackson. One of the earliest land battles of the Civil War, the Battle of Carthage was a Southern victory that gave Confederate-allied forces temporary control of southwest Missouri. The Battle of Carthage State Park at the eastern edge of Carthage commemorates the battle, and a downtown museum is also dedicated to preserving the history of the battle. The so-called Second Battle of Carthage, little more than a skirmish, occurred in October 1863.

Carver, George Washington —George Washington Carver was a botanist and educator who is known for his research and promotion of alternative crops to cotton, such a peanuts and soybeans. Born into slavery near Diamond, Missouri, during the Civil War, Carver overcame his humble beginnings to become a famous scientist and the president of Tuskegee Institute.

Cascade, Missouri—Cascade is an unincorporated community in northeast Wayne County. It was settled in the 1880s and prospered around the turn of the twentieth century, boasting a railroad depot, a bank, and several stores. However, little remains to suggest the town's former prosperity.

Casey House—Built about 1855, the Casey House was one of the first houses built in Mountain Home, Arkansas. Today it is maintained by the Baxter County Historical and Genealogical Society, and it is on the National Register of Historic Places.

Cassville, Missouri—Cassville is a town of about 3,265 people and the seat of Barry County. It was established as the county seat in 1845 when Barry County was reduced to its current size by the creation of Lawrence County. Cassville served briefly as Missouri's Confederate state capital during the fall of 1861, and it was a Union post throughout the latter part of the Civil War. Cassville is home to the Cassville R-4 Schools.

Catawissa, Missouri—Catawissa is an unincorporated community in eastern Franklin County a few miles south of Pacific at the northeast edge of the Ozarks. It was founded about 1840 and got a post office in 1860. Mass murderer Bertha Gifford lived at Catawissa when she was arrested in 1928.

Cate Brothers Band—The Cate Brothers Band is a singer/song-writer/musician duo, consisting of twin brothers Earl and Ernie Cate. Born in Fayetteville, Arkansas, and reared in Springdale, they grew up singing country-style rock and roll and were influenced by Ronnie Hawkins, whose band the Hawks spawned Bob Dylan's backup band the Band. The Cates infused their sound with soul, funk, and rhythm and blues, and they became popular performers at clubs and dances during the 1960s and later successful recording artists.

Cathedral Cave—Located near Leasburg, Missouri, Cathedral Cave was operated during the 1930s as a commercial cave in competition with nearby Onondaga Cave, but it is now part of Onondaga Cave State Park with tours offered only on a limited basis.

Cattle Drives—Beginning in the mid-1840s, cattle were driven from Texas along the Shawnee Trail (aka Texas Trail) through eastern Indian Territory to markets in Missouri. In northeast Indian Territory, one branch of the trail turned toward Springfield and St. Louis, and a little farther along, another branch veered toward Sedalia, while the main trail continued north to Kansas City. The Shawnee Trail's peak use occurred during the years immediately before and after the Civil War, but by the early 1870s, the drives had shifted farther west to railroad shipping points in Kansas like Wichita and Abilene.

Caulfield, Missouri—Caulfield in an unincorporated community in western Howell County that was formed in 1930 and named for Missouri governor Henry Stewart Caulfield.

Cave City, Arkansas—Cave City is a town of about 1,900 people located primarily in southern Sharp County but straddling the Independence County line. It was named for the large Crystal River Cave located directly beneath the town, which was a tourist cave promoted for its curative waters during the 1880s. The town was formed in 1891, and today it also incorporates the previous communities of Cedar Grove, Loyal, and Flat Rock. A local landmark, the Crystal River Tourist Court, which was built in 1934 near the cave's entrance, is said to be the oldest motor court in Arkansas. The town boasts of the sweetest watermelons in Arkansas and hosts a watermelon festival each year. Cave City is home to the Cave City School District.

Cave Restaurant—Formerly called Caveman Restaurant, Cave Restaurant is a well-known restaurant located inside a cave near Richland, Missouri.

Cave Spring, Missouri—Cave Spring is an unincorporated community in northwest Greene County. It got its name from a spring that flows from a cave-like depression at the site. Having been founded in the 1840s, it is one of the oldest settlements in the county and was also one of the more important ones during the mid to late 1800s. Today, just a few houses constitute the town.

Cave Spring Park and Current River Cavern—Located just east of Van Buren, Missouri, on U.S. Highway 60, Cave Spring Park and Current River Cavern is a commercial park offering tours of Current River Cavern (formerly Big Spring Onyx Cavern), camping, and other outdoor activities.

Cave Springs, Arkansas—Cave Springs is a town of about 1,700 people in Benton County at the west edge of Rogers and Springdale. The area was settled and called Cave Springs in the 1800s because of two caves in the vicinity and the water that flows from one of them. However, the first Cave Springs post office was not established until 1908, and the town was incorporated in 1910.

Cayuga, Oklahoma—Cayuga is a community of about 140 people in eastern Delaware County on the eastern-most arm of Grand Lake. It was established in the old Seneca Reserve of Indian Territory in the 1880s by the so-called "Millionaire Indian," Mathias Splitlog. Located at the site of a large spring, the settlement was called Cayuga or Cayuga Springs in honor of Splitlog's wife's tribe. The Cayuga Mission Church that Splitlog built at the southern edge of the community was dedicated in 1896, and it is still holding services today.

Cecil, John—John Cecil was the first elected sheriff of Newton County, Arkansas, serving from 1846 to 1850 and again from 1856 to 1858. During the Civil War, he was a Confederate guerrilla leader in northwest Arkansas, and the Union burned the town of Jasper while searching for him and his band.

Cedar County, Missouri—Cedar County is located in the western part of the state on the western outskirts of the Ozarks. It was formed in 1845 from parts of Dade and St. Clair counties and named for Cedar Creek, one of the principal streams in the area. Stockton was named the county seat the following year.

Cedar Springs, Missouri—Cedar Springs is a small community in northern Cedar County at the northwest edge of the Ozarks. It grew up in the 1880s as mineral-water resort, but almost nothing of it remains today.

Cedarville, Arkansas—Cedarville is a town of about 1,395 population in Crawford County at the southern edge of Ozarks. It is home to the Cedarville Public Schools.

Center Creek—Center Creek is a 26.5-mile stream that forms in southeast Jasper County, Missouri, near Sarcoxie and meanders westward across the county to the Kansas state line, where it joins Spring River.

Centerton, Arkansas—Centerton is a town of about 10,000 people in Benton County. Named for its location in the center of the county, it was established in the early 1900s as a railroad stop and processing center for the county's apple industry, and it was once known as the Apple Capital of the World. It declined during the mid-1900s but has since rebounded because of the dramatic growth in northwest Arkansas in recent years. It is home to the Centerton Gamble Elementary School, which is part of the Bentonville School District.

Centertown, Missouri—Centertown is a village of about 280 people in northwest Cole County.

Centerville, Missouri—Centerville is the county seat of Reynolds County. With about 200 people, it is one of the least populous county seats in the state. It is home to the K-8 Centerville R-1 School District. High school students travel to either Ellington or Lesterville.

Central Bible College—Central Bible College was a private, coed Bible college, affiliated with the Assemblies of God Church and located in Springfield, Missouri, from 1922 until 2013, when it merged with nearby Evangel University.

Central City, Missouri—Central City is an extinct town west of Joplin. During the height of the lead and zinc mining boom during the late 1800s and early 1900s, Central City had a population approaching 1,000 people, but almost nothing of the town remains today.

Chadwick, Missouri—Chadwick is an unincorporated community in eastern Christian County. A settlement called Log Town was established just east of present-day Chadwick in 1842. When a railroad came through the area in 1883 to serve its booming lumber industry, Log Town was abandoned, and the people and businesses moved to the new town of Chadwick on the line of the railroad. It was named for railroad foreman John. F. Chadwick. In the mid to late 1880s, Chadwick was a center of activity for the Christian County Bald Knobbers. Chadwick is home to the Chadwick R-1 Schools.

Chamois, Missouri—Chamois is a town of about 400 people in northern Osage County. Founded in 1856, it is the home of the Osage County R-1 School District.

Charity, Missouri—Charity, also known as Hogeye, is an unincorporated community in southern Dallas County.

Chateau on the Lake—Located on Table Rock Lake, Chateau on the Lake is one of the larger, better-known resorts and convention centers in the Branson area.

Cherokee Advocate—*The Cherokee Advocate* was a weekly newspaper published from 1844 to 1906 in both English and Cherokee at Tahlequah, Oklahoma.

Cherokee Bay, Skirmish at—The Skirmish at Cherokee Bay was a minor action of the Civil War involving the Third Missouri State Militia Cavalry under Captain Abijah Johns and an unknown Confederate party near Cherokee Bay in Randolph County, Arkansas, on May 8, 1864. Captain Johns reported one man missing and claimed to have killed twelve Southerners.

Cherokee County, Kansas—Cherokee County, located in the extreme southeast corner of Kansas, is the only county in the state lying partly in the Ozarks. It was formed in 1866 and given its name because a large portion of the Cherokee Neutral Lands were contained within its boundaries. Columbus was named the county seat in 1869 after a disputed contest between Columbus and Baxter Springs.

Cherokee County, Oklahoma—Located at the western edge of the Ozarks, Cherokee County was created from the Cherokee Nation's Tahlequah District at Oklahoma's 1906 Constitutional Convention and named for the Cherokee Nation. Tahlequah, which was also the capital of the Cherokee Nation, was named the county seat.

Cherokee Indians—The Cherokee Indians are a Native American people who historically lived in the southeastern United States. Some of the tribe migrated to Arkansas in 1817, and much of the remainder was removed along the infamous Trail of Tears during the late 1830s to reservations in present-day Oklahoma. The circumstances surrounding the removal split the tribe into two factions, the Treaty Party and the Anti-Treaty Party. The division turned violent after the tribe's arrival in the Indian Nation when three leaders of the Treaty Party were killed by the opposing faction on June 22, 1839. The Treaty Party retaliated, and each side continued to carry out raids on the other sporadically over the next several years. The antipathy was revived when the Civil War broke out, with the Treaty Party generally siding with the Confederacy and the Anti-Treaty Party generally aligning with the U.S. Tahlequah, Oklahoma, is the headquarters of the Cherokee Nation today.

Cherokee Landing State Park—Cherokee Landing State Park is a 146-acre Oklahoma state park south of Tahlequah on Lake Tenkiller.

Cherokee Male and Female Seminaries—The Cherokee Male and Female Seminaries were boarding schools opened in 1851 by the Cherokee tribal government and operated, with an interruption for the

Civil War, until the early 1900s. The male school was located near Tahlequah and the female school near Park Hill.

Cherokee National Historical Society—The Cherokee National Historical Society is an organization established in the mid-1960s to preserve and promote Cherokee history and culture. Its headquarters, called the Cherokee Heritage Center, is located at Park Hill.

Cherokee State Park—Cherokee State Park is a 43-acre Oklahoma State Park on the western shore of Grand Lake in Mayes County.

Cherokee Village, Arkansas—Cherokee Village is a town of about 4,670 people, located primarily in northwest Sharp County but spilling over into Fulton County. It was formed in 1954 as a summer resort and, by the early 1960s, had developed into Arkansas's leading retirement community. Cherokee Village incorporated in the late 1990s.

Cherry Tree, Oklahoma—Cherry Tree is a community of about 885 people in southern Adair County.

Chesapeake, Missouri—Chesapeake is a village on State Highway 174 in eastern Lawrence County. It was once a thriving little village, but about the only enterprise at the location today is a state fish hatchery.

Chewey, Oklahoma—Chewey is a community of about 135 people in northwest Adair County.

Childress, William—William Childress is a journalist and author whose column "Out of the Ozarks," published in the *St. Louis Post-Dispatch*, was twice nominated for a Pulitzer Prize. Some of his other works include a book by the same title, *Out of the Ozarks*, and a family memoir entitled *Ozark Odyssey*. Childress lived many years in McDonald County, Missouri, but now lives in California.

Christ of the Ozarks—Christ of the Ozarks is a statue of Jesus Christ atop Magnetic Mountain on the grounds surrounding the Great Passion Play amphitheater at Eureka Springs, Arkansas. About seven stories tall and weighing about two million pounds, it is one of the Five Sacred Projects founded by Gerald L.K. Smith and his wife, Elna M. Smith and overseen by the Elna M. Smith Foundation. The statue was dedicated in 1966. (See Great Passion Play and Gerald Lyman Kenneth Smith)

Christie, Ned—Ned Christie was a Cherokee Indian who was accused of killing a deputy U.S. marshal in 1887 at Tahlequah,

Oklahoma. He successfully evaded arrest for five years before he was finally killed by a posse of sixteen U.S. marshals in 1892. He is often mentioned as a notorious outlaw, but he is considered a hero by many Cherokee Indians.

Christie, Oklahoma—Christie is a community of about 220 people in Adair County, Oklahoma. Although the notorious Ned Christie lived in the area of present-day Adair County, the community of Christie was apparently named for another Christie family.

Christmas Day Massacre—The so-called Christmas Day Massacre (aka Wilson Massacre) occurred on December 25, 1863, southwest of Doniphan, Missouri, when Major James Wilson and a Union detachment of the Third Missouri State Militia, on a mission to free over a hundred Union prisoners captured a few days earlier at Centerville in Reynolds County, surprised and killed thirty-five Southern soldiers at the camp of Colonel Timothy Reeves's Fifteenth Cavalry Regiment. According to local tradition, a number of civilians present for the holiday gathering were also killed. Near the beginning of General Sterling Price's invasion of Missouri in the fall of 1864, Wilson and several of his men were captured and turned over to Reeves, who had them executed by firing squad southwest of Washington in Franklin County for the killing of his men the previous fall. Union officials in St. Louis, in turn, retaliated by executing a like number of Confederate prisoners there.

Cincinnati, Arkansas—Cincinnati is an unincorporated community in Washington County near the Oklahoma border. Originally called Buzzard Roost and later Silvia, Cincinnati thrived during the late 1800s but declined during the twentieth century. Cincinnati has a population of about 100. It was hit by a devastating tornado on New Year's Eve of 2010.

Clarksville, Arkansas—Clarksville is a town of about 9,250 people and the seat of Johnson County. Although it is home to the University of the Ozarks, it is, strictly speaking, not part of the Ozarks, since it is located in the Arkansas River Valley, but most residents consider the town's northern limits to be at the edge of the Ozarks.

Clearwater Lake—Clearwater Lake is a reservoir on the Black River near Piedmont, Missouri. The dam was completed in 1948, and the lake covers 2.5 square miles.

Cleburne County, Arkansas—Cleburne County, located in north-central Arkansas in the southern part of the Ozarks, was established in 1883 from territory taken from Independence, Van Buren, and White counties. Named for Confederate general Patrick Rowayne Cleburne, it was the last county formed in Arkansas. Sugar Loaf, now Heber Springs, was named the county seat.

Cleburne County Draft War—The Cleburne County Draft War was a violent encounter during the summer of 1918 between local officials and Jehovah's Witnesses, then called Russellites, who were resisting conscription into military service during World War I. On July 7, Sheriff Jasper Duke led a small posse to the rural home of Tom Adkisson, whose son Bliss was several months delinquent in registering for the draft. A shootout ensued during which posse member Porter Hazlewood was killed. With both sides reinforced, the gunfight was renewed later the same day before the Russellites fled into the countryside. They were rounded up or turned themselves in over the next few days, and Bliss Adkission was convicted of second degree murder in the case.

Clementine, Missouri—Clementine was a small community along old Route 66 at the western edge of Phelps County. It became known as "Basketville" because of the handcrafted baskets sold at a roadside store there, but the community died out after I-44 was built.

Cleora, Oklahoma—Cleora is a community of about 1,115 people on the north shore of Grand Lake in northwest Delaware County. A post office was established at the site in 1900, and the place was named for Cleora Ann Lunday, a sister of the postmaster. When the railroad came through the area in 1910, most of the town moved a short distance to where the train depot was located. Some of the townspeople moved again to nearby higher ground when Grand Lake was built in the 1930s, but others simply moved away.

Clever, Missouri—Clever is a town of about 2,140 people in western Christian County. It was established in the 1890s but was not platted and officially organized until the first decade of the 1900s after a railroad was laid out through the town. The town has grown rapidly in recent years, the population more than doubling between 2000 and 2010. Clever is home to the Clever R-5 Schools. Television actor Robert Mandan was born at Clever.

Clifty, Arkansas—Clifty is an unincorporated community in northern Madison County. Major League Baseball player Arky Vaughan was a native of Clifty.

Climax Springs, Missouri—Climax Springs is a town in western Camden County. It was founded during the mineral-water craze of the 1880s at the site of a large spring, and it enjoyed several years of popularity as a resort. The town continued to thrive after its popularity as a resort declined, but the town, too, declined during the latter part of the twentieth century. Today it has a population of less than 100, but it is still home to the Climax Springs R-4 School District.

Clinton, Arkansas—Clinton is a town of about 2,600 people, the county seat of Van Buren County, and the most populous community in the county. A post office was established at the site in 1833, and the town was named the county seat in 1844. It was first incorporated in 1851. An EF-4 tornado struck Clinton in 2008, killing three people and destroying many homes and buildings. The town is home to the Clinton Public Schools.

Clinton, Bill—William Jefferson "Bill" Clinton was president of the United States from 1993 to 2001 and previously a longtime governor of Arkansas. Although he was not born in the Ozarks, he taught law in the early to mid-1970s at the University of Arkansas at Fayetteville, and he and his wife, Hillary Rodham Clinton, were married there in 1975.

Clinton House Museum—Located in Fayetteville, Arkansas, the Clinton House Museum preserves the home where Bill and Hillary Rodham Clinton first lived after they were married.

Clover Bend, Arkansas—Clover Bend is an unincorporated community in southern Lawrence County. Although it was never an incorporated town, it is the oldest settlement in the county and was briefly the county seat during Reconstruction. It was first settled during the 1820s as a landing on the Black River and was named after the many bends on the river in the area. A New Deal program revitalized Clover Bend during the Depression, but the community experienced a gradual downturn after funds for the program dried up. The Clover Bend Schools closed in 1983, and the Clover Bend Historic Preservation Association was soon formed to preserve the community as the Clover Bend Historic District.

Clum, Ed—Ed Clum was the perpetrator of one of the most notorious crimes in Ozarks history when he murdered his friend J. J. White and White's seventeen-year-old fiancée, Ella Bowe, south of Pierce City, Missouri, in 1886. White had run off with Clum's wife, leaving their home in New York state to settle in Missouri. When Mrs. Clum grew gravely ill, her husband was summoned, and upon his arrival at the White farm near Pierce City, he bore the insult of his betrayal at first and even maintained a charade of friendship with White. After Clum's wife died, however, and White announced his intention to marry Miss Bowe, Clum killed them both and was hanged for the double murder the next spring on the public square in Cassville.

Hanging of Ed Clum at Cassville, 1887. *Courtesy Fields' Photo Archives.*

Cobbites—The Cobbites were a bizarre and fanatical religious group that settled near Searcy in White County, Arkansas, in 1876 under the leadership of a Reverend Cobb. They believed that sanctification could only come through Cobb to the women and then to the rest of the group through the women, and among their strange practices was walking back and forth on rooftops blindfolded to prove that they were protected by God. The group dissolved after a curious visitor to their settlement was murdered and two of the Cobbites were killed in retaliation by a mob.

Coffee, John T.—A lawyer and state legislator from Dade County, Missouri, before the Civil War, John T. Coffee became a colonel in the Missouri State Guard at the beginning of the war. When the State Guard began to dissolve in late 1861 and early 1862, Coffee balked at entering Confederate service and remained in southwest Missouri with the remnants of his regiment recruiting and carrying on an irregular, guerrilla-type warfare. He finally joined the Confederacy late in 1862, at least nominally. However, he never fully adapted to Confederate service and continued to operate independently much of the time.

Colcord, Oklahoma—Colcord is a town of about 820 people in southern Delaware County. The community of Row, a predecessor of Colcord, was established in the 1890s and was a thriving little town when a road (later known as State Highway 116) was built about a mile to the south and a new town platted along the new road. Known as Little Tulsa, the new town grew during the 1920s, and in the 1928 its name was changed to Colcord in honor of area ranch owner Charles Francis Colcord. The towns feuded for some time, but Colcord eventually absorbed most of the residents of Row. Colcord is home to the Colcord Public Schools and the Talbot Library and Museum, which preserves the history of northeast Oklahoma.

Cole Camp, Missouri—Cole Camp is a town of about 1,120 people in northeast Benton County in the northern outskirts of the Ozarks. It was laid out in 1857 and named after Cole Camp Creek, a nearby stream which, in turn, got its name because a family named Cole had reportedly camped there. Cole Camp hosts several annual festivals, including an Oktoberfest each October, which highlight the town's German heritage. It is home to the Cole Camp R-1 School District.

Cole Camp, Skirmish at—The Skirmish at Cole Camp was a Civil War action that occurred on June 19, 1861, at Cole Camp in Benton County, Missouri, between a Union home guard force of about 500 men and a battalion of Missouri State Guard recruits numbering about 350. The Southerners routed the home guards, clearing a path for Governor Claiborne F. Jackson and his larger Missouri State Guard force, who were retreating toward southwest Missouri after their defeat at the Battle of Boonville on June 17.

Cole County, Missouri—Located in central Missouri bordering the south bank of the Missouri River, Cole County was formed in 1820 from Cooper County and named for pioneer Stephen Cole. The county seat was located at Marion but was moved in 1828 to Jefferson City, which had been named the state capital in 1826.

College of the Ozarks—College of the Ozarks is a private, Christian, liberal-arts college located at Point Lookout, Missouri, just south of Branson. It was established in 1906 as a high school, became a junior college in 1956, became a four-year college in 1965, and changed its name from School of the Ozarks to College of the Ozarks in 1990. Many students at CofO, sometimes called "Hard Work University," pay no tuition but instead earn their education through a work-study program.

Aerial view of College of the Ozarks. *Courtesy Wikimedia.*

Collins, Missouri—Collins is a village of about 160 people in southeast St. Clair County. Located at the intersection of U.S. Highways 13 and 54, it was once a thriving community with a K-12 public school, but now its main commerce consists of a few businesses at the junction, which depend on passing motorists for their survival.

Collins Kids—The Collins Kids (Lorrie and Larry Collins) was a sister-brother rockabilly music act from Tahlequah, Oklahoma, that became famous during the 1950s with appearances on *The Ozark Jubilee*, *The Adventures of Ozzie and Harriet*, and other national TV and radio programs.

Coleman, William O.—William O. Coleman was a Missouri State Guard and Confederate officer who conducted guerrilla warfare in south central Missouri during the Civil War.

Columbia, Arkansas—Columbia was an important settlement during the early 1800s that was located on Fourche Creek about eight miles north of present-day Pocahontas in Randolph County. It is sometimes called the second oldest settlement in northeast Arkansas and was the site of the first Baptist Church in Arkansas. It began to decline after Pocahontas was made the county seat of newly formed Randolph County in the mid-1830s.

Combs, Cass and Eastern Railroad—Originally called the Black Mountain and Eastern, the Combs, Cass and Eastern Railroad was a logging railroad that operated from 1913 to the late 1920s from Combs, Arkansas, to Cass, Arkansas, in Madison and Franklin counties. It had the distinction of being the last railroad built in northwest Arkansas, reaching the highest elevation of any railroad in the region, and having the youngest railroad president in the United States, future U.S. senator J. William Fulbright, who took over from his father at the age of eighteen.

Commerce, Oklahoma—Commerce is a town of about 2,470 people in Ottawa County. It started as a mining camp called Hattonville in 1906. Its first post office, established in 1913, was called North Miami. However, the name was changed to Commerce the next year, and a new North Miami sprang up between Commerce and Miami. Famous baseball player Mickey Mantle grew up in Commerce. The town is home to the Commerce Public Schools.

Competition, Missouri—Competition is an unincorporated community in southeast Laclede County. It was founded before the Civil War as Newburg, but the name was changed to Competition shortly after the war when the town wanted to establish a post office and a town named Newburg already existed. Competition was a thriving village during the late 1800s and early 1900s and had a high school for several years, but today the community scarcely survives.

Community and Conflict—Community and Conflict is a digital collection of letters, diaries, court cases, and other material pertaining to the Civil War in the Ozarks and the Trans-Mississippi theater. The collection is the collaborative effort of numerous libraries, museums, and historical organizations throughout the region and beyond. The website (www.ozarkscivilwar.org) is maintained by the Springfield-Greene County Library District.

Compton, Neil Ernest—See the Ozark Society.

Concord, Arkansas—Concord is a town of about 255 people in northeast Cleburne County. Wayne Raney, a country singer and harmonica player known for the song "Why Don't You Haul Off and Love Me," was born at Wolf Bayou near Concord and attended school at Concord. The town is home to the Concord School District.

Confederate Cemetery, Fayetteville—The Fayetteville Confederate Cemetery was established in Fayetteville in 1878 by the Southern Memorial Association of Washington County as a burial place for Confederate veterans or Confederate soldiers who had been killed during the Civil War. The first burials were re-interments of soldiers who had been killed in area battles like Pea Ridge and initially buried near where they died. The Confederate Cemetery is located about a mile and half from the Fayetteville National Cemetery, and it is still under the care of the Southern Memorial Association, thought to be the oldest organization of its type in continual operation. A similar Confederate Cemetery in Springfield, Missouri, was established in 1871 adjacent to the National Cemetery there, but it is now part of the Springfield National Cemetery.

Connor Hotel Collapse—The nine-story Connor Hotel, which was being prepared for demolition in Joplin, Missouri, to make way for a public library, collapsed prematurely on November 11, 1978, burying three workers beneath the rubble. The collapse and the subsequent rescue effort made national headlines, especially when one of the workers was found alive three and a half days later. The other two, it was ascertained, had died instantly.

Conway, Missouri—Conway is a town of about 800 people in southwest Laclede County. It was laid out in 1869 and named for the first storekeeper. Conway holds an annual festival, usually in September, called Old Fashioned Days. The town is home to the Laclede County R-1 School District, which includes Conway High School.

Conway County, Arkansas—Only the northern part of Conway County, located along the Arkansas River, is in the Ozarks.

Cook, Alfred—Alfred Cook was a Confederate guerrilla leader in the Taney County, Missouri, area during the Civil War.

Cook, Bill—Bill Cook was a notorious mass murderer from Joplin, Missouri. In early January of 1951, he killed five members of an Illinois family, whom he had flagged down along Route 66, and he dumped their bodies in an abandoned mine shaft in Joplin. Later he was executed in California for killing a man there.

Mass murderer Bill Cook. *Courtesy Jim Hounschell.*

Cookson, Oklahoma—Cookson is a small community in southeastern Cherokee County. A post office was established at the site about 1895, and it was reportedly named after the first postmaster, John H. Cookson.

Cookson Hills—The Cookson Hills are a western extension of the Boston Mountains, which in turn constitute the southern portion of the Ozarks. In other words, the Boston Mountains are called the Cookson Hills in Oklahoma.

Cook Station, Missouri—Cook Station is an unincorporated community in southern Crawford County. It was named after Christopher Columbus Cook, who settled in the area in the 1850s. The settlement became known as Cook Station after the Civil War when a branch railroad from Cuba to Salem was constructed through the area. The name became official in 1874 when the community was granted a post office. The village prospered during the early 1900s but has declined since the train stopped coming through and the school closed during the mid-1900s.

Cooper, Douglas H.—Douglas Cooper was a Confederate general during the Civil War. He led his Indian brigade at the Battle of Pea Ridge and commanded all Southern forces at the First Battle of Newtonia in September 1862.

Cooper County, Missouri—Cooper County, located at the north edge of the Ozarks along the Missouri River, was organized in 1818 from territory taken from Howard County and named for brothers Benjamin and Sarshall Cooper. Boonville became the county seat the following year.

Copeland, Lori—Lori Copeland is a best-selling author of romance and Christian romance novels. She lives in Springfield, Missouri.

Copeland, Oklahoma—Copeland is a community of about 1,630 people located on the Grand Lake of the Cherokees in Delaware County. Also called Copeland Switch, it was founded as a railroad town and named for local resident D.R. Copeland.

Corsicana, Missouri—Corsicana is a small community in western Barry County. Originally called Gadfly, it was the site of a Union outpost during the Civil War and was a thriving little village after the war. The name was changed to Corsicana in 1876, and soon afterward the town began to decline.

Cosmic Cavern—Cosmic Cavern is a commercial cave located about six miles northeast of Berryville, Arkansas. The cave features two lakes, and, at 64 degrees year-round, it is the warmest cave in the Ozarks.

Stalactites inside Cosmic Cavern. *Courtesy of Cosmic Cavern.*

Cotter, Arkansas—Cotter is a town of about 1,080 people located on the White River in eastern Baxter County. A post office was established at the site in 1902, and people began to settle there in anticipation of the coming of the Missouri-Pacific Railroad. The town was incorporated in 1905 and named after William Cotter, a railroad official. The town is home to the Cotter Public School District.

Couch, Missouri—Laid out by and named for G.W. Couch, Couch is an unincorporated community in southern Oregon County about eight miles north of the Arkansas line. It is home to the Couch R-1 Schools.

Courtois Creek—Courtois Creek (pronounced Coort-a-way) is a stream approximately 39 miles long that rises in northern Iron County, Missouri, and flows generally northward through Washington and into Crawford County, where it joins Huzzah Creek just a mile or two from the latter's confluence with the Meramec River. It shares its name with the nearby community of Courtois.

Covenant, the Sword, and the Arm of the Lord—The Covenant, the Sword, and the Arm of the Lord is a militia-style group that was active in northern Arkansas during the 1970s and 1980s. Started by minister James Ellison, the group supported the American Christian Patriot Movement, whose followers tend to vilify Jews and non-whites as children of Satan and are generally hostile to any government above the county level. A member of the Covenant, the Sword, and the Arm of the Lord killed an Arkansas State Police trooper in 1984 and was eventually executed for the crime. In 1985, law enforcement raided the group's compound in Marion County, resulting in numerous indictments against members of the group.

Crabb, Benjamin—Benjamin Crabb was colonel of the Nineteenth Iowa Volunteer Infantry during the Civil War and was post commander at Springfield at the time of the Battle of Springfield in January 1863.

Crane, Missouri—Crane is a town of about 1,400 people located on Crane Creek in northern Stone County. Dating from the late nineteenth century, it was originally called Hickory Grove but around 1890 changed its name to match the creek it was located on when citizens sought a post office and discovered that another Missouri town named Hickory Grove already existed. Crane is home to the Crane R-3 School District and to an annual celebration called the Crane Broiler Festival.

Crane Creek—Crane Creek, a tributary of the James River, is located in Stone County, Missouri, and flows through the town of Crane. There is also a Crane Creek in Hickory County near Hermitage.

Crawford County, Arkansas—Crawford County is located in the northwest part of the state bordering Oklahoma. It was created in 1820 and named for William F. Crawford, who was then the U.S. secretary of the treasury. Van Buren was named the county seat in 1837. Approximately the northern two-thirds of the county is located in the Ozarks, with the rest lying in the Arkansas River Valley.

Crawford County, Missouri—Located in the east central part of the state, Crawford County was formed in 1829 from a part of Gasconade County and named for William H. Crawford, a U.S. senator from Georgia. The county seat of Steelville was laid out in 1836. Three early courthouses burned, and the original portion of the current courthouse was built in 1885-1886.

Crescent College and Conservatory—The Crescent College and Conservatory was an exclusive boarding school for young women that operated out of the Crescent Hotel from 1908 to 1928.

Crescent Hotel—The Crescent Hotel is a historic hotel in Eureka Springs, Arkansas. Opened in 1886 as a luxury resort hotel, it was used during different periods of the first half of the twentieth century as a women's college and as a "cancer hospital" run by a quack doctor. Said by some to be haunted by ghosts, the hotel was in a state of disrepair during the mid-twentieth century but has since been restored.

Crescent Hotel, circa 1886. *Courtesy Wikimedia.*

Crittenden, Thomas Theodore—Thomas Theodore Crittenden served in southwest Missouri as a Union colonel in the Seventh Missouri State Militia during the mid-part of the Civil War. He was also governor of Missouri from 1881 to 1885.

Crocker, Missouri—Crocker is a town of about 1,000 people on Highway 17 in northern Pulaski County. It was founded in 1869 as a station along the Southwest Pacific Railroad. Today, it is home to the Crocker R-2 Schools.

Crooked Creek Structure—See Weaubleau-Osceola Structure

Crop Farming—Corn was the primary crop grown by early settlers in the Ozarks, but crops like wheat, sorghum, flax, cotton, tobacco, and hemp were grown in various parts of the region as well. Until the late 1800s, most farming was general farming on small acreages, meaning that a variety of crops were raised, mostly for the needs of the farmer's own family or for sale locally. The rise of specialization and large-scale commercial farming generally coincided with the coming of railroads, but general farming still dominated until about the 1940s. See also Apple Industry, Tomato Industry, and Strawberry Industry.

Cross Roads, Skirmish at—The Skirmish at Cross Roads was a minor Civil War action that occurred on March 27, 1864, southwest of Batesville, Arkansas, between a detachment of the Eleventh Missouri Cavalry and Confederate guerillas under a man named Smith. The guerrilla band was scattered and several of them killed.

Cross Timbers, Missouri—Cross Timbers is a small town on Highway 65 in Hickory County. At one time it had a high school and was a thriving little community, but it barely survives nowadays.

Crushed Stone Mining—Crushed stone mining of limestone and other rock formations has been carried out in quarries throughout the Ozarks, particularly the Boston Mountain sub-region of the Ozarks in northern Arkansas, since the 1800s.

Crystal Bridges Museum—Crystal Bridges Museum is a museum of American art in Bentonville, Arkansas, established largely through the effort and philanthropy of Alice Walton, daughter of Wal-Mart founder Sam Walton. Opened in 2011, Crystal Bridges takes its name from the nearby Crystal Spring and the bridge construction incorporated into the design of the museum building.

Crystal Cave—Crystal Cave is a cave in Greene County, Missouri, located on Highway H about six miles north of Springfield. The cave was opened to the public in 1893 and remained open for tourists for well over a hundred years, until it closed about 2010. There is also a Crystal Cave in Joplin that operated as a commercial cave in the early 1900s, but, out of safety concerns, the entrance was filled in and the cave closed many years ago.

Crystal Caverns—Crystal Caverns is a former show cave near Cassville, Missouri, that is now leased by the Missouri Caves and Karst Conservancy.

Crystal City, Missouri—Crystal City is a town of about 4,900 people in Jefferson County on the Mississippi River. It and its neighbor, Festus, are often called the Twin Cities. Although some maps show the Ozarks extending all the way to the Mississippi River in the area around Crystal City and Festus, other maps do not, and the citizens of the area usually do not think of themselves as residing in the Ozarks.

Cuba, Missouri—Cuba is a town of about 3,500 people located in Crawford County on old Route 66. The town was founded prior to the Civil War and was named for the island of Cuba. Called the Route 66 Mural City, Cuba is known for its numerous murals painted on the town's buildings, several of which celebrate visits to the town by well-known people like President Truman and Amelia Earhart. Cuba was the site of the first Adopt a Highway program in Missouri. Today, the town hosts an annual festival called the Route 66 Cuba Fest, and it is home to the Crawford County R-2 Schools.

Cummings, Robert—Robert "Bob" Cummings was a film and television actor. He was known for movies like *Dial M for Murder* during the 1940s and 1950s and for his television career during the 1950s, notably the *Bob Cummings Show*. Cummings was born and grew up in Joplin, Missouri, and briefly attended Drury College in Springfield.

Cureall, Missouri—Also known as Cureall Springs, Cureall is a historic community in Howell County that sprang up about fourteen miles southwest of West Plains during the mineral water craze of the early 1880s. The Cureall Cemetery is about the only thing left to mark the location.

Current View, Missouri—Current View is a small village in southern Ripley County near the Arkansas border. The area was originally called Buck Skull and was the site of the historic Pitman Ferry, which crossed the Current River at the Missouri-Arkansas line along the old Military Road. Several skirmishes were fought at or near the site on the Arkansas side in Randolph County during the Civil War. Today, the area on the Missouri side is called Current View, while a small community on the Arkansas side is named Pitman.

Current River—The Current River forms at Montauk State Park in southwest Dent County and flows in a southeasterly direction through southeastern Missouri into Arkansas, where it empties into the Black

River near Pocahontas. The Current is popular for canoeing, fishing, and other outdoor activities.

Current River Float Trip of Governor Hadley—In 1909, Missouri governor Herbert S. Hadley took a float trip on the Current River that drew national attention and spurred the popularity of float fishing on Ozarks streams.

Current River State Park—Current River State Park is a Missouri state park located on the Current River north of Eminence in Shannon County at the site of a former corporate retreat. Most of the buildings at the park date from the late 1930s and early 1940s.

Curtis, Samuel R.—Samuel R. Curtis was a Union general during the Civil War. Commanding the Army of the Southwest, he drove the Confederates out of Springfield, Missouri, in February of 1862 and pursued them into Arkansas, where he led the victorious Federals at the Battle of Pea Ridge in March. Curtis also commanded the Army of the Frontier during Sterling Price's 1864 invasion of Missouri.

Cushing, Charles Phelps—Charles Phelps Cushing was a Kansas City newspaperman during the first half of the twentieth century who was known for his photographs of the Ozarks and Ozarks people.

Cushman, Arkansas—Cushman is a town of about 450 people in northwest Independence County. It was established in the 1880s as a center for the area's manganese mining. Originally called Minersville, it changed its name to Cushman when the town was incorporated in 1906. Cushman's estimated population exceeded 2,000 during the boom mining years around World War I, but mining and the town declined during the Depression and after World War II. Cushman formerly had its own school district but was annexed into Batesville after the 2008-2009 school year.

D

Dablemont, Larry—Larry Dablemont is an outdoor writer who lives in the Bolivar, Missouri, area. His weekly column appears in various newspapers across the Ozarks, and he has written several books about the Ozarks outdoors.

Daboll, Raymond Franklin—Raymond Franklin Daboll, often known as R.F.D., was one of the most talented calligraphers in

America. His work included ads in national magazines, book covers, and newspaper mastheads. He moved to Independence County, Arkansas, in 1952 and proclaimed himself the "Ozarkalligrapher." He died in 1982 and is buried at Batesville.

Dade County, Missouri—Dade County was formed in 1841 from territory taken from Greene County, and Greenfield was shortly afterwards named the county seat because of its central location. The county was named for Major Francis L. Dade, who was killed during the Second Seminole War.

Dadeville, Missouri—Dadeville is a town in eastern Dade County, Missouri. It was established before the Civil War as Melville, and during the war, it was raided twice by Confederate bushwhackers under Kinch West. In 1865, the name of the town was changed to Dadeville, supposedly because postal workers kept getting it confused with another town named Millville. Home to the Dadeville R-2 School District, Dadeville has a current population of slightly over 200.

Dailey, Janet—Janet Daily was the author of numerous best-selling romance novels. She lived the last thirty-five years of her life in Branson, Missouri, and died there in 2013.

Dairy Farming—Early settlers in the Ozarks often had one or two cows, along with a variety of other animals, which they milked to supply dairy products for their own families, but high-quality dairy cattle did not arrive in the region in large numbers until about 1900. Commercial dairying began shortly afterwards, and the Ozarks, particularly the southwest Missouri area around Springfield, soon became one of the most important dairy centers in the country. By 1940, nearly every town with a railroad and a population of 1,500 people or more had a creamery. However, the industry began to decline in the Ozarks during the 1950s as large dairy operations started shifting to lands in the West. Today, most cattle farmers in the Ozarks raise beef.

Daisy Airgun Museum—The Daisy Airgun Museum is located in downtown Rogers, Arkansas. The museum preserves the history of Daisy airguns and displays Daisy memorabilia. The corporate headquarters of Daisy Outdoor Products, maker of Daisy airguns, is also located in Rogers.

Daisy Airgun Museum in Rogers. *Courtesy Daisy Outdoor Products.*

Dallas County, Missouri—Located north of Springfield in southwest Missouri, Dallas County was organized about 1841 as Niangua County from territory taken from Polk County, but it was renamed Dallas in late 1844 after George M. Dallas, who was then the vice-president-elect of the United States. After Dallas County issued bonds in 1869 to finance a railroad through the county, the railroad was never built, and the county and its citizens, refusing to pay the bonds, became involved in a noted dispute with bondholders that lasted until 1919, when a compromise was finally reached.

Dalton, Arkansas—Dalton is a small community in north Randolph County. It is the site of the Rice-Upshaw house, which was built circa 1826 and is one of the two oldest standing structures in Arkansas.

Damascus, Arkansas—Damascus is a town of about 385 people located on U.S. Highway 65 on the Faulkner-Van Buren county line.

Daniel, Lucy J.—Lucy J. Daniel was a stone carver who sculpted the Liberty of Freedom statue at Pea Ridge National Military Park, which was dedicated at a reunion of Civil War veterans in 1889.

Dark, John William "Bill"—Bill Dark was Confederate guerrilla from Searcy County, Arkansas, who terrorized Searcy and other counties of north central Arkansas from June 1862 until his death in January of 1863. In the distorted legend of Bill Dark that has been handed down, perpetuated partly by folksinger Jimmy Driftwood,

Dark was a deserter from the Confederate army and a ruthless "jayhawker," a term usually applied to Union partisans, and he was, in fact, killed by a member of a Southern home guard unit. The scant available documentary evidence shows, however, that Dark was an irregular Confederate in Colonel John T. Coffee's command.

Daugherty, James Alexander—James Alexander Daugherty was a miner, bank president, civic leader, and politician from Carterville, Missouri. He was a U.S. Congressman from southwest Missouri from 1911 to 1913, while serving simultaneously as president of the First National Bank of Carterville.

Daugherty, Roy "Arkansas Tom"—Roy "Arkansas Tom" Daugherty was a notorious outlaw who operated in Oklahoma and southwest Missouri during the late 1800s and early 1900s. He spent time in prison for his part in the Doolin gang's shootout at Ingalls, Oklahoma Territory, during the 1890s, robbed several banks in southwest Missouri around 1920, and was killed in a shootout with police at Joplin in 1924.

Davidsonville, Arkansas—Davidsonville was a historic town located in present-day Randolph County. Founded in 1815, it was, while still a part of Missouri Territory, the site of the first post office in what would become Arkansas and later was the site of the first courthouse in Arkansas Territory. It was abandoned by the 1830s. Today, the site is preserved by the Davidsonville Historic State Park.

Davis, Lowell—See Red Oak II.

Davisville, Missouri—Davisville is an unincorporated community in the Mark Twain National Forest in southeast Crawford County. The post office, officially named Pucky Huddle, is located inside the Davisville General Store, an old-time general store where you can still find about anything you want.

Day, Clyde "Pea Ridge"—Clyde "Pea Ridge" Day was a colorful baseball pitcher who had two stints in the Major Leagues from 1924 to 1931. He grew up in Pea Ridge, Arkansas, which gave him his nickname. Known for his celebratory yells while on the mound, he was also nicknamed the "hog-calling pitcher." He committed suicide in 1934 after unsuccessful surgery to restore his pitching arm.

Deane, Ernie—Ernest Cecil "Ernie" Deane was an Arkansas journalist best known for his "Arkansas Traveler" column published in the *Arkansas Gazette* during the 1950s and 1960s and his "Ozarks

Country" column published in the *Morning News of Northwest Arkansas* (formerly the *Springdale Morning News*) from 1970 until shortly before his death in 1991. He was also the author of several books about Arkansas and the Ozarks.

Decatur, Arkansas—Decatur is a town of about 1,700 people in western Benton County. The settlement dates from at least 1869, when a Baptist church was organized at the site. The place was known then as Corner Springs, but when the community applied for a post office in 1882, the name Corner Springs was rejected, and the place was renamed Decatur after War of 1812 naval hero Stephen Decatur. The town has hosted a popular barbecue festival each summer for many years. Decatur is home to the Decatur School District.

Decaturville, Missouri—Decaturville is an unincorporated community in Camden County, on State Highway 5 south of Camdenton. It was founded before the Civil War and named for Stephen Decatur, U.S. naval hero of the War of 1812.

Decaturville Dome—See Weaubleau-Osceola Structure.

Delassus, Missouri—Delassus (aka De Lassus) is a small community in St. Francois County. It was laid off in 1869 by A. D. De Lassus.

Delaware County, Oklahoma—Located in the northeastern part of the state, Delaware County was established at statehood in 1907 from the Delaware District of the Cherokee Nation. The district and the county were named after the Delaware tribe, which inhabited the area in small numbers prior to the arrival of the Cherokee. Grove was the first county seat, but Jay became the permanent county seat a few years later.

Delaware Town, Missouri—Originally a Delaware Indian village, Delaware Town, located on the James River about seven miles east of Billings, was the first white settlement in the Springfield Plateau.

Dellinger, Samuel Claudius—Samuel Claudius Dellinger was curator of the University of Arkansas Museum for 30 years. He was very interested in archaeology, and his field crews collected many artifacts from the Ozarks. He also helped organize the first Ozarks folklore meeting in Arkansas in 1928.

Delta, Missouri—Delta is a town of about 440 people in southern Cape Girardeau County. Originally called Deray, it is home to the Delta R-5 Schools.

Dennard, Arkansas—Dennard is a community of about 530 people on U.S. Highway 65 in northern Van Buren County.

Dennis, Oklahoma—Dennis is a community of about 185 people located on Grand Lake of the Cherokees in Delaware County about six miles southwest of Grove. A post office was established at the site in 1914 and named after local resident Peter Dennis.

Dent County, Missouri—Dent County, located in the south central part of the state, was founded in 1851 from territory taken from Crawford and Shannon counties and named for Lewis Dent, the new county's first representative to the state legislature. Salem was laid out as the county seat shortly afterwards, and the first courthouse was built in 1853. This courthouse, like many throughout Missouri, was burned during the Civil War.

Denton, Arkansas—Denton was a historic community located about six miles west of Powhatan in Lawrence County. One of the county's earliest communities, it was established before the Civil War and grew into a thriving town in the late 1800s. It gradually declined throughout the first half of the twentieth century until today about the only thing that remains is the nearby Bethel Cemetery, where many former residents were buried.

Denton, Ivan—Ivan Denton was a pioneering Ozarks woodcarver specializing in wildlife and western scenes. Considered one of the most prominent artists in Arkansas, he lived most of his life in Crawford County and died there in 2013.

Des Arc, Missouri—Des Arc is a village of about 175 people in southern Iron County. The area was settled during the early 1800s, but the village was not named Des Arc until 1871 or incorporated until 1889.

De Soto, Missouri—De Soto is a town of about 6,500 people in southern Jefferson County. The first settler arrived in the area in 1803. Named for explorer Hernando De Soto, the town was organized in 1857 and incorporated in 1869. Jay Nixon, 55th and current governor of Missouri, was born and reared in De Soto. The town was also the birthplace of famous Major League Baseball player Whitey Ford. De Soto is called the Fountain City because of its artesian wells. It is home to the De Soto Public School District 73.

De Soto, Hernando—Hernando de Soto was a Spanish explorer who, around 1540, led the first European expedition deep into the territory of what would become the United States. He and his men were the first documented Europeans to cross the Mississippi River and the first to set foot in what would become Arkansas. They ranged at least as far north as the Arkansas River and perhaps into the southern portion of the Ozarks.

Devil's Backbone Wilderness Area—Named for a long, narrow ridge known locally as the Devil's Backbone and managed by the U.S. Forest Service, the Devil's Backbone Wilderness Area encompasses about 6,700 acres of protected wilderness within the Mark Twain National Forest near Dora, Missouri.

Devil's Den—Located in southwestern Webster County, Missouri, Devil's Den is a large sinkhole, actually a small collapsed cave, enclosed by steep rock except for a single narrow passageway. A small lake at one end of the enclosure is about 300 feet in diameter, and the enclosure itself covers about an acre. The water level is said sometimes to rise and sink mysteriously, irrespective of whether there has been recent rain in the area.

Devil's Den State Park—Devil's Den State Park is a state park in southern Washington County, Arkansas, in the Lee Creek Valley. It was built in 1933 by the Civilian Conservation Corps and is open year-round for outdoor activities like hiking and picnicking. The Devil's Den Cave, now closed to the public, is located at the site.

Waterfall at Devil's Den State Park. *Courtesy Wikimedia.*

Devil's Elbow, Missouri—Devil's Elbow is an unincorporated village located on old Route 66 in Pulaski County. Situated on the Big Piney River, it was named for a sharp bend in the river.

Devil's Honeycomb—See Hughes Mountain Natural Area

Devil's Tollgate—See Taum Sauk Mountain

Devil's Well—Located near Akers in northwest Shannon County, Missouri, Devils' Well was formed when the roof of a cave containing an underground lake collapsed. The result is a large sinkhole with an opening in the bottom through which one can view the lake. A trail leads from Devil's Well to Cave Spring on the Current River.

Dewey Short Visitor Center—Located near Table Rock Dam southwest of Branson, Missouri, the Dewey Short Visitor Center tells the story of Table Rock Lake and Ozarks rivers.

Diamond, Missouri—Diamond is a town of about 900 people in Newton County. It is known for its proximity to the George Washington Carver National Monument. Diamond Grove, a forerunner to Diamond, was a small community located about two or three miles northwest of the present town. Diamond is home to the Diamond R-4 Schools.

Diamond Cave—Diamond Cave is a large cave on Henson Creek near Jasper, Arkansas. Presumably named for the brilliant display caused by the mineral water that drips from the ceiling, Diamond Cave was discovered during the mid-1800s. It opened for tours in 1925 and was very popular during the twenties and thirties. It closed to commercial tours during the mid-1990s.

Diamond City, Arkansas—Diamond City is a town of about 800 people in northern Boone County. It is located on the banks of Bull Shoals Lake at the former site of Dubuque, a historic town that dissolved after the Civil War. Diamond City sprang up as a resort town after the lake was completed in 1952. Originally called Sugar Loaf, the town became Diamond City in the 1960s.

Diamond Grove Prairie Conservation Area—Diamond Grove Prairie Conservation Area preserves a tallgrass prairie remnant of the grassland that covered much the Springfield Plateau years ago. It is located northwest of Diamond, Missouri, in an area where a community named Diamond Grove was once situated.

Diggins, Missouri—Diggins is a village in southern Webster County with a population of about 300. It was platted in 1887 as a town along the Kansas City, Springfield and Memphis Railroad and was a thriving little community until about the time of the Depression. The family of Sam Walton, founder of Wal-Mart, lived at Diggins prior to Sam's birth. Nowadays, Diggins is known for the concentration of old order Amish families who live in the area.

Dillard Mill State Park—Dillard Mill State Historic Site, located on Huzzah Creek at the small community of Dillard in southern Crawford County, Missouri, interprets one of the state's best preserved grist mills. The site also offers hiking, picnicking, and other outdoor activities. The community of Dillard was founded in 1887 and named after Joseph Dillard Cottrell, operator of a previous mill on the site, which burned in the 1890s. The present mill was completed in 1908.

Dinsmore, Hugh Anderson—Born in Benton County, Hugh A. Dinsmore was a lawyer and politician from northwest Arkansas, and he represented the area in the U. S. Congress from 1893 to 1905.

Disfarmer, Michael—Michael Disfarmer was an eccentric photographer from Heber Springs, Arkansas, who gained national recognition for his work several years after his 1959 death. Born Michael Meyer to a German immigrant farm family, he changed his name as an adult to Michael Disfarmer, presumably as an expression of rebellion against his family and his rural upbringing, because "meier" means "dairy farmer" in German.

Disney, Oklahoma—Disney is a community of about 310 people in Mayes County. It is also called Disney Island, because the north part of the town is surrounded by Grand Lake and the southern limit is formed by a wide stream. In the 1930s, during construction of Pensacola Dam, which created Grand Lake, many workers were based in and around Disney, and the town bustled with activity. Today, Disney is a recreation area on the lake.

Disney-Little Blue State Park—Disney-Little Blue State Park is a 32-acre Oklahoma state park offering access to Grand Lake at Disney.

Dixon, Missouri—Dixon is a town of about 1,550 people in northern Pulaski County. It was laid out in 1869 as a railroad town. Former Major League Baseball player Morrie Martin was born at Dixon, and former NBA basketball player John Brown attended Dixon High School. Dixon is home to the Dixon R-1 Schools.

Dodge, Oklahoma—Dodge is a community of about 95 people in eastern Delaware County near the Arkansas border. It was established along the railroad about 1900.

Doe Run, Missouri—Doe Run is an unincorporated community in southern St. Francois County. In the late 1880s, it prospered as a lead mining town and had a population of about 1,000 people, but its population is now about 300.

Doe Run Company—See Viburnum, Missouri.

Dogpatch USA—Dogpatch USA was a theme park that operated in Newton County, Arkansas, south of Harrison on Highway 7, from 1968 until 1993. Based on the comic strip "Li'l Abner" by Al Capp, it sought to recreate the fictional, hillbilly town of Dogpatch, as depicted by the cartoonist.

Dogwood Canyon Natural Park—Located near Lampe, Missouri, Dogwood Canyon is a 10,000-acre, commercial, wilderness park offering wildlife tours and outdoor activities like fishing and hiking.

Doniphan, Missouri—Doniphan is the county seat of Ripley County. It was settled about 1847 and became the county seat in 1849 when Carter County was formed and Ripley's former county seat, Van Buren, became the seat of the new county. The town was named for Alexander Doniphan, colonel of Missouri troops during the Mexican War. Doniphan was burned by Union troops in September of 1864 but was rebuilt after the Civil War. It has a population today of about 2,000 people and is home of the Doniphan R-1 School District.

Donnelly, Phil M.--Phil M. Donnelly was governor of Missouri from 1945 to 1949 and again from 1953 to 1957. He was born and raised in Lebanon and died there in 1961.

Doolin, Bill—Bill Doolin was a member of the Dalton gang who went on to form his own outlaw gang, sometimes called the Wild Bunch. His gang's most notorious action in the Ozarks was the holdup of a bank in May of 1894 at Southwest City, Missouri, during which one citizen of the town was killed.

Doolittle, Missouri—Doolittle is a town of about 630 people in Phelps County. Originally called Centertown because it was halfway between Rolla and Newburg, the community boomed during construction of nearby Fort Leonard Wood in the early 1940s, when it was incorporated and renamed in honor of World War II general Jimmy Doolittle.

Dora, Missouri—Dora is an unincorporated community in northeast Ozark County. It was established about 1880 and named after the first postmaster's daughter. Today, Dora contains several businesses and churches and is home to the Dora R-3 School District.

Douglas County, Missouri—Douglas County was formed in 1857 from territory taken from Ozark County. It later added territory from Taney and Webster counties and lost territory to Howell County. The county seat moved several times before Ava was finally selected as the county seat in 1871.

Dr. Smith's Champion Hoss-Hair Pullers—Dr. Smith's Champion Hoss Hair Pullers was a string band organized in 1926 by Dr. Henry Harlin Smith to promote tourism in the Izard County, Arkansas, area. It became marginally famous before disbanding in 1930.

Drake Constitution—The Drake Constitution was a state constitution passed in Missouri at the end of the Civil War which immediately outlawed slavery and disenfranchised former Confederates and Confederate sympathizers, requiring them to take an oath of allegiance to the United States before they could vote or hold certain jobs like teacher, preacher, or lawyer. Named after its chief proponent, Charles Drake, the new constitution contributed to post-war conflict in the Missouri Ozarks during the late 1860s and early 1870s and tended to prolong the bitterness left over from the war.

Dresbach, Glenn Ward—Glenn Ward Dresbach was an internationally known poet when he moved to Eureka Springs, Arkansas, in 1941. He continued to write poetry, including many poems about the Ozarks, after his arrival in Eureka Springs. His wife, Beverly Githens Dresbach, was also a noted poet and a journalist. She was active in promoting the culture of Eureka Springs.

Drew, Thomas Stevenson—Thomas Stevenson Drew was a farmer, schoolteacher, and politician from Randolph County, Arkansas. He was elected as the state's third governor in 1844 and served until 1849, when he resigned because of financial difficulties.

Drey, Leo—Leo Drey was a St. Louis businessman and philanthropist who began acquiring Missouri lands, mostly in the heart of the Ozarks in south-central and southeast Missouri, in the early 1950s for preservation, until his total holdings amounted to almost 160,000 acres, making him the largest private landowner in the state. In 1962 he formed the L-A-D Foundation to protect natural areas and began donating land to the foundation, including a donation in 2004 of about 146,000 acres, constituting most of Pioneer Forest. Today, the foundation oversees about 150,000 acres, including a lot of land that has been leased to the state of Missouri at virtually no charge for use as natural areas or state parks. Drey died in 2015 at the age of 98.

Driftwood, Jimmy—Jimmy Driftwood, born James Corbett Morris, was a prolific folk songwriter and singer best known for the "Battle of New Orleans" and "Tennessee Stud." Born in 1907 at Timbo in Sharp County, Arkansas, he lived in north central Arkansas most of his life. He helped found the Ozark Folk Center at Mountain View.

Droughts—See precipitation extremes.

Drury-Mincy Conservation Area—Comprising about 5,600 acres, the Drury-Mincy Conservation Area is a state-owned conservation area in southern Taney County, Missouri. It was the site of the Department of Conservation's first deer preserve.

Drury University—Drury University is a private, liberal-arts institution of higher learning in Springfield, Missouri. Founded in 1873 by the Congregational Church, the school is still affiliated today with the United Church of Christ, successor of the Congregational Church. Originally called Springfield College, it was renamed Drury College shortly after its founding in honor of its largest benefactor, Samuel Drury, and it became Drury University in 2000. Drury has a total enrollment of about 3,550, including part-time and graduate students.

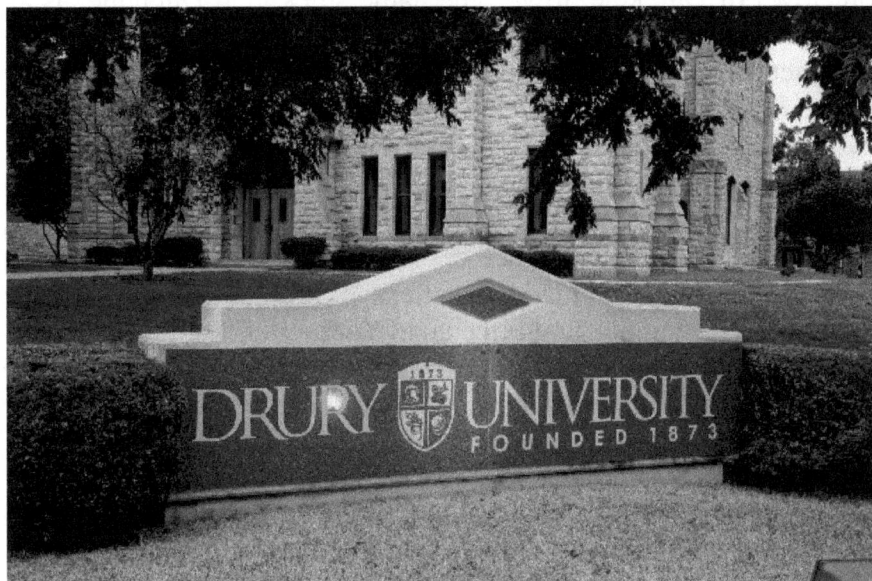

Drury University sign and campus building. *By Jim Mayfield, Courtesy Drury University.*

Dry and Dusty, Missouri—Dry and Dusty was the name of a school and a church in southwest Laclede County, so named because they were located on a stretch of the Old Wire Road that was notoriously dusty during dry weather, but the area was also very muddy during rainy weather.

Dry counties—Arkansas is one of a number of states in the United States that allows counties or other local jurisdictions to go "dry" by prohibiting the sale of alcoholic beverages. Even in the "wet" counties, municipalities are allowed to ban alcohol sales through a local option election. Thus, in the Arkansas Ozarks, counties where alcohol sales are legal exist side by side with dry counties and partially dry counties.

Dubuque, Arkansas—Dubuque was a town on the White River about two miles south of the Missouri line in present-day Boone County. A settlement called Sugarloaf Prairie, named for nearby Sugarloaf Creek, existed at the site as early as 1818. The site became an important river crossing, and a town grew up during the 1840s. In 1851, a northbound steamboat on the White River had to stop at the settlement because low waters would not allow it to proceed farther north, and the boat captain suggested the name Dubuque after his hometown of Dubuque, Iowa. The name stuck, and Dubuque, as an important crossing and the northernmost port on the White River, saw much activity during the Civil War, with North and South fighting over its occupation. Devastated by the war, the town declined rapidly after the war until virtually nothing of it remained by 1870.

Dug Springs, Battle of—The so-called Battle of Dug Springs was a Civil War engagement on August 2, 1861, near present-day Clever, Missouri, between the advance of Union general Nathaniel Lyon's Army of the West and a detachment of troops representing the advance of General Sterling Price and General Ben McCulloch's pro-Southern "Western Army." After some initial skirmishing, the Southerners fled in confusion, and there were few casualties on either side. The action was a precursor of the Battle of Wilson's Creek fought eight days later between the same forces.

Duenweg, Missouri—Duenweg is a town in Jasper County about three miles east of Joplin. Founded during the lead and zinc mining boom in southwest Missouri during the late 1800s, it has a current population of about 1,100. It once had its own high school but consolidated with Joplin in the 1960s.

Duncan, Virginia Maud Dunlap— In 1925, pharmacist and newspaper editor Virginia Maud Dunlap Duncan, running with an all-female city council, won election as mayor of Winslow, Arkansas, and a so-called "Petticoat Government" was installed.

Dunklin, Daniel—Daniel Dunklin was a frontier lawyer and politician from Potosi, Missouri, who served as the fifth governor of the state from 1832 to 1834. Dunklin County in southeast Missouri is named for him.

Dunnegan, Missouri—Dunnegan is an unincorporated community in Polk County. It was founded in the 1880s as a station along the Kansas City, Clinton and Springfield Railroad and named Dunnegan Springs after the Dunnegan family, early settlers in the area, but "Springs" was later dropped.

Duquesne, Missouri—Duquesne is a town in Jasper County at the eastern edge of Joplin. It was founded during the mining boom of the late 1800s. Much of the community was wiped out by the Joplin tornado of 2011, but the town has largely rebuilt and today has a population of about 1,700 people.

Durham, Arkansas—Durham is an unincorporated community in eastern Washington County. It is the home of Terra Studios, maker of the glass figurine known as the Bluebird of Happiness.

Dusenbury, Emma Hays—Emma Hays Dusenbury was an outstanding traditional singer, many of whose songs were collected in the 1920s and 1930s by folksong collectors like Vance Randolph. She lived for a while during her early life near Gassville in Baxter County, Arkansas, but later moved to the Ouachita Mountains of west-central Arkansas.

Dutch Mills, Arkansas—Dutch Mills is an unincorporated community in western Washington County. It was originally named Hermannsburg after German immigrant Johann Hermann, who settled there in the early 1850s. Other German settlers followed, and American settlers in the area started calling the place Dutch Mills, a name that stuck even after the last of the Germans were run out during the Civil War.

Dutchtown, Missouri—Dutchtown is a village of about 95 people in southern Cape Girardeau County. Martin Rodner, a former Hessian soldier, settled in the area in 1801, and an influx of Swiss and German immigrants followed in the 1830s. They called their settlement Spencer, but it soon became known by other area residents as Dutchtown, because many English-speaking settlers called Germans "Dutch," a corruption of "Deutsch," the German word for "German."

E

Eagle Rock, Missouri—Eagle Rock is an unincorporated community on Highway 86 in Barry County. Located on Table Rock Lake, it is a resort area with a campground and a public marina.

Earle, Fontaine Richard—Fontaine Richard Earle was a major in the Thirty-fourth Arkansas Infantry (CSA) who fought at Prairie Grove and other actions in the Trans Mississippi theater. He served as president of Cane Hill College before and after the war.

Eau de Vie, Missouri—Located in southern Christian County, Eau de Vie was one of numerous resort towns that sprang up in the Ozarks during the mineral water craze of the 1880s, and like a lot of them, Eau de Vie faded almost as quickly as it sprang up until nothing remained to indicate it ever existed.

Ebenezer, Missouri—Ebenezer is a community in northern Greene County. One of the oldest communities in the county, it was established in the 1830s, and was, at one time, a thriving town, with several general stores and other businesses. It was also home to Ebenezer College, which merged with Scarritt College of Neosho to form the Morrisville-Scarritt College in 1909. Today, little remains of Ebenezer to suggest its glory days of yesteryear.

Edgar Springs, Missouri—Edgar Springs is a village of about 200 people located in Phelps County at the eastern edge of Fort Leonard Wood on Highway 63. At the time of the 2000 census, Edgar Springs was the closest community to the mean center of United States population.

Edom, Clifford C.—Often called the "father of photojournalism," Clifford C. Edom was a longtime professor of photojournalism at the University of Missouri. He retired to the Missouri Ozarks, and he and his wife compiled a book entitled *Twice Told Tales and an Ozark Photo Album with Emphasis on Taney County, Missouri* in 1987. An annual photography contest sponsored by the Ozark Writers League is named after Edom.

Edwards, John—John Edwards was a Civil War officer and a politician. As colonel of the Eighteen Iowa Infantry, he served in southwest Missouri and northwest Arkansas during the war, including a brief stint as commander of the post at Springfield during the spring and early summer of 1863. After the war, he settled at Fort Smith, Arkansas, and he ran for Congress in 1870. He was seated as the apparent victor and represented northwest Arkansas for about a year before the result of the election was successfully challenged by his opponent.

Egypt Mills, Missouri—Egypt Mills is an unincorporated community in eastern Cape Girardeau County. A post office was established at the site in 1899. It is home to the Neil Holcomb R-4 School District.

El Camino Real—Laid out in 1789, the El Camino Real was a road that ran from New Madrid, Missouri, to St. Louis. A marker commemorating the road was placed in 1917 by the Daughters of the American Revolution along the route of the old road in Ste. Genevieve.

Eldon, Missouri—Eldon is a town of about 4,550 people in northwest Miller County just off U.S. Highway 54. It was laid out in the early 1880s with the coming of a railroad. It is home to the Eldon School District.

Eldon, Oklahoma—Supposedly named for Eldon, Illinois, Eldon is a town of about 370 people in Cherokee County east of Tahlequah at the intersection of U.S. Highway 62 and State Highway 51. A post office was established at the site in 1911.

Eldridge, Missouri—Eldridge is an unincorporated community in northern Laclede County. A post office was established at the site in 1876. The first store was opened in 1884 by a black man named Alfred Eldridge, and the town was named after him.

Elephant Rocks State Park—Located in northeast Iron County, Elephant Rocks State Park is home to one of the most curious geologic formations in Missouri. Giant reddish boulders of granite stand end to end like a caravan of circus elephants. Picnic facilities are available in the park.

Eleven Point River— The Eleven Point River is a 138-mile tributary of Spring River. It forms in south central Missouri near Willow Springs, nearly doubles its flow when Greer Spring merges with it north of Alton in Oregon County, and continues south into Arkansas, where it empties in the Spring River southwest of Pocahontas.

Elk—The eastern subspecies of elk was native to the Ozarks but was wiped out by the time of the Civil War, mostly because of clearing of land. The Rocky Mountain subspecies of the big animal was brought from Colorado and introduced in the public lands around the Buffalo River beginning in 1981. The elk have since thrived enough that they can now be hunted on a limited basis. A similar elk restoration program began in southeast Missouri in 2010.

Elk River—Elk River is a 35-mile tributary of the Neosho River that forms at the confluence of Big Sugar Creek and Little Sugar Creek at Pineville in McDonald County, Missouri, and flows generally west into Oklahoma, where it joins the Neosho as part of the Grand Lake of the Cherokees.

Elkhorn Tavern, Battle of—See Battle of Pea Ridge

Elkins, Arkansas—Elkins is a town of about 2,650 people in eastern Washington County comprising the historic communities of Harris and Hood. The Hood post office was established in 1885 and the Harris post office in 1888. In 1892, the name of Hood was changed to Elkins, and years later Harris became part of Elkins. Major League Baseball player Jim King was born in Elkins in 1932. A one-lane bridge on Mount Olive Road in Elkins was a centerpiece of the 1982 TV miniseries *The Blue and the Gray*. Elkins is home to the Elkins School District.

Elkland, Missouri—Elkland is a small, unincorporated community in northwest Webster County. It was the site of a notorious crime in 1987, when James Schnick killed six of his relatives and tried to frame his nephew, who was one of the victims, for the murders.

Elkton, Missouri—Elkton is a community in southern Hickory County. It was the hometown of Sally Rand, the famous fan dancer.

Ellington, Missouri—Ellington is a town of slightly over 1,000 people in southern Reynolds County. The infamous Tri-State Tornado of 1925 first touched down near Ellington. Today, the town is home to the Southern Reynolds County School District and the Reynolds County Museum.

Ellis, Roy—Roy Ellis was president from 1926 to 1961 of the college known today as Missouri State University. This is the longest tenure of any president in the history of the institution. The campus in Springfield has a building named after Dr. Ellis, and the university offers a scholarship that was established in his honor.

Ellsinore, Missouri—Ellsinore is a town in eastern Carter County founded in the late 1880s along the Cape Girardeau and Southwestern Railroad (aka Houck Railroad). Today it has a population of about 450 people and is home to the East Carter County School District.

Ellis, Clyde Taylor—Clyde Taylor Ellis was politician from northwest Arkansas during the 1930s and 1940s. He was born near Garfield in Benton County and went to school at Garfield and Fayetteville. He served in the U. S. House of Representatives from 1939 to 1943 and was a leader in the country's rural electrification movement. He died in 1980 and is buried at Arlington National Cemetery.

Elmer, William P.—William P. Elmer was a politician from Salem, Missouri, who served in the U.S. House of Representatives from 1943 to 1945.

Elsey, Missouri—Elsey is an unincorporated community in Stone County about halfway between Crane and Galena. It was platted about 1901 by O.F. Douglas and given the name Douglas. However, a post office called Elsey after two women by that name already existed at the site, and the town soon adopted the name of the post office.

Emerson, John Wesley—John Wesley Emerson was an officer in the Union army during the Civil War. After the war, he was a prominent lawyer at Ironton, Missouri, a Missouri Circuit Court judge, and a U.S. marshal. He also founded the Emerson Electric Company and authored a book about General Grant's Mississippi Valley campaign.

Eminence, Missouri—Eminence, a town of about 500 people, is the seat of Shannon County and home to the Eminence R-1 School District. Originally founded as a frontier community prior to the Civil War on a bluff overlooking the Current River several miles north of its present location, it was burned by Union soldiers during the war and rebuilt near the center of the county. Located near the Current and the Jacks Fork rivers, Eminence today is considered the "Canoe

Capital of the World" and one of the top outdoor sports towns in America.

Empire City, Kansas—Empire City is a former town in the southeast corner of Kansas that was annexed by Galena in the early 1900s. After lead was discovered on Short Creek in 1879, the two towns sprang up almost simultaneously, and a rivalry between them almost erupted in violence.

Empire District Electric Company—Formed in 1909 and based in Joplin, Missouri, the Empire District Electric Company is a utility company that provides services, primarily electricity, to approximately 215,000 customers in southwest Missouri, southeast Kansas, northeast Oklahoma, and northwest Arkansas.

Enrolled Missouri Militia—The Enrolled Missouri Militia was a Union militia force organized in Missouri in 1862. It was a part-time force that operated locally. Its primary purpose was to augment the Missouri State Militia in defending the state from Confederate threats and to free up the Missouri State Militia for offensive operations. The Enrolled Missouri Militia played an important role in several military actions in the Ozarks, including the Battle of Springfield.

Erie, Missouri—See Oregon, Missouri.

Etterville, Missouri—Etterville is an unincorporated community in Miller County, located on U.S. Highway 54 northeast of Eldon.

Eureka Springs, Arkansas—Eureka Springs is a town of about 2,070 people in Carroll County and one of its two county seats. Claims that the springs of the area had curative powers had been made since before the Civil War, but the town was not established until July 1879, after a man who was supposedly cured of a crippling disease by the waters of Basin Spring started heavily promoting the place. People flooded to Eureka Springs, and by the end of 1879, the town had a reported population of near 10,000. Eureka Springs is still a popular resort and vacation spot, and its entire downtown area is on the National Register of Historic Places. Eureka Springs is home to the Eureka Springs School District.

Eureka Springs Baby—The Eureka Springs Baby, also called the Petrified Indian Baby, was supposedly a fossilized human child that was "discovered" at Eureka Springs in 1880 by Arkansas merchant Henry Johnson, who displayed his find around Eureka Springs, charging a fee for people to view it, before taking his show on the road. Although Johnson's story was not without skeptics from the very beginning, it was not until 1948 that the Eureka Springs Baby was revealed as nothing more than a statue fashioned by a tombstone carver with whom Johnson was in cahoots.

Eureka Springs Bank Robbery—The infamous Eureka Springs bank robbery was, in a sense, not a robbery but an attempted one that went awry. After the remnants of the Henry Starr gang held up the First National Bank of Eureka Springs on September 27, 1922, armed citizens shot it out with the five crooks as they tried to escape. Three of the robbers were killed and the other two captured.

Citizens pose after thwarting Eureka Springs Bank heist. *Bank of Eureka Springs Historical Museum.*

Evangel University—Evangel University, originally called Evangel College, was established in 1955 in Springfield, Missouri, on the grounds that had previously been O'Reilly General Hospital, a World War II government hospital built to treat wounded soldiers. Affiliated with the Assemblies of God Church, Evangel became the first Pentecostal liberal arts college chartered in America. It opened with an initial class of eighty-seven students and now has a student body over 2,000.

Evangel University. *Photo by the author.*

Evansville, Arkansas—Evansville is an unincorporated community in southwest Washington County near the Oklahoma border.

Evening Shade, Arkansas—Evening Shade is a town of about 400 located on U.S. Highway 167 in Sharp County. The town was fictionalized in the television show entitled *Evening Shade* that starred Burt Reynolds and aired during the early 1990s.

Everton, Missouri—Everton is a town of slightly over 300 people located on U. S. Highway 160 in southeast Dade County. It was established as a point on the Kansas City, Fort Scott and Memphis Railroad when the railroad was built in 1881. A post office and country store about a mile northeast of Everton, where the Springfield to Fort Scott road crossed the Boonville to Sarcoxie road and appropriately called Crossroads, was a predecessor to Everton. Everton is home to the Everton R-3 Schools.

Ewing, Thomas, Jr.—Thomas Ewing, Jr. was a Union general during the Civil War. He is perhaps best remembered in Missouri for his infamous Order No. 11, issued in 1863, which decimated several counties in the western part of the state, but he was also the Union commander at the Battle of Pilot Knob in the eastern Ozarks in the fall of 1864.

Exeter, Missouri—Exeter is a town of about 800 people in Barry County. A post office named El Paso west of the present-day town was a predecessor to Exeter. The town was platted in 1880 and incorporated as a village the following year with an eye toward becoming the county seat, a goal that was never realized. The name of the town derives from Exeter, England. Exeter is home to the Exeter R-6 School District.

Experimental forests---Experimental forests are timbered lands established primarily for the purpose of scientific research. The U.S. Forest Service maintains two experimental forests in the Arkansas Ozarks, the Henry R. Koen Experimental forest near Jasper and the Sylamore Experimental Forest near Mountain View, and one in the Missouri Ozarks, the Sinkin Experimental Forest in southeast Dent County.

F

Fagan, James F.—James F. Fagan was a Confederate general during the Civil War. He fought at the battles of Cane Hill and Prairie Grove and commanded a division during Sterling Price's 1864 invasion of Missouri.

Fagg, Pink—Joel Pinkney "Pink" Fagg was a notorious gambler from Springfield, Missouri, who, during the 1880s, tried to kill his wife at Carthage, Missouri, assaulted a man with a gun at Pierce City, Missouri, and, after a stint in prison, killed a man at Fort Smith, Arkansas.

Fairdealing, Missouri—Fairdealing is an unincorporated community in eastern Ripley County. The origin of its unusual name is a matter of conjecture. One story holds that a passing stranger commented that he got a fair deal in a business transaction at the place, and the name stuck. Another legend claims that after a thief stole a horse at the place but left the saddle, he was said to have dealt fairly.

Fair Grove, Missouri—Fair Grove is a town in northeast Greene County, Missouri, that was established prior to the Civil War. Perhaps best known for the Fair Grove Heritage Reunion (formerly known as the Fair Grove Arts and Crafts Festival) held each fall, Fair Grove has a current population of about 1,500 people, and it is home to the Fair Grove R-10 School District.

Fair Play, Missouri—Fair Play is a town of about 475 people in western Polk County. A man named Owen had a store near the current town site, and he called the place Oakland. However, when he applied for a post office, he was informed that there was already an Oakland in Missouri. About the same time, two other men donated some land just north of the store for a town site, and Mr. Owen suggested that they just "call it fair play." Fair Play is home to the Fair Play R-2 Schools.

Fairfield, Oklahoma—Fairfield is a community of about 370 people in Adair County near the Arkansas border.

Fairfield Bay, Arkansas—Fairfield Bay is a town of about 2,340 people on the Van Buren-Cleburne county line, primarily in Van Buren. A resort community located on the banks of Greers Ferry Lake, Fairfield Bay did not exist until several years after the lake was formed in the mid-1960s.

Fairland, Oklahoma—Fairland is a town of about 1,025 in Ottawa County at the western edge of the Ozarks. It was laid out in 1889 along the Frisco Railroad. Fairland is home to the Fairland Public Schools.

Fairview, Missouri—Fairview is a town of about 380 people in southeast Newton County. It was at one time a thriving community with its own high school, but it declined during the latter half of the twentieth century. Fairview was the hometown of financier and hotel developer John Q. Hammons.

Falcon, Missouri—Falcon is an unincorporated community in eastern Laclede County on Highway 32. A post office was established at the site in the early 1900s, and the name "Falcon" was assigned by the U.S. Postal Service. Falcon is home to the Gasconade C-4 School District, a K-8 district.

Falling Water Falls—See Ozark National Forest

Fanning, Missouri—Fanning is a small community that lies along Old Route 66 in Crawford County. It was named for John Fanning, the local railroad agent when the railroad was built through the area in the mid-nineteenth century. It is home to the Fanning 66 Outpost, which claims that the rocking chair outside its business is the world's largest.

Fantastic Caverns—Fantastic Caverns is a commercial cave just north of Springfield, Missouri, on State Highway 13. It offers a totally ride-through tour. Originally called Knox Cave, it was discovered during the 1860s, and it was first explored in 1867. Twelve women from Springfield were among the first explorers, although they were not the very first, as legend holds. Besides its use as a show cave at various times throughout its history, the cave has also served as a speakeasy during Prohibition and as a venue for concerts during the 1950s. It was first called Fantastic Caverns in 1951, and Jeep-drawn trams were first introduced in the late 1960s.

Jeep-drawn tram pulls tourists through Fantastic Caverns. *Courtesy of Fantastic Caverns.*

Fantasy World Caverns—Formerly known as Stark Caverns, Fantasy World Caverns is a commercial cave located near Eldon in Miller County, Missouri. It has been a commercial cave since the early 1950s and was extensively explored many years before that.

Far West Seminary—The Far West Seminary was a collegiate level educational institution that was planned for northwest Arkansas in the mid-1840s. It failed, however, because of political opposition, economic hard times, and a fire in 1845 that destroyed the building at Mount Comfort in Washington County where it was going to be located. The same year, the Ozarks Institute was built upon the ashes of the burned-out building as a school for boys, a counterpart to the nearby Fayetteville Female Seminary, and the institute provided education to students for the next quarter century.

Farmington, Arkansas—Farmington is a town of about 6,000 people at the west edge of Fayetteville in Washington County. Originally called Engles Mill, it was renamed Farmington shortly after the Civil War because the area was considered prime farm land. The town is home to the Farmington School District.

Farmington, Missouri—Farmington is a town of about 16,250 people and the seat of St. Francois County. The area was originally called Murphy's Settlement after David Murphy, the first white settler, who arrived in the late 1790s. In 1822, Murphy donated land for the town as a prospective county seat for Francois County, and it was shortly afterwards named Farmington. Like its counterpart in Arkansas, the town was given its name because of the agriculture in the region. During the late 1800s and early 1900s, Farmington was home to Carleton College, the Elmwood Seminary, and the Farmington Baptist College, and it is currently home to the Farmington R-7 School District.

Farmington State Hospital—The Farmington State Hospital is one of several state hospitals for mental patients throughout Missouri. They were originally called insane asylums, but the name was changed in 1903, the same year that the Farmington facility received its first patients.

Fassnight Park—Fassnight Park is a historic twenty-eight-acre park in Springfield, Missouri. The park and swimming pool were opened during the 1920s, and the bathhouse and other stone structures were built by the WPA during the 1930s. Fassnight Creek runs through the park.

Faubus, Orval Eugene--Orval Faubus served as governor of Arkansas from 1955 to 1967. He is best known for his stand against integration of the Little Rock School District, which led to the Little Rock Crisis in 1957, during which President Eisenhower intervened by sending U.S. troops to ensure the first black students were allowed to attend Little Rock Central High School. Faubus was born and grew up in rural Madison County, Arkansas, near Huntsville, and he first held political office as circuit clerk and recorder of Madison County.

Orville Faubus, on right, and Bill Clinton. *Courtesy the Arkansas Traveler.*

Faulkner County, Arkansas—Located in the central part of the state, Faulkner County borders the Arkansas River, and only the northern part can rightfully be considered in the Ozarks.

Fayetteville, Arkansas—Fayetteville is a city of about 75,000 people and the county seat of Washington County. After Washington County was formed in 1828, the current site of Fayetteville, then called Washington Courthouse, was selected as the county seat. The next year, the settlement was renamed Fayetteville after Fayetteville, Tennessee, the hometown of two of the commissioners who located the county seat. Fayetteville was incorporated in 1841. It is the home to the Arkansas Air Museum, the Northwest Arkansas Mall, the University of Arkansas, a Veterans Administration medical c enter, Washington Regional Medical Center, and the Fayetteville Public Schools, the oldest public school district in the state. Among the well-known people born in or closely associated with Fayetteville are NBA basketball player Mike Conley, Jr., artist Donald Roller Wilson, and noted black poet George Ballard.

Fayetteville and Cane Hill, Skirmish between—The Skirmish between Fayetteville and Cane Hill (also called the Skirmish at

Fayetteville or the Skirmish at Cane Hill) occurred on November 9, 1862, several miles north of Cane Hill and on the northern outskirts of Cane Hill. Forces engaged were a large scouting party under Union colonel William Cloud and Confederate troops from Colonel Emmett MacDonald's Missouri Provost Guard. The Federals drove off the Confederates and captured their flag and supplies.

Fayetteville Female Academy—Founded by Sophia Sawyer, the Fayetteville Female Academy was an institution of higher learning for young women chartered in 1836 in Fayetteville, Arkansas.

Fayetteville, Battle of—The Action at Fayetteville, sometimes called the Battle of Fayetteville, was a Civil War battle that took place on April 18, 1863, when Confederate general William L. Cabell, with about 900 cavalrymen, attacked the Union post at Fayetteville, where Colonel M. LaRue Harrison commanded about 1,100 men. The fighting took place mostly in the heart of present-day Fayetteville. The battle is sometimes cited as a Union victory, since the Confederates withdrew after being unable to take the post, but the outcome was indecisive, since the Union army, fearing another attack, abandoned Fayetteville just a few days later.

Feaster, Elbert—Elbert Feaster was a major in the Missouri State Guard near the beginning of the Civil War and later a Confederate captain. He was from Benton County, and in the spring of 1862 while he was recruiting in his home territory preparatory to joining the Confederate army, his forces skirmished with Federal troops near the St. Clair County line.

Featherstonhaugh, George William—George William Featherston-haugh, the first U.S. government geologist, was appointed to do a geological survey of Arkansas in 1834. He bought a horse and wagon at St. Louis and set off generally following the Southwest Trail, which Highway 67 roughly approximates today. He entered Arkansas Territory in what is now Randolph County at Hix Ferry (later Pitman's Ferry) on the Current River and continued to Little Rock. He was also one of the first people to leave an accurate record of what life was like for early settlers in the region.

Fellows Lake—Located about five miles north of Springfield, Missouri, Fellows Lake is an 860-acre manmade reservoir that serves as a water source for the city. Constructed in 1955 when the Little Sac

River was dammed, it is also a popular spot for fishing and other outdoor activities.

Ferguson, Tom R.—Tom R. Ferguson is a rodeo cowboy who was named World All-Around Champion six consecutive years from 1974 to 1979. He was born in Tahlequah, Oklahoma, and has lived most of his adult life in Miami, Oklahoma.

Festus, Missouri—Festus is a town of about 11,600 people in Jefferson County. See Crystal City.

Fifty Six, Arkansas—Fifty Six is a town of about 165 people in northern Stone County. When the community was established about 1920, the first storekeeper applied for a post office and reportedly offered Pleasant Hill as his first choice for a name and Fifty Six, the name of the local school district, as his second. The government selected Fifty Six, since a Pleasant Hill, Arkansas, already existed.

Finley River—The Finley River, or Finley Creek, is a tributary of the James River, located mainly in Christian County, Missouri. It begins in Webster County, flows in a generally southwest direction through Christian County and empties into the James River just across the county line in Stone County. It is popular for fishing, and the lower part is also used for floating.

First Arkansas Cavalry (Union)--Composed largely of Union refugees from northwest Arkansas, the First Arkansas Cavalry was organized at Cassville, Missouri, by Captain Marcus LaRue Harrison, the post quartermaster, and mustered into service at Springfield, Missouri, during the summer of 1862. Harrison was promoted to colonel in command of the regiment, which saw action at Prairie Grove later in 1862, at Fayetteville in 1863, and as a counter-guerrilla force in northwest Arkansas and southwest Missouri throughout the remainder of the war.

Fisher Cave—Fisher Cave is a tour cave located at Meramec State Park near Sullivan, Missouri.

Fisher's Cave—Fisher's Cave is an undeveloped river cave located in Sequiota Park in Springfield, Missouri. Also known as Springdale Cave, it was a popular summer resort around the turn of the twentieth century, was a state park and fish hatchery from 1920 to 1959, and became part of the city of Springfield in 1969.

Fish and Fishing—The Ozarks are home to at least 200 different species of fish. Commercial fishing played an important role in the early settlement and development of the area, and today fishing is one of the top recreational activities in the region.

Flanders, Robert B.—A former professor at Missouri State University in Springfield, Robert B. Flanders was the co-founder of *Ozarks Watch Magazine* and chairman of the university's Department of Ozark Studies for several years.

Flat Creek—Flat Creek is a tributary of the James River that forms in Barry County, Missouri, flows through Barry, and empties into the James in western Stone County. It was reportedly named for the flat land through which it flows. A township and a small community in Barry County are named after the creek.

Flat River, Missouri—See Park Hills, Missouri

Fleagle, Jake—Jake Fleagle and his brother Ralph were leaders of the Fleagle gang, notorious bank robbers in the 1920s. After the gang held up a bank in Colorado in May of 1928, killing a bank cashier and his son, Ralph Fleagle and two other gang members were captured and hanged in the summer of 1930. Meanwhile, Jake Fleagle hid out near Ridgedale, Missouri, for several months and was finally mortally wounded in a showdown with police at Branson in October of the same year.

Flemington, Missouri—Flemington is a village in northern Polk County with a population of about 150 people. It was established along the line of the Frisco Railroad that was extended from Bolivar to Kansas City in 1898, and it was named after Robert L. Fleming, who gave the land for the town site.

Fletcher, John Gould—See Ozark Folklore Society

Flint Creek—Flint Creek is a tributary of the Illinois River that forms in northwest Arkansas and flows into Oklahoma, where it joins the Illinois.

Flint Creek, Oklahoma—Flint Creek is a community of about 600 people in Delaware County, named for the nearby creek.

Flippin, Arkansas—Flippin is a town of about 1,360 people on U.S. Highway 412/62 in Marion County near the south shore of Bull Shoals Lake. A place known as the Barrens, located just outside present-day Flippin, was settled in the early 1800s. It became known as Flippin Barrens after Thomas H. Flippin and his family moved to the area in 1837. The town moved to its current location closer to the railroad around 1900 and was officially incorporated as Flippin in

1921. Flippin is home to Ranger Boats and to the Flippin Public Schools.

Florence, Missouri—Florence is an unincorporated community in the northern Ozarks of Morgan County. It was founded about 1840 and was a thriving little village until the Civil War, when it was raided by Confederate bushwhackers. Several citizens were killed and several store buildings burned. Although the community carried on after the war, it has never regained its previous prosperity.

Floyd, Charles "Pretty Boy"—Pretty Boy Floyd was an outlaw during the gangster era of the 1920s and 1930s who grew up in the Cookson Hills of Oklahoma. One of his more notable crimes in the Ozarks was his kidnapping of Polk County sheriff Jack Killingsworth at Bolivar, Missouri, on June 16, 1933. Floyd and his sidekick, Adam Richetti, drove Killingsworth to Kansas City before turning him loose, and the next day, the two desperadoes reportedly helped carry out the infamous Union Station massacre in Kansas City.

Floyd, John C.—John C. Floyd represented northwest Arkansas in the U.S. House of Representatives from 1905 to 1915. He grew up in Benton County and practiced law at Yellville.

Foggy River Boys—The Foggy River Boys was a gospel music group that was popular in the Ozarks in the 1940s, with live shows on KWTO radio in Springfield. The group evolved into the Jordanaires, who became famous as a backup group for Elvis Presley, and there was also a later incarnation of the Foggy River Boys, which also became well known.

Ford, Edsel—Edsel Ford was a distinguished Arkansas poet who died in 1970 at the age of 41. Ford published numerous poems in national journals and magazines, and he edited a poetry column entitled "The Golden Country" for the *Ozarks Mountaineer* during the late 1950s and the 1960s. He is perhaps best remembered in the Ozarks today for his sonnet "Return to Pea Ridge," which was read at the dedication of the Pea Ridge National Military Park in 1962 and which is still inscribed on a plaque there.

Fordland, Missouri—Fordland is a town with a population of about 800 in southern Webster County. It was laid out along the Kansas City, Springfield and Memphis Railroad in 1882 and named for landowner Joseph Ford. Fordland is home to the Fordland R-3 Schools.

Forsyth, Missouri—Forsyth is a town of about 2,260 people and the seat of Taney County. The county was formed in 1837, and Forsyth became the seat shortly afterwards. Forsyth was an important shipping point on the White River prior to the Civil War. During the war, it was the site of a skirmish in July of 1861, when Federal forces under General Thomas W. Sweeny drove out a detachment of Rebels and captured the town, damaging some of the buildings with cannon fire in the process. Some buildings were again damaged in 1863 when Rebels vacated the town and set fire to it in an attempt to burn it down rather than surrender it into the hands of the Union. In 1950, virtually the whole town of Forsyth was moved to the high banks overlooking the White River when Bull Shoals Lake was created, flooding the previous town site. Forsyth is home to the Forsyth R-3 School District.

Fort Ancient (aka Old Spanish Fort)--Fort Ancient is an earthworks near present-day Hoberg in Lawrence County, Missouri. It is believed to have been built by Indian mound builders, long before white men settled in the area. However, it is often known locally as the Old Spanish Fort.

Fort Gibson, Oklahoma—Fort Gibson is a town of about 4,200 at the western edge of the Ozarks on the Cherokee-Muskogee county line. From 1824 to 1890, it was the site of a U.S. Army post, which is now commemorated at the Fort Gibson Historic Site.

Fort Gibson Lake—Covering about 12,000 surface acres, Fort Gibson Lake is a reservoir north of Fort Gibson, Oklahoma, that was created in the early 1950s by the damming of the Grand River. Sequoyah State Park, featuring Western Hills Guest Ranch, is located on the lakeshore.

Fort Leonard Wood, Missouri—Fort Leonard Wood is a U. S. Army base covering almost 63,000 acres in Pulaski County. The main entrance is located about two miles south of Interstate 44. When the fort was built at the beginning of World War II, several small communities in the county were wiped off the face of the map. Fort Leonard Wood serves as a training center for service men and women in the chemical, engineering, transportation, and military police fields.

Foster, Ralph D.—Ralph D. Foster was a broadcasting pioneer whose radio station KWTO in Springfield, Missouri, was known especially during the 1940s and 1950s for its live country music performances by entertainers like Porter Wagoner and Chet Atkins. The success of the station led to creation of the TV show *Ozark Jubilee*, which enabled Springfield to challenge Nashville during the fifties as the live country music capital of the world.

Fourche River—A 32.4-mile tributary of the Black River, the Fourche River, or Fourche Creek as it is often called, rises in Ripley County, Missouri, and flows south into Randolph County Arkansas, where it empties into the Black near Pocahontas.

Fox, Nettie Pease—Nettie Pease Fox was a nationally known revivalist and proponent of spiritualism who started a spiritualist newspaper and gave a series of spiritualist lectures in Springfield, Missouri, during the late 1870s.

Franklin, Arkansas—Franklin is a town of about 200 people in Izard County.

Franklin, Connie, Alleged murder of—In March of 1929, Connie Franklin, a thirty-two-year-old drifter and former mental patient who claimed to be twenty-two, disappeared from the area of St. James, Stone County, Arkansas, and his sixteen-year-old girlfriend claimed he had been killed by a gang of men and that they had also raped her. The subsequent investigation into the case was widely covered in the national media, and the scandal served to reinforce negative stereotypes about Arkansas, especially when the alleged victim turned up alive just as the case was getting ready to go to trial. See *Ghost of the Ozarks: Murder and Memory in the Upland South* by Brooks Blevins.

Franklin County, Missouri—Located southwest of St. Louis in the east central part of Missouri, Franklin is one of the oldest counties in the state, having been organized in 1818 under territorial law. The first county seat was located near the Missouri River, but the county seat was moved to Union in 1825. Franklin County originally encompassed a large swath of southern Missouri, but when Gasconade County was detached in 1820, Franklin County was reduced to near its current size.

Frauenthal, Max—A German immigrant noted for his courage as a Confederate soldier during the Civil War, Max Frauenthal later donated land for the town of Heber Springs (then Sugar Loaf) and helped found the town and its county, Cleburne, which was named after Confederate general Patrick R. Cleburne.

Fredericktown, Missouri—Located in the eastern Ozarks, Fredericktown is the county seat of Madison County. It was laid out in 1819 shortly after the county was formed. Fredericktown has a population of about 4,000 people, and it is home to the Fredericktown R-1 School District.

Freeburg, Missouri—Freeburg is a village of about 435 people on U.S. Highway 63 in southern Osage County about halfway between Jefferson City and Rolla. It is home to the Holy Family School and the Sacred Heart School, which are both K-8 Catholic-affiliated schools.

Freeman, Dale—Dale Freeman is a former editor of the *Springfield News-Leader* and the author of *How to Talk Pure Ozark: In One Easy Lesson.*

Freeman, Thomas R.—Thomas R. Freeman was a Missouri State Guard and Confederate officer who carried on guerrilla warfare in south central Missouri during the Civil War.

Fremont, Missouri—Fremont is an unincorporated community in western Carter County. It was established in the late 1880s along the Current River branch of the Frisco Railroad. It was originally going to be called McDonald after the man who laid out the town for the railroad. However, the post office rejected the name, and the town was named Peggy instead, after the wife of an early settler. In 1907, the name was changed to Fremont. Fremont, along with several other Carter County communities, thrived as a lumber town during the late 1800s and early 1900s. At one time, it had its own school district, but it consolidated with Van Buren many years ago.

Freistatt, Missouri—Freistatt is a village of about 200 people in Lawrence County. The Ernte-Fest, a popular festival held each August just outside Freistatt, celebrates the German heritage of the area.

Fremont, John C.—John C. Fremont was a famous explorer, military officer, and the first Republican candidate for President. While commanding the Union's Western Department in the fall of 1861, he and his army marched through the Missouri Ozarks to Springfield, where he briefly established his headquarters before being relieved of duty.

General John C. Fremont. *Courtesy Library of Congress.*

French, Alice—Alice French, whose penname was Octave Thanet, was a well-known magazine writer during the late 1800s and early 1900s, and some of her best writing, portraying life in Arkansas, was based on time she spent at her winter home in Lawrence County at the edge of the Ozarks.

Freund, Henry Louis and Elsie Mari Bates—Henry Louis Freund and his wife, Elsie Marie Bates Freund, were artists who established a summer art school at Eureka Springs in 1940 and helped turn the town into a haven for artists and writers. Louis Freund had already gained fame during the 1930s for his depictions of life in the Ozarks when he purchased Hatchet Hall, Carrie Nation's former home in Eureka Springs, in 1939. The couple were married there the same year and started their art school there the next year.

French Village, Missouri—French Village is an unincorporated community in northeast St. Francois County that was laid out in 1825 by French colonists.

Friendship Community—The Friendship Community was one of several failed communist communities started by Alcander Longley in Missouri during the late 1800s. Founded in 1872, the Friendship Community was located about four miles west of Buffalo and lasted until about 1877.

Frisco Highline Trail—The Frisco Highline Trail is a biking and walking trail on the roadbed of a former railroad between Bolivar and Springfield, Missouri.

Fristoe, Missouri—Fristoe is an unincorporated community in southern Benton County on U.S. Highway 65. Another community by the same name was a forerunner of Warsaw and was located about three-fourths of a mile east of where Warsaw was later founded. Both the current Fristoe and the historic one were named for Markham Fristoe, a prominent early resident who helped get an act passed through the Missouri legislature to build a road from Jefferson City to Springfield with a ferry crossing of the Osage River at present-day Warsaw.

Frohna, Missouri—One of several communities in Perry County settled by German immigrants in 1839, Frohna is a town of about 255 people in the southeastern part of the county.

Fruit Experimentation Station—The State Fruit Experimentation Station is an operation of the Agriculture Department of Missouri State University dedicated to improving fruit crops in Missouri. The primary site of the operation is a 190-acre farm located near Mountain Grove, Missouri.

Fulbright Industries—Fulbright Industries was a furniture manufacturing business located at Fayetteville, Arkansas, that produced distinctive, modern furniture during the 1940s and 1950s. It was owned by the family of U.S. senator Bill Fulbright.

Fulbright, J. William "Bill"—Bill Fulbright was a U. S. senator from Arkansas from 1945 to 1975 and was noted during the 1960s and 1970s for his outspoken opposition to the Vietnam War. Fulbright was born in Sumner, Missouri, but grew up in Fayetteville and attended the University of Arkansas. In 1939, he became president of the university at the age of 34 and then served one term as a U. S. congressman representing northwest Arkansas before being elected to the Senate.

Fulbright, Roberta Waugh—The mother of Senator Bill Fulbright, Roberta Waugh Fulbright was an influential bank president, newspaper publisher, and civic leader in Fayetteville, Arkansas. As publisher of the *Fayetteville Daily Democrat* (later the *Northwest Arkansas Times*), she wrote a column entitled "As I See It," in which she campaigned for local projects like a new hospital and commented on the local and national political scene. She was largely credited with getting her son elected to the U. S. Senate in 1944.

Fuller, Claude Albert—Claude Albert Fuller was a lawyer and politician from Eureka Springs, Arkansas. He served in the U.S. House of Representatives from 1929 to 1939.

Fulton County, Arkansas—Located in the north central part of the state bordering Missouri, Fulton County was formed in 1842 from territory taken from Izard County and named for William Fulton, Arkansas's first junior U. S. senator. Salem was laid out as the county seat in 1844.

Funk, Erwin Charles—Erwin Charles Funk was a well-known editor of the *Rogers Democrat* in Rogers, Arkansas, during the first third of the twentieth century and was an influential citizen in the community until his death in 1960.

Futrall, John Clinton—John C. Futrall started the football program at the University of Arkansas and was its first coach from 1894 to 1896. He also served as president of the university from 1914 until his death in 1939, and the school's first student union was named in his honor.

Fyan, Robert W.—Robert W. Fyan was a military officer, lawyer, and politician from Marshfield, Missouri. He was a Union officer during the Civil War, served as the prosecutor in Wild Bill Hickok's trial for killing Dave Tutt in 1865, and later was a U.S. congressman representing southwest Missouri.

G

Gad's Hill, Missouri—Gad's Hill is a small village in Wayne County. It was laid out in 1872 along the St. Louis, Iron Mountain and Southern Railroad. The James-Younger gang staged its first train robbery at the Gad's Hill station in January of 1874.

Gainesville, Missouri—Gainesville is the county seat of Ozark County. It has a population of about 650 people, and it is home to the Gainesville R-5 School District and the Ozark County Historium. The town also hosts a popular annual festival called Hootin and Hollarin.

Galbraith, Art—Art Galbraith was a well-known old-time fiddle player from Springfield, Missouri. He died in 1993.

Galena, Kansas—Galena is a town of about 3,000 people in the extreme southeast corner of Kansas at the western edge of the Ozarks. It was founded in 1877 as a booming lead mining camp. Galena is home to the Galena Unified Schools 499.

Galena, Missouri—Galena, a town of about 450 people, is the seat of Stone County. Originally called Jamestown, it was named the county seat shortly after county formation in 1851, and the name was changed to Galena a couple of years later. (There was also a previous Jamestown in Stone County near the present site of Cape Fair that was destroyed by flood waters in 1844 and never rebuilt.) Galena is home to the Galena R-2 School District.

Garfield, Arkansas—Garfield is a town of about 500 people, located in Benton County northeast of Rogers on Highway 62.

Garrison, Missouri—Garrison is an unincorporated community in southeast Christian County on State Highway 125. It was founded in the early 1880s and named for "Uncle George" Garrison, who opened the first store there and later became the first postmaster.

Garrott House—Built in 1842 by pioneer George Case, the Garrott House is the oldest surviving structure in Batesville, Arkansas, and the first Batesville structure to be listed on the National Register of Historic Places (1971).

Gasconade, Missouri—Gasconade is a town of about 225 people in northern Gasconade County near the confluence of the Gasconade and Missouri rivers. It was the first seat of Gasconade County.

Gasconade Bridge Train Disaster—The Gasconade Bridge train disaster was a railroad accident that occurred at Gasconade in northern Gasconade County, Missouri on November 1, 1855. The Pacific Railroad had just completed a road from St. Louis to Jefferson City, and an inaugural train carrying about 600 dignitaries and other invited guests west from St. Louis fell into the Gasconade River when the bridge over the river collapsed, killing 31 people and injuring hundreds in the biggest railroad accident in Missouri history.

Gasconade County, Missouri—Located in east central Missouri, Gasconade County was formed in 1820 from territory taken from Franklin County. At the time it was organized, Gasconade County included all of Missouri west of Franklin County between the Missouri River and a latitude going through present-day Licking, but other counties were later formed from the original area of Gasconade. The county's name comes from a French term that means "boastfulness" or "to boast," and it was applied by early French settlers to the Indians they met in the area. Some people, including many residents, do not consider the northern portion of the county part of the Ozarks.

Gasconade River—The Gasconade River begins around Hartville, Missouri, in Wright County and flows in a north-northeasterly direction through Laclede, Pulaski, Phelps, Maries, Osage, and Gasconade counties to the Missouri River. At approximately 280 miles long, it is the longest river completely within the state of Missouri. It is also considered one of the crookedest rivers in the world, as its length covers only about 120 miles "as the crow flies."

Gassville, Arkansas—Gassville is a town of about 2,100 people in Baxter County. Located near the White River, it was originally called Turkey's Neck because of the shape of the river. In 1878, a post office was established and called Gassville, because, according to legend, the postmaster had a reputation as an incessant talker or a "gasser." A local feud resulted in the notorious 1892 murder of Baxter County sheriff Abraham Byler by Jesse Roper near Gassville. The town was incorporated in 1903.

Gateway, Arkansas—Gateway is a town of about 120 people in Benton County just south of the Missouri border at the intersection of State Highway 37 and U.S. Highway 62.

Gentry, Arkansas—Gentry is a town of about 3,150 people in western Benton County. It was founded in 1894 when a railroad was constructed through the area, and it quickly became a shipping point for apples and other fruit grown in the area. It was even called Orchard for a while but was incorporated in 1898 as Gentry, named for the first president of the railroad. When the orchard industry began to decline during the Depression, Gentry shifted its focus to poultry and other industries. The town is home to the Gentry Public School District and the Ozark Adventist Academy.

Gerald, Missouri—Gerald is a town of about 1,350 people in western Franklin County. "Fitz" was dropped from the name of some early settlers named Fitzgerald to give the community its name. Gerald was incorporated as a village in 1907, although it existed as an unincorporated community years earlier. It became a fourth-class city in 1947. Gerald formerly had a high school but now has only an elementary that is part of the Gasconade R-2 School District.

George Washington Carver National Monument—The George Washington Carver National Monument is located at Carver's birthplace three miles west of Diamond, Missouri. It is dedicated not only to preserving the birthplace but also to educating the public about science, nature, and other topics relating to Carver and his life.

Moses Carver home at George Washington Carver National Monument. *Photo by the author.*

Gerstacker, Friederich—Friederich Gerstacker was a popular nineteenth-century German author who wrote extensively about his travels through the backwoods of pre-Civil War Arkansas, including parts of the Ozarks,

Gibson baskets—Made for four generations by the Gibson family of northwest Arkansas, Gibson baskets are split white oak baskets woven from thin, flexible splints and assembled without nails. Gibson baskets were begun in the 1880s by Christopher Columbus "Lum" Gibson, and a collection of baskets made by his son, George Gibson, is on display at the Smithsonian Institution's Museum of American History. Lum's great grandson Terry Gibson continues the Ozarks craft of basket making from his workshop near Fayetteville.

Gibson, Robert Edward Lee—Robert Edward Lee Gibson was a minor poet and songwriter from Steelville, Missouri, who enjoyed limited popularity around the turn of the twentieth century.

Gifford, Bertha—Bertha Gifford was an infamous mass murderer who poisoned up to seventeen people near Catawissa, Missouri, over a period of about fifteen years ending with her arrest in 1928. She confessed to three murders and was suspected in numerous others. Most of her victims were children. She was found not guilty by reason of insanity and was committed to a mental institution.

Gilbert, Arkansas—Gilbert is a town in Searcy County with a 2010 population of 28 people, making it one of the smallest municipalities in the country. Built in 1901, the Gilbert General Store, under the name Mays Store, is on the National Register of Historic Places. Because of its secluded location, the town was chosen in 1920 as the site for a colony of the Incoming Kingdom Missionary Unit, a utopian religious group.

Gilchrist, Ellen—Ellen Gilchrist is an award-winning American novelist, short story writer, and poet. She is known for works like *Victory Over Japan*, a short story collection which won the National Book Award for Fiction in 1984. She is currently a professor of creative writing at the University of Arkansas.

Gilliland, Charles Leon—Born near Mountain Home, Arkansas, Charles Leon Gilliland was the youngest Medal of Honor recipient of the Korean War.

Gilmore, Robert K.—Robert K. Gilmore was a professor at what is now Missouri State University, co-founder in 1987 of *Ozarks Watch Magazine*, and author of *Ozark Baptisms, Hangings, and Other Diversions*.

Ginger Blue, Missouri—Ginger Blue is a village of about 60 people in McDonald County, Missouri. It was the site of a well-known resort for many years during the twentieth century.

Glade Top Trail—Missouri's only National Forest Scenic Byway, Glade Top Trail is a 23-mile driving trail that weaves through parts of Douglas, Ozark, and Taney counties.

Glass, David—David Glass is the former chief executive officer of Walmart and the current owner of the Kansas City Royals. He grew up in Mountain View, Missouri, and graduated from Southwest Missouri State University in Springfield (now Missouri State), where Glass Hall is named after him.

Glen Allen, Missouri—Glen Allen is a village of about 85 people in Bollinger County. It was established 1870 as a stop on the St. Louis, Iron Mountain and Southern Railroad. It was the site of one of Alcander Longley's utopian communities during the late 1800s.

Glenn, Wayne—Wayne Glenn, known as the Old Record Collector, has been a disc jockey on Springfield, Missouri, radio station KTXR-FM since 1977. He plays music from his extensive collection of older songs, and he is also known for having authored several books about the Ozarks, particularly his native Christian County.

Godsey, Townsend—Townsend Godsey was a photojournalist during the mid to late 1900s noted for his articles and photos of Ozarks people and places. The Townsend Godsey Archives are housed at the College of the Ozarks in Point Lookout, Missouri.

Goingsnake District—Goingsnake was one of eight districts of the Cherokee Nation. It was comprised mainly of present-day Adair County, Oklahoma.

Goingsnake Massacre—Resulting from a jurisdictional dispute between the U.S. government and the Cherokee court system, the Goingsnake Massacre was a gunfight on April 15, 1872, near present-day Christie, Oklahoma, that broke out between Cherokee Indians and U.S. marshals during Zeke Proctor's trial for killing Polly Beck. The shootout left eight U.S. marshals and three Cherokee Indians dead.

Gold, Gracie—Gracie Gold is an American figure skater who finished fourth in Figure Skating Ladies at the 2014 Sochi Olympics. She grew up and took her first skating lessons in Springfield, Missouri.

Golden, Missouri—Golden is an unincorporated community in southeastern Barry County. Its proximity to Table Rock Lake makes the vicinity of Golden a thriving resort area.

Golden City, Missouri—Golden City is a town of about 750 people in eastern Barton County. Established in the late 1860s as a stop on the Butterfield Stagecoach Line, it is home today to the Golden City R-3 School District.

Goodwill Family—The Goodwill Family was a popular gospel music group in the Ozarks during the mid-twentieth century. Its members included Slim Wilson, his sister Martha, and Martha's son, Speedy Haworth.

Goodman, Missouri—Goodman is a town of about 1,250 people in northern McDonald County. Goodman High School won the Class S Missouri State Basketball championship in 1964. A couple of years later, the school district consolidated with Neosho, and Goodman is still home to an elementary school that is part of the Neosho district.

Gordonville, Missouri—Gordonville is a village of about 390 people in southern Cape Girardeau County. Established in 1875, it is the home of Gordonville Elementary School.

Gowrow—The gowrow is a legendary monster said to haunt the backwoods of northwest Arkansas. The story of the gowrow probably owes its existence to a tall tale that appeared in the *Arkansas Gazette* on January 31, 1897, but folklorist Vance Randolph said in his *We Always Lie to Strangers: Tall Tales from the Ozarks* that the gowrow's existence had been reported as early as the 1880s.

Graham, Josephine Hutson—Josephine Hutson Graham was a folklorist and prolific artist perhaps best known for her authentic, primitive paintings depicting rural, Depression-era life in the White River country of Arkansas. Born in Jackson County, Arkansas, in 1915, she died in 1999.

Granby, Missouri—Granby is a town of about 2,100 people on U. S. Highway 60 in eastern Newton County. It was established during the 1850s as a booming lead mining camp and was considered the lead mining capital of the world in the years immediately prior to the Civil War. The mining boom continued after the war but slackened in the latter part of the nineteenth century as lead was discovered in other parts of southwest Missouri, and it petered out altogether in the twentieth century. Granby advertises itself as the Oldest Mining Town in the Southwest, it is home to the Granby Miners Museum, and it hosts an annual festival called Old Mining Town Days. High school students from Granby attend East Newton High School, located near Newtonia.

Grand Falls   Grand Falls is a waterfall on Shoal Creek at the south edge of Joplin, Missouri. Billed as the largest continuously flowing natural waterfall in Missouri, Grand Falls was once the site of an electrical power plant and a park that drew hundreds of visitors, but today it serves mainly as a hangout for young people and a curiosity for the occasional tourist.

Grand Gulf State Park—Located near Thayer, Missouri, Grand Gulf State Park preserves and presents the largest collapsed cave system in the Ozarks. Sometimes called the "Little Grand Canyon," the gulf is almost a mile long, about 120 feet deep, and 50 to 200 feet wide.

Grandin, Missouri—Grandin is a town of about 250 people in southeastern Carter County. It was established in the late 1880s by the Missouri Lumber and Mining Company and named for the two principal stockholders of the company, E.B. Grandin and George Grandin. The town grew to become one of the largest lumber milling centers in the country and at one time had a population of about 2,500, but the town declined dramatically after its lumber industry died during the Depression era.

Grand Lake of the Cherokees (aka Grand Lake)—Grand Lake of the Cherokees, familiarly known simply as Grand Lake, is a man-made reservoir on the Grand River in northeast Oklahoma in the western foothills of the Ozarks. It was created by construction of Pensacola Dam, which was completed in 1940 and named after the nearby community of Pensacola. Covering 46,500 acres, Grand Lake is popular for fishing, water skiing, and other water sports.

Grand River—Grand River is another name for the lower section of the Neosho River, a 463-mile tributary of the Arkansas River. The Neosho forms in east central Kansas and flows southward into Oklahoma. In Oklahoma, below its confluence with the Spring River near Miami in Ottawa County, it is known as the Grand River. It empties into the Arkansas River near Muskogee.

Graniteville, Missouri—Graniteville is an unincorporated community in Iron county about six miles north of Ironton. It was established in the mid-1870s and named for the nearby granite quarries. The town boomed for a while in the late 1800s during the peak of the area's granite mining. Graniteville is best known today as the site of Elephant Rocks State Park.

Gravely, Joseph J.—Joseph J. Gravely was a military officer and a politician from Cedar County, Missouri. During the Civil War he commanded the Eighth Missouri State Militia Cavalry. After the war, he served one term in the U.S. House of Representatives and later was lieutenant governor of Missouri.

Gravette, Arkansas—Gravette is a town of about 2,325 people in northern Benton County near the Missouri state line. Nebo, a forerunner to Gravette, was established in the area in the 1870s, but storeowner E.T. Gravett moved his business slightly west in the early 1890s, and the town of Gravette was laid out there in 1893 along the proposed line of the Kansas City, Pittsburg, and Gulf Railroad. It was named after Gravett, who had owned the land where the town was platted. Among the notable people from Gravette is former Major League Baseball player Gene Stephens, who was born there in 1933. When U.S. Highway 71 ran through Gravette, it was called the "Gate Community" because it was considered the gateway to northwest Arkansas from Missouri and surrounding states. Gravette is home to the Gravette Public Schools.

Gravois Mills, Missouri—Gravois Mills is a village of about 145 people in southern Morgan County on the Gravois Creek or northern arm of the Lake of the Ozarks. It was laid out in 1884 on Gravois Creek near some mills, and it thus took its name from its location.

Graydon Springs, Missouri—Located in southwest Polk County, Graydon Spring started as a health resort in the 1880s. The town hardly flourished, but in the mid twentieth century a Girl Scout camp called Camp Wakahni was started at the site. The camp was abandoned early in the twenty-first century, but a movement is underway to restore it.

Gray Summit, Missouri—Gray Summit is a community of about 2,700 people located along I-44 in northeast Franklin County at the northeast edge of the Ozarks. It was laid off in the late 1800s and named after Daniel Gray, who had opened a hotel at the site in 1845, and because it was the highest point along the Missouri Pacific Railroad in the region.

Great Passion Play—The Great Passion Play is an outdoor drama based on the life, death, and resurrection of Jesus Christ that is presented during the summer at Eureka Springs, Arkansas. Opened in 1968, it is one of the Five Sacred Projects founded by Gerald L.K. Smith and his wife, Elna M. Smith, on the grounds surrounding the outdoor amphitheater. (See Gerald Lyman Kenneth Smith)

Great Railroad Strike of 1922—The Great Railroad Strike of 1922, often called the Railway Shopmen's Strike, was a nationwide strike of approximately 400,000 railroad workers during the summer of 1922. It particularly affected Springfield, Missouri, home of the Frisco Railroad's shops.

Green Forest, Arkansas—Green Forest is a town of about 2,800 people in Carroll County. It was established before the Civil War and originally called Scott's Prairie after the first settler in the area, but it was renamed Green Forest in 1895. It is the home of the Green Forest Public Schools.

Greene County, Missouri—Greene County was formed in 1833 from territory taken from Crawford and Wayne counties, and it was named for Nathaniel Greene of Revolutionary War fame. Springfield was named the county seat in 1835. Greene County became the parent county of several later counties that were formed from its territory, including Barry, Polk and Taney

Greenfield, Missouri—Greenfield was established and named the seat of Dade County shortly after the county was formed in 1841. Greenfield has many historic buildings constructed during the late 1800s, including most of those on the public square. The town was home to Ozark College, a Presbyterian institution of higher learning, from 1882 until 1902. Greenfield has a current population of about 1,400 and is home to the Greenfield R-4 Schools.

Greenfield, Raid on—On the morning of October 6, 1863, Colonel Jo Shelby, during his noted raid into Missouri, drove the Union militia out of Greenfield and took possession of the town. The Confederates ransacked the place, set fire to the courthouse, and then marched out of town a few hours after entering it.

Greenland, Arkansas—Greenland is a town of about 1,300 people just south of Fayetteville in Washington County. Incorporated in 1910, it has grown rapidly in recent years. It is home to the Greenland School District.

Greenville, Missouri—Greenville was laid out in 1819 as the seat of Wayne County. The county was named for General Anthony Wayne, and Greenville was named for Fort Greenville, Ohio, the site where Wayne signed a treaty with a confederation of Native Americans ending the Northwest Indian War. Greenville today has a population of about 500, and it is home to the Greenville R-2 School District.

Greenwood, Alfred Burton—Alfred Burton Greenwood was an early settler of Benton County, Arkansas, who served three terms in the U.S. House of Representatives during the 1850s. During the Civil War, he was appointed by Jefferson Davis as the Confederate tax collector in Arkansas.

Greer, Dabbs—Robert William "Dabbs" Greer was a film and television actor who was born in Fairview, Missouri, and grew up in nearby Anderson. He died in 2007.

Greers Ferry, Arkansas—Greers Ferry is a town of about 900 on the north shore of Greers Ferry Lake in western Cleburne County. It was established in 1968, primarily by citizens who had been displaced from their homes by construction of the lake and dam. The town is perhaps best known for the recreational opportunities offered by the lake. Greers Ferry is home to the West Side School District.

Greers Ferry Lake and Dam—Greers Ferry Lake is a reservoir created by the damming of the Little Red River in western Cleburne County, Arkansas. The dam and lake were created primarily as a flood control measure, but they also supply hydroelectric power. Construction occurred between 1959 and 1962, and the dam was dedicated on October 3, 1963, by President John F. Kennedy. The lake is often cited as one of the top ten cleanest and clearest lakes in North America. One of its features is Sugar Loaf Mountain, which rises from an island in the middle of the lake.

Greer Spring—Greer Spring is located in Oregon County, Missouri, about eight miles north of Alton in the Mark Twain National Forest. It is the second largest spring in the state with an average discharge of about 220 million gallons of water per day.

Grove, Oklahoma—Grove is a town of about 6,625 people in Delaware County on the banks of the Grand Lake of the Cherokees. The area was known by a variety of names, including Grove Springs, until a post office was established at the site in the 1880s and called simply Grove. Grove was the only incorporated town in Delaware

County at the time of Oklahoma statehood in 1907, and it became the county seat. However, the seat was moved to Jay a few years later. Sailboat Bridge, the second-largest bridge in Oklahoma, spans Grand Lake just north of Grove. Grove is home to the Grove Public Schools. Area resident and noted country musician Jana Jae holds an annual fiddle camp and festival at Grove each year.

Grovespring, Missouri—Grovespring is a small community on State Highway 5 in northwest Wright County. It was established about 1885 and got its name from its location in a grove near a spring. Today, Grovespring is home to an elementary school, a church, a senior center, and two or three businesses.

Guerrillas, Civil War—During America's Civil War, guerrillas were irregular soldiers who generally fought for the South but were not affiliated with or only loosely affiliated with the Confederate army. They were prevalent throughout most of Missouri and also inhabited northern Arkansas. Sometimes called bushwhackers, they waged a war of sabotage and plunder and usually did not wear uniforms or else donned the uniform of the enemy. Union sympathizing guerrillas also existed in the Ozarks, especially in northern Arkansas, but they were fewer in number than Southern-sympathizing guerrillas.

Guion, Arkansas—Guion is town of about 90 people in Izard County. Located on the White River, the area was originally settled as a landing in the mid-1800s. The small town that grew up at the river landing was called Louis until 1903, when the name was changed to Guion. After the coming of a railroad in 1902, the town thrived as a business center during the early twentieth century but declined during the mid-1900s. The local school consolidated with Mount Pleasant in 1968. Today, Guion is noted mostly for its nearby sand mines.

Gunter, Lando—Lando Gunter was leader of an outlaw gang that pulled off a string of robberies and other crimes in the Missouri Ozarks and in eastern Oklahoma during the early 1930s. Known as the "Ozark Bandit," he was captured at his mother's house near Dora, Missouri, in 1935. Convicted of bank robbery and kidnapping, he was sentenced to 25 years in prison.

Gunter, Thomas M.—Thomas M. Gunter was a soldier, attorney, and politician from Fayetteville, Arkansas. He was a colonel in the Confederate Army during the Civil War, and he represented northwest Arkansas in the U.S. House of Representatives from 1874 to 1883.

H

Hackney, Thomas—Thomas Hackney was a lawyer and politician from Carthage, Missouri. He served as a U.S. congressman from southwest Missouri from 1907 to 1909.

Ha Ha Tonka State Park—Ha Ha Tonka State Park is a Missouri state park about five miles south of Camdenton on the Niangua arm of the Lake of the Ozarks. It has several nature trails and contains Ha Ha Tonka Spring. Perhaps the most notable feature of the park is a stone mansion or "castle" that was begun in 1905 by Robert McClure Snyder and completed during the 1920s by his sons. It was used as a

Ruins of castle at Ha Ha Tonka State Park. *Courtesy Wikimedia.*

hotel until it was ruined by fire in 1942. The state purchased the grounds and castle in 1978 and opened the property as Ha Ha Tonka State Park. The castle has since been partially restored. Ha Ha Tonka was named for a small community at or near the same site around the turn of the twentieth century. It was earlier known as Gunter.

Halbrook, William Erwin—Born in Van Buren County, William Erwin Halbrook was a prominent educator in the Arkansas Ozarks during the first half of the twentieth century and helped modernize the schools of the region, especially Boone County, where he served as country superintendent of schools for a number of years.

Halfway, Missouri—Halfway is a town of about 175 people in eastern Polk County. Prior to the Civil War, the town's first postmaster named the place because of its location halfway between Bolivar and Buffalo. Halfway is home to the Halfway R-3 School District.

Hall, David—David Hall was an African-American pioneer and leader of a free black community that settled in Marion County, Arkansas, prior to the Civil War. Although ostensibly barred by state law from living in Arkansas, the group was allowed to settle in Marion County with little interference from local whites, and at least 129 free blacks lived in the county at one time. An 1852 murder case involving a white man and a free black man marked the beginning of the community's decline, and the African-Americans were finally driven from the state altogether by Arkansas's 1859 expulsion law, "An Act to Remove the Free Negroes and Mulattoes from the State."

Hall, Doug—A native of Neosho, Missouri, Doug Hall is an oil painter known especially for his paintings of Native Americans, such as his mural of the First Battle of Newtonia depicting their involvement in that battle.

Hall, Durward—Durward Hall was a medical doctor and a politician from Springfield, Missouri. He served from 1961 to 1973 in the U.S. House of Representatives, where he was sometimes called "Dr. No," because of his propensity for voting "no."

Halltown, Missouri—Halltown is a community of about 175 people in northeast Lawrence County. Located along old Route 66, it was a booming little town during the highway's heyday and was known as the "Antique Capital of the World" because of the many antique shops located there, but Halltown has declined since construction of Interstate 44. It once had a high school, but students from the area now go to Miller Schools.

Hammerschmidt, John Paul—John Paul Hammerschmidt is a politician from Harrison, Arkansas. He served thirteen terms in the U.S. House of Representatives as a congressman from northwest Arkansas, retiring in 1993.

Hamilton, Jodie—Jodie Hamilton committed the most notorious crime in the history of Texas County, Missouri, and one of the most notorious ever in the Missouri Ozarks. In October of 1906, he shot sharecropper Carney Parsons with a shotgun blast in front of his family and finished him off by bludgeoning him with the gun. He also beat the man's wife to death when she tried to come to her husband's aid. Then he beat in the brains of the couple's three kids, killing all three. Hamilton was captured shortly afterwards and hanged at Houston in December of 1906. His execution turned into a spectacle, as the convict prayed, sang songs, and exhorted the young people present not to stray from the narrow path as he had done.

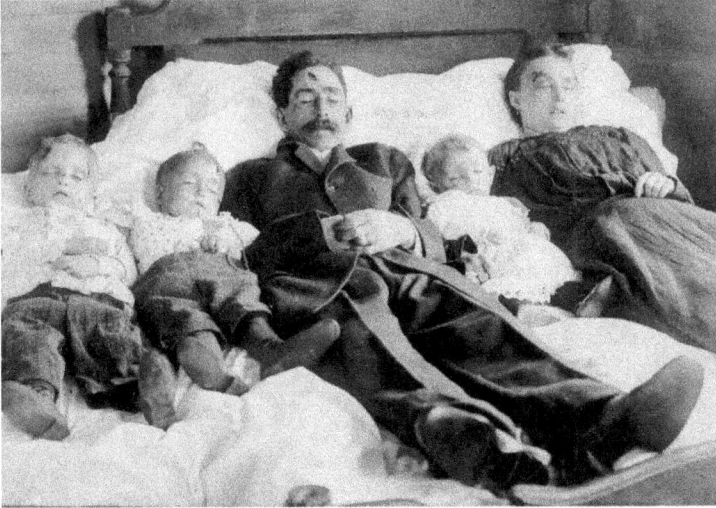

Parsons family, victims of Jodie Hamilton. *Courtesy Texas County Genealogical and Historical Society.*

Hamlin, Courtney W.—Courtney W. Hamlin was a lawyer who represented southwest Missouri in the U.S. Congress from 1903 to 1905. He grew up in Crawford County and later lived at Bolivar and Springfield.

Hammons, John Q.—John Q. Hammons was a businessman and property developer who grew up in Fairview, Missouri, and spent most of his life in Springfield, where several structures, including Hammons Field, John Q. Hammons Arena, and Hammons Tower (the tallest building in the Ozarks) bear his name. He died in 2013.

Hancock, Mel—Mel Hancock was a politician from Springfield who represented southwest Missouri in the U.S. House of Representatives from 1989 to 1997, but he is perhaps best remembered for his previous work in getting the Hancock Amendment, a tax limitation bill, passed through the Missouri state legislature.

Har-Ber Village—Har-Ber Village is an antique museum in the form of a reconstructed, turn-of-the-twentieth-century town located about three miles southwest of Grove, Oklahoma at the edge of Grand Lake. It features authentic buildings, furnishings, tools, and other items from the late 1800s and early 1900s. In 1968, Harvey and Bernice Jones created the village, which was originally their summer home, by purchasing old buildings and artifacts and bringing them to the location. The village is open to the public as a tourist destination.

Replica of one-room schoolhouse at Har-Ber Village. *Photo by the author.*

Hardy, Arkansas—Hardy is a town of about 775 people in northern Sharp County at the Fulton County border. The town grew up along the railroad in the 1880s. In the 1890s, Hardy was named the seat of Sharp County's northern district and retained that status until the 1960s, when the county's dual county seats (the other one being Evening Shade) were dissolved and Ash Flat was named the county seat. During the early part of the twentieth century, Hardy became a tourist and resort destination, and the area still draws many vacationers today. Hardy is home to the Highland Public Schools.

Harington, Donald—Donald Harington was an award-winning American author known for such novels as *The Architecture of the Arkansas Ozarks*. Most of his novels were set in the fictional town of Stay More, which was loosely based on Drakes Creek, Arkansas, east of Fayetteville, where Harington spent summers as a child. Harington taught at the University of Arkansas for twenty-two years prior to his death in 2009.

Harmonial Vegetarian Society—The Harmonial Vegetarian Society was an experimental community founded about 1857 by physician James E. Spencer in Benton County, Arkansas, about two or three miles east of Maysville. The site was known as Harmony Springs, while the group was called the Harmonial Vegetarian Society.

Patterned after the earlier Oneida Community in New York state, the group professed Christianity but was scorned by many locals for not keeping the Sabbath and other supposed violations of moral code. The group was already in decline by the time Arkansas troops took over its grounds as a training area at the beginning of the Civil War.

Harper, Tess—Tess Harper is a film and TV actress, known for roles in such movies as *Tender Mercies* and *Crimes of the Heart*. She grew up in Mammoth Spring, Arkansas, and attended Southwest Missouri State College (now Missouri State University) in Springfield.

Harrington, M. R.—M.R. Harrington was a pioneering archeologist who studied Indian sites in Arkansas during the 1910s and 1920s. During the early twenties, he led an expedition that investigated rock shelters in Benton, Carroll, Madison, Marion, and Newton counties of Arkansas and in McDonald County, Missouri. Harrington published an article about this work in 1924, but his book on the subject, *The Ozark Bluff-Dwellers*, was not published until 1960.

Harrison, Arkansas—Harrison is the seat of Boone County. It was laid out as the county seat at the time Boone County was organized in 1869, and it was named for M. LaRue Harrison, the former Union officer who platted it. As the largest town in Boone County, with a population of about 13,500, Harrison is the commercial center for the county and for much of north central Arkansas. It is home to the Harrison School District.

Harrison, David—David Harrison is a nationally known children's author and poet who lives in Springfield, Missouri, where an elementary school is named after him. He is poet laureate of Drury University and was one of the founders of and first inductees into the Springfield-based Writers Hall of Fame.

Harrison Flood—In May of 1961, downtown Harrison and much of the southwest part of the town flooded when Crooked Creek, which flows through the town, raged out of its banks. Four people were killed, over 300 buildings were destroyed or damaged, and approximately 100 vehicles were destroyed, many of them picked up by the churning waters and reportedly tossed about like matchsticks.

Harrison Race Riots—The Harrison Race Riot of 1905 began after a mob broke some prisoners, including two black men, out of the county jail, took them to the edge of town, whipped them, and ordered them to leave. The mob then returned to town and rampaged through the black district of Harrison, driving much of the African-American population out of town. A similar riot occurred four years later after a black man allegedly assaulted a white woman, but by then most of Harrison's formerly thriving black community had already left. After the second riot, only one black person remained in Harrison.

Harrison Railroad Riot—The Harrison Railroad Riot was a two-year outbreak of anti-union violence against striking workers of the Missouri and North Arkansas Railroad. Supported by city government, local business interests, and the Ku Klux Klan, the violence culminated with the lynching of a striking worker just outside Harrison, Arkansas, in January of 1923 and the forced exodus of the strikers to Missouri.

Harrison, Marcus LaRue—M. LaRue Harrison was a colonel during the Civil War who recruited and led the First Arkansas Cavalry (Union). Composed mostly of refugees from Arkansas, the unit operated in southwest Missouri and northwest Arkansas. A trained engineer, Harrison also designed the fortifications at Springfield.

Harrison, William Neal—William Neal Harrison was a novelist, short story writer, and screenwriter noted especially for writing the screenplay for the 1975 movie *Rollerball* based on his short story and for starting the University of Arkansas creative writing program.

Hartville, Missouri—Hartville is a town of about 615 people and the seat of Wright County. Named for early settler Isaac Hart, who donated land for the town site, Hartville already existed as a small village at the time Wright County was formed in 1841, and it was named the county seat. Hartville was virtually destroyed during the Civil War but was soon rebuilt after the war. The town is home to the Hartville R-2 School District.

Hartville, Battle of—The Battle of Hartville was a Civil War engagement that occurred January 9-11, 1863 at Hartville, Missouri. Minor skirmishing on the 9th and 10th led up to the main action on January 11, when Confederate forces under brigadier general John S. Marmaduke fought a four-hour battle with Union forces under Colonel Samuel Merrill. Although Merrill eventually withdrew and the battle is, therefore, considered a Confederate victory, Marmaduke sustained more casualties (slightly over 100, whereas the Union had slightly less than 100), and the Southerners were compelled to retire to Arkansas almost immediately after the battle.

Harvey, William Hope "Coin"—Coin Harvey was a businessman, lawyer, and silver miner who won fame during the 1890s promoting the free silver cause. In 1894, he published a successful book called *Coin's Financial School* which presented his arguments in favor of silver and gave him his nickname, and during the 1896 presidential race he campaigned throughout the country for silver candidate William Jennings Bryan. He is best known in the Ozarks as the founder of the Monte Ne resort in Benton County, Arkansas, where he himself was nominated for president in 1931 as the candidate of the Liberty Party.

Harviell, Missouri—Harviell is an unincorporated community south of Poplar Bluff in Butler County. It was established about 1873 as a railroad town and named for local landowner Simeon Harviell.

Hastings, William Wirt—William W. Hastings was a lawyer and politician who was born in Benton County, Arkansas, and lived much of his adult life in Tahlequah, Oklahoma. He represented the eastern part of Oklahoma in the U.S. House of Representatives from 1915 to 1921 and from 1923 to 1935.

Havens, Harrison E.—Harrison E. Havens was a lawyer, newspaper editor, and politician from Springfield, Missouri. He served southwest Missouri in the U.S. House of Representatives from 1871 to 1875.

Haw Creek Falls Recreation Area—Haw Creek Falls Recreation Area is a campground in the Ozark National Forest in northern Johnson County, Arkansas, which features its namesake waterfall.

Hawksley, Oz—Designated by Missouri as a master conservationist, Oscar "Oz" Hawksley is perhaps best known for his book *Missouri Ozarks Waterways*.

Hawkins, Ronnie—Ronnie Hawkins is a Juno Award-winning rockabilly singer who is considered influential in the evolution of rock music in Canada. Born in 1935 at Huntsville, Arkansas, he moved to Fayetteville at age nine and went to high school there. His music career started in Arkansas, but he soon moved to Canada. He is crediting with helping develop numerous musicians through his backing band, the Hawks. The members of the most noted incarnation of the Hawks, including Levon Helm and Robbie Robertson, formed the legendary group the Band after leaving Hawkins.

Haworth, Speedy—A nephew of Slim Wilson, Speedy Haworth was a country and gospel singer who achieved success during the 1940s,

1950s, and 1960s as a member of the Goodwill Family and the Tall Timber Trio. He was a backup musician for Porter Wagoner and other famous performers and a cast member of the *Ozarks Jubilee* and the *Slim Wilson Show*.

Hazelgreen Volcanics See Weaubleau Osceola Structure

Hazeltine, Ira S.—Ira S. Hazeltine was a lawyer, orchardist, and U. S. congressman from Greene County Missouri. He served one term in the U. S. House as a member of the Greenback Party from 1881 to 1883.

Headlee, Samuel S., Killing of—Samuel S. Headlee was a Southern sympathizer and minister of the Methodist Episcopal Church South who was killed by Northern sympathizers in July of 1866 when he tried to preach at a church in northwest Webster County, Missouri, that was held by the Methodist Episcopal Church North. The rancor aroused by the Civil War lingered in the Ozarks (and elsewhere) long after the war officially ended, and sometimes the bitter feelings spawned violent incidents such as this one.

Sketch by Nic Frising depicting murder of Rev. Samuel S. Headlee. *Author's collection.*

Headquarters House Museum—The Headquarters House Museum is a museum of the Washington County (Arkansas) Historical Society housed in the historic Headquarters House at Fayetteville. The house was built in 1853 and served in the Civil War as a headquarters for both the Union and Confederate armies during their respective occupations of Fayetteville.

Headrick-Lail Murder Case—The murder of James Lail by John Headrick near Jackson, Missouri, in 1898, and the subsequent hanging of Headrick for the crime is perhaps the most notorious murder case in the history of Cape Girardeau County. It is commemorated even today by a mural painted inside the courthouse.

Heber Springs, Arkansas—Located in the southeastern Ozarks, Heber Springs is the county seat of Cleburne County. First called Sugar Loaf Springs, it was founded as a resort at the site of some mineral water springs (present day Spring Park). When the postal service rejected the name Sugar Loaf, the local post office took the name Heber Springs after the son of an early owner of the town site, but the town continued to be called Sugar Loaf for several more years. President Kennedy visited Heber Springs in 1963 for the dedication of Greers Ferry Dam. Heber Springs has a current population of about 6,500 people, and it is home to the Heber Springs School District and the Greers Ferry National Fish Hatchery.

Hector, Arkansas—Hector is a town of about 500 people in central Pope County at the southern edge of the Ozark National Forest. The town was reportedly named for President Grover Cleveland's dog by the President himself when post office officials grew frustrated with the town's inability to settle on a name.

Heerwagon, Paul Martin—Paul Martin Heerwagon was an interior decorator who worked out of his studio in Fayetteville, Arkansas, from 1911 to 1931. Some of his noteworthy projects include the Arkansas state capitol in Little Rock, the Peabody Hotel in Memphis, Tennessee, and the Strand Theatre in Shreveport, Louisiana.

Hemmed-In Hollow Falls—Hemmed-In Hollow Falls is a single-drop waterfall in the Ponca Wilderness Area of the Buffalo National River in Newton County, Arkansas. At 209 feet, it is the tallest waterfall between the Rockies and the Appalachians.

Henderson, Missouri—Henderson is an unincorporated community in southwest Webster County, just north of Rogersville. During the late 1800s, it was a flourishing little town with a peak population of about 300 people. It was known particularly for the Henderson Academy, a school that had an enrollment of about 120 students in 1880.

Henley, Jesse Smith—Born in Searcy County, Arkansas, Jesse Smith Henley was a federal district judge in Arkansas during the mid-twentieth century who presided over a number of desegregation cases and who reformed the state's prison system. He died in Harrison in 1997.

Hensley, Violet Brumley—Sometimes called the "Stradivarius of the Ozarks," Violet Brumley Hensley is a musician and fiddle maker who has received wide recognition for her handcrafted fiddles.

Hercules Glades Wilderness Area—Hercules Glades is a 12,300-acre wilderness area in eastern Taney County, Missouri, within the Mark Twain National Forest.

Hermann, Missouri—Located on the south side of the Missouri River, Hermann is a town of about 2,450 people and the seat of Gasconade County. It was settled by Germans in 1837 and became the county seat in 1842. Hermann celebrates both its German heritage and its status as the center of Missouri's wine industry with an annual Oktoberfest held each weekend in October. Hermann is home to the Gasconade County R-1 Schools.

Hermitage, Missouri—Hermitage was laid out in 1847 as the seat of Hickory County. It has a population of about 470 people and is home to the Hermitage R-4 School District.

Herron, Francis Jay—Francis J. Herron was a Union officer during the Civil War. He served as a captain at the Battle of Wilson's Creek and as a lieutenant colonel at the Battle of Pea Ridge. He was promoted to brigadier general and led two divisions of the Army of the Frontier at the Battle of Prairie Grove in December 1862. He was later promoted to major general.

Hess, Joan Edmiston—Joan Edmiston Hess is a well-known author of mystery novels who grew up in northwest Arkansas, and many of her books are set in the Arkansas Ozarks. She has won numerous awards, including the American Mystery Award for best traditional novel of 1989.

Hickok, James B. "Wild Bill"—James Butler "Wild Bill" Hickok was a famous gunfighter and lawman of the Old West. He was stationed at Springfield, Missouri, during the latter part of the Civil War, and his shootout with Davis Tutt on the Springfield square in July of 1865 is widely considered the first Wild West gunfight.

James Butler "Wild Bill" Hickok. *Author's collection.*

Hickory County, Missouri—Hickory County was formed in 1845 from territory taken from Benton and Polk counties. It was named in honor of Andrew Jackson, who was nicknamed Old Hickory. A site for the permanent county seat was selected in 1846 or 1847 and named Hermitage after Jackson's home in Tennessee.

High Point, Missouri—High Point is an unincorporated community in southern Moniteau County six miles south of California at the northern edge of the Ozarks. Founded prior to the Civil War after lead was discovered nearby, it takes its name from the fact that it is the most elevated point in the county.

High, Fred—Fred High was a preserver of Ozarks folklore and music, and many of his folksongs were also recorded by others. In addition, he wrote three self-published books, including *It Happened* *in the Ozarks*, which contribute to the folklore of the region. A lifelong resident of Carroll County, he was well known throughout northern Arkansas during the twentieth century until his death in 1962.

Highfill, Arkansas—Highfill is a town of about 560 people in central Denton County. It is home to the Northwest Arkansas Regional Airport.

Highland, Arkansas—Highland is a town of about 1,050 people in northern Sharp County. In 1962, when the Ash Flat and Hardy school districts consolidated, they built a high school halfway between the two towns on U.S. Highway 62 and called the consolidated district the Highland School District. The town of Highland grew up around the new high school.

Highlandville, Missouri—Highlandville is a town of about 910 people in central Christian County. It was settled during the late 1800s. Highlandville is served by the Spokane R-7 School District, which has a Highlandville mailing address.

Hildebrand, Sam—During the Civil War, Sam Hildebrand was a notorious Confederate guerrilla from St. Francois County, Missouri. He became an outlaw after the war and continued to terrorize southeast Missouri until he was killed in 1872 just across the Mississippi River in Illinois.

Hillbilly—"Hillbilly" is a term that has often been used to refer to white people of Appalachia and the Ozarks in a derogatory sense, implying that they are poor, ignorant, and largely uncivilized. Fueled by news stories of mountain feuds, such as the one between the Hatfields and the McCoys in the 1880s, the stereotype of the hillbilly developed during the late 19th century and early 20th century.

Hillsboro, Missouri—Hillsboro is located in Jefferson County at the northeast edge of the Ozarks. Originally called Monticello, the town was established in the late 1830s as the county seat, and the name was changed to Hillsboro shortly afterwards. Hillsboro has a population of about 2,850, and it is home to the Hillsboro R-3 School District.

Hills of Home: The Rural Ozarks of Arkansas—*Hills of Home: The Rural Ozarks of Arkansas* is a mostly photographic book that was originally published in 1975 by Roger and Bob Minick, offering a nostalgic look at the Arkansas Ozarks.

Hindman, Thomas Carmichael—Thomas C. Hindman was a U.S. congressman from northeast Arkansas for one term prior to the Civil

War and a Confederate general during the war. In 1862, he briefly commanded the Trans Mississippi Department. Later in the year, as commander of the District of Arkansas, he led the Confederate forces at the Battle of Prairie Grove.

Hindsville, Arkansas—Hindsville is a town of about 75 people in northwest Madison County. Lake Hindsville, one of the oldest man-made lakes in Arkansas, is nearby.

Hiwasse, Arkansas—Hiwasse is an unincorporated community of about 500 people in northern Benton County. It was established about 1900 as a settlement along the railroad that ran west from Bentonville into Indian Territory, and the area was known for its apple production during the first part of the twentieth century. It is home to the historic Holloway House, also called the Pioneer House or Hiwasse Hotel.

Hobbs State Park-Conservation Area—Hobbs State Park-Conservation Area is a natural park with limited development located east of Rogers, Arkansas, near Beaver Lake. It has hiking trails and wildlife viewing areas, among other features. Covering over 12,000 acres, it is Arkansas's largest state park in land area.

Hoberg, Missouri—Hoberg is a village of about 55 people in Lawrence County about three miles southwest of Mount Vernon. It was laid out in 1903 on land owned by Daniel Withams and Henry Hoberg along the line of the Missouri Pacific Railroad. It flourished briefly during the early 1900s, attaining a population of about 200, but it has since declined.

Holden, Bob—Bob Holden was the 53rd governor of Missouri, serving from 2001 to 2005. He was reared on a farm near Birch Tree, Missouri, and attended what is now Missouri State University in Springfield.

Holiday Island—Holiday Island is a planned retirement and vacation community at the edge of Table Rock Lake in northern Carroll County, Arkansas.

Holland, Colley B.—Colley B. Holland was a Union officer who rose to the rank of brigadier general commanding the Enrolled Missouri Militia in southwest Missouri during the Civil War. A resident of Springfield, Missouri, he is perhaps best remembered for his role in defense of the town during the Battle of Springfield in January of 1863.

Hollister, Missouri—Hollister is a town of about 4,425 people in western Taney County. It was established as a crossroads settlement on the west bank of Turkey Creek in the 1880s. It was named Hollister when Reuben Kirkham, who opened at store at the site in the early 1900s, applied for a post office in 1904. It was named after Hollister, California, where Kirkham had formerly lived. Hollister was developed in the early 1900s as a planned, English-style village, and many of the town's older buildings of Elizabethan or mock Tudor style still exist. The town is home to the Hollister R-5 Schools.

Honey Branch Cave—A former show cave, Honey Branch Cave is now part of the Garden of Dreams, a commercial, outdoor wedding venue east of Sparta, Missouri.

Honey Creek State Park—Located near Grove, Honey Creek State Park is a 30-acre Oklahoma state park offering access to Grand Lake.

Horseshoe Bend, Arkansas—Horseshoe Bend is a town of about 2,185 people located primarily in the northeast corner of Izard County but spilling over slightly into Sharp and Fulton. It was developed in the 1960s and early 1970s as a retirement community and named for a loop or bend in the Strawberry River, on which it is located. It is the largest town in Izard County.

House of Lords—The House of Lords was a noted restaurant, saloon, and gambling house at Joplin, Missouri, during the mining boom of the early 1900s. It also reputedly housed a brothel on an upstairs floor.

Houston, Missouri—Houston is a town of about 2,100 people and the seat of Texas County. The county was organized in 1845, and Houston was laid out as the county seat the following year and named for Sam Houston, president of the Republic of Texas and later a U.S. senator from Texas. The town was destroyed during the Civil War but rebuilt afterward. A city park at Houston is named after famous clown Emmett Kelly, who grew up nearby. Houston is home to the Houston R-1 Schools.

Howell County, Missouri—Howell County was organized in 1857 from parts of Oregon and Ozark counties. West Plains was named the county seat, and a courthouse was built. It and most of the rest of West Plains were destroyed during the Civil War, but the courthouse and the town were rebuilt after the war.

Hoxie, Arkansas—Hoxie is a town of about 2,780 people in eastern Lawrence County at the edge of the Ozarks. It was formed in the late

1870s when a railroad wanted to come through the area and leaders of the nearby town of Walnut Ridge could not agree on a location. Henry and Mary Boas offered some of their land south of Walnut Ridge for the road, and Hoxie, named for a railroad executive, grew up around the railroad. Hoxie gained national attention in 1955 when its public school became the fourth school in Arkansas to desegregate, and the case was profiled in *Life Magazine*. Hoxie is home to the Hoxie Public Schools.

Hubbard, Cora—Dubbed the "Second Belle Starr" in newspaper headlines, Cora Hubbard was a female bandit who helped rob a bank at Pineville, Missouri, in 1897.

Bank robber Cora Hubbard. *Courtesy McDonald County Library.*

Hubbard, Joel D.—Joel D. Hubbard was a doctor, lawyer, and politician from Morgan County, Missouri, who served in the U.S. House of Representatives from 1895-1897.

Hubble, Edwin—Edwin Hubble was a famous astronomer after whom the Hubble Space Telescope is named. He is known, among other reasons, for "Hubble's Law," which suggests that the universe is expanding. Hubble was born in Marshfield, Missouri, in 1889.

Hudson, George—George Hudson was one of several notorious outlaws who came out of Granby, Missouri, during the post-Civil War era. He was known to have killed five men in four separate affrays and was rumored to have killed at least a couple more, but he avoided conviction by intimidating witnesses. His most notorious crime was the unprovoked murder of a Joplin dentist in 1886. Although acquitted of the crime, he was widely considered guilty. Hudson was finally killed in 1892 by a Colorado lawman sent to Missouri to arrest Hudson on an old assault charge in Colorado.

George Hudson, second from left, at Granby, Missouri. *Photo courtesy of Granby Miners Museum.*

Hudspeth-Watkins Murder Case—The notorious Hudspeth-Watkins murder case involved a series of events surrounding the disappearance of George Watkins in Marion County, Arkansas, in December of 1886. Watkins's wife, Rebecca, who had been romantically involved with the couple's hired hand, Andy Hudspeth, was suspected of plotting with Hudspeth to kill her husband, and Hudspeth was charged with murder for carrying out the deed. Rebecca died before coming to trial for her part in the crime, while Hudspeth was convicted of murder and eventually hanged, even though

Watkins's body was never found. After the execution, a specious report surfaced that Watkins had been found alive living in Kansas.

Hughes, Langston—See Joplin, Missouri.

Hughes Mountain Natural Area—A property of the Missouri Department of Conservation, Hughes Mountain Natural Area preserves 462 acres at the site of Hughes Mountain in southeast Washington County. The Devil's Honeycomb, polygonal columns of stone up to three feet tall that resemble a honeycomb when viewed from above, is located on Hughes Mountain.

Hulston Mill—Hulston Mill is a historic mill in Dade County, Missouri, that was established in 1840 and played an important role during the Civil War in processing grain for troops. The mill is located at Hulston Mill Historic Park a mile or two from its original site and about seven miles east of Greenfield. The park hosts an annual Civil War encampment called Hulston Mill Civil War Days.

Humansville, Missouri—Humansville is a town of about 1,050 in northwest Polk County. A post office was established at the site shortly before the Civil War and named for James Human, a prominent early citizen of the area. The town was incorporated in 1873. Humansville is home to the Humansville R-4 School District.

Humansville, Skirmish at—A skirmish occurred at Humansville, Missouri, on March 26, 1862, involving several companies of Missouri State Militia on the Union side and three or four hundred guerrillas and rebel recruits under Colonel James M. "Polk" Frazier of Cedar County. The action resulted in few casualties, but Colonel Frazier, who was killed, was one of them. Humansville was also the site of a brief skirmish during Confederate colonel Jo Shelby's cavalry raid into Missouri during the fall of 1863.

Hunt, Johnnie Bryan—Johnnie Bryan Hunt, usually known as J.B. Hunt, was the founder of J.B. Hunt Transport Services. Born in 1927 near Heber Springs, Arkansas, Hunt started the company in the 1960s, and by 1980 it had grown into the largest publicly held trucking company in America. The company is still based in Lowell, Arkansas, where Hunt lived at the time of his death in 2006.

Hunter, David—David Hunter was a Civil War general who briefly led the Union forces at Springfield, Missouri, in the fall of 1861.

Hunter, Missouri—Hunter is an unincorporated community in southeast Carter County. Like its neighbor Grandin, Hunter was established in the late 1880s by the Missouri Lumber and Mining Company and was a booming lumber milling town for many years. Hunter achieved its highest population of about 700 in 1920. It now has a population of less than 200.

Hunting—While hunting is not distinctive to the Ozarks, it is perhaps a more ingrained part of the region's culture than in many other areas of the United States. Hunting was a way of life and a means of survival for most early settlers, and hunting is still very popular as an outdoor sport today. By way of illustration, Missouri is traditionally one of the leading states in the country in terms annual deer harvest, and the counties of Howell, Oregon, and Texas in the southern Missouri Ozarks are usually among the leading counties in the state. Other game, such as rabbits, squirrels, raccoons, and various kinds of wild birds, are also regularly hunted in the Ozarks. See White-tailed deer.

Huntsville, Arkansas—Huntsville is a town of about 2,350 people and the seat of Madison County. It was founded in the late 1820s and named by some settlers who had migrated from the Huntsville, Alabama, area. It became the county seat after Madison County was formed in 1836. The Trail of Tears passed through Huntsville. During the Civil War, Huntsville was the site of what became known as the Huntsville Massacre. (See entry below.) Governor Orville Faubus lived at Huntsville and built his mansion there in the late 1960s. Legendary musician Ronnie Hawkins, whose band the Hawks later formed the Band, was born in Huntsville. The town is home to the Huntsville School District.

Huntsville Massacre—The so-called Huntsville Massacre occurred on January 10, 1863, at the height of the Civil War, when nine men who were being held prisoner at the guardhouse in Huntsville by the Union army were taken out and executed just beyond the town limits. The reason for the executions is not definitely known, although it may have been in response to the ambush of a Union escort just outside town by Confederate guerrillas a few weeks earlier.

Hurley, Missouri—Hurley is a town of about 180 people located on Spring Creek in Stone County. The first business was a mill, and the place was called Spring Creek Mill. When the community got its first post office around the turn of the twentieth century, however, it was renamed Hurley. Hurley is home to the Hurley R-1 School District.

Hurley Arch (aka James River Arch)—Located on the James River east of Hurley, Missouri, the Hurley Arch is a natural rock bridge formed by the erosion of an arch-shaped opening through the limestone rock.

Hurricane River Cave—Hurricane River Cave is a commercial cave located near Pindall, Arkansas, on U.S. Highway 65 in Searcy County. The cave offers extreme or wild cave tours, involving difficult climbing and crawling, in addition to regular tours.

Hutchinson, Asa— Born in Bentonville, Asa Hutchinson represented northwest Arkansas in the U.S. House of Representatives from 1997 to 2001 and served as head of the Drug Enforcement Administration from 2001-2003. He was elected governor of the state in 2014.

Hutchinson, Tim—The older brother of Asa Hutchinson, Tim Hutchinson represented northwest Arkansas in the U.S. House of Representatives from 1993 to 1997 and was a U.S. senator from Arkansas from 1997 to 2003. He was reared near Gravette and currently lives in Washington, DC.

Huzzah, Missouri—Huzzah is an unincorporated community in eastern Crawford County along Huzzah Creek in the Mark Twain National Forest.

Huzzah Conservation Area—Managed by the Missouri Department of Conservation, the Huzzah Conservation Area is a 6,225-acre area in Crawford County that is popular for outdoor activities like camping, fishing, and hiking.

Huzzah Creek—Located in Crawford County, Missouri, Huzzah Creek is a 23.4 mile tributary of the Meramec River.

I

Iberia, Missouri—Iberia is a town of about 735 people in southeastern Miller County. A post office named Iberia was established about a mile from the present town around 1840. The town was platted and the post office moved just prior to the Civil War. The town went by the nickname Rock Town for a while because of a rock-throwing incident during or near the time of the Civil War, and it was also known as Oakhurst for a few years. Incorporated in 1875, Iberia was home to the Iberia Normal School during the late nineteenth and early twentieth centuries, and today it is home to the Iberia R-5 School District.

Ichord, Richard Jr.—Richard Ichord Jr. was a lawyer and politician from Texas County, Missouri. He served in the U.S. House of Representatives from 1961 to 1981.

Illinois River—The Illinois River is a 145-mile tributary of the Arkansas River. It forms in Washington County, Arkansas, southwest of Fayetteville, flows west and then southwest through eastern Oklahoma, and joins the Arkansas about twenty miles southeast of Muskogee.

Imboden, Arkansas—Imboden is a town of about 685 people in northwest Lawrence County. The area was settled long before the Civil War, and the town, incorporated in 1887, was named for an early settler. Imboden made news in 1912 when the town elected a twenty-one-year-old paraplegic, who used a goat-cart to get around, as its mayor, making him the youngest mayor in the United States at the time. Imboden is home to the Sloan-Hendrix School District.

Incoming Kingdom Missionary Unit—The Incoming Kingdom Missionary Unit was a utopian religious group founded by the Reverend John Adams Battenfield at Gilbert in Searcy County, Arkansas, shortly after World War I. Battenfield predicted the civilized world would end, perhaps as early as 1923, because of a world-wide war between Protestants and Catholics, and he urged the faithful to retreat to secluded, mountainous communities, from where they would emerge after the holocaust and establish the Millennial Kingdom of God. Community members were expected to share their possessions and to learn Hebrew, the chosen language of God. The first unit began at Gilbert in September 1920, and within a few months seventy "colonists" had joined the community. However, problems arose, partly because members were reluctant to share their belongings as Battenfield's vision dictated, and the movement quickly died out after 1923 passed with no holocaust.

Independence County, Arkansas—Independence County was formed in 1820 from territory taken from Lawrence County and named in honor of the Declaration of Independence. Batesville was platted the next year as the county seat.

Indian Creek—Indian Creek is a 27.4 mile tributary of the Elk River that forms in Newton County, Missouri, and flows southwest into

McDonald County, where it empties into the Elk near Lanagan. It is popular for camping, fishing, and paddling.

Indian Expedition (1862)—Led by Colonel William Weer, the Indian Expedition of 1862 was a Union military expedition from Baxter Springs, Kansas, into the Cherokee Nation with an aim of restoring the Indian Territory, which was largely controlled by the Confederacy, to the Union. It was not successful in all its objectives but did succeed in organizing three Indian regiments for the Union.

Indians in the Ozarks—When European settlers first began arriving in the Ozarks in the late 1700s and early 1800s, the region was inhabited by Native Americans, primarily the Osage tribe, but including also the Delaware, Kickapoo, Shawnee, and other tribes. The Indians were forced to sign a series of treaties in the early 1800s removing them to reservations in Kansas and present-day Oklahoma. Also see Trail of Tears.

Indian Soldiers in the Civil War—Native Americans fought in the Civil War on the western edges of the Ozarks, notably at the First Battle of Newtonia, one of the few actions of the war in which regiments composed primarily of Indians fought on opposite sides.

Indian Springs, Missouri—Indian Springs was a resort that sprang up in northern McDonald County, Missouri, near the present-day community of McNatt during the mineral-water craze of the 1880s. The place was short-lived, and nothing of it remains.

Indian Territory—Indian Territory, often called the Indian Nation or just the Nation, was an area generally comprising eastern Oklahoma that was set aside by the Federal government during the mid-1800s for American Indians, such as the Cherokee, who were being removed from their ancestral homelands in the eastern United States.

Ingenthron, Elmo—Elmo Ingenthron was an author and educator who died in Taney County, Missouri, in 1988. He was a school superintendent in the Taney County area and authored several books on regional history, including *Borderland Rebellion: A History of the Civil War on the Missouri-Arkansas Border* and *Land of Taney*.

Inspiration Point—See Opera in the Ozarks.

Interstate 44—Interstate 44 is a major highway that runs from St. Louis, Missouri, to Wichita Falls, Texas, and generally follows the path of historic Route 66. The Missouri part of the highway is mostly in the Ozarks.

Interstate 44 Truck Explosion—In September of 1970, a truck, owned by Tri-State Motors, Inc. of Joplin and carrying over twenty tons of dynamite, exploded a few miles west of Springfield on I-44 when a sniper shot into the rig. The explosion, which killed the driver, shook the earth for miles around and left a hole about thirty feet wide and forty feet deep in the highway. Tri-State Motors was the object of a Teamsters strike at the time, and some of the firm's trucks had previously been fired upon. One man later received a 90-year prison sentence for second-degree murder in the case, and another man got a ten-year sentence.

Ionia, Missouri—Ionia is a village of about 90 people located on the border of Benton and Pettis counties. It was laid out in 1866.

Irish Settlement—See Wilderness, Missouri.

Iron—The southeast Missouri Ozarks has a long history of mining for iron ore, as evidenced by the many place names in the region bearing the word "iron." Currently, the only underground iron mine in the United States is located in Washington County, Missouri, as most iron ore is extracted by surface mining.

Iron County, Missouri—Located in southeastern Missouri, Iron County was formed in 1857 from territory taken from several surrounding counties. The difficulty encountered in finding enough territory for the county without reducing the surrounding counties too much accounts for the unusual, upside-down L shape of the county. Ironton was laid out as the county seat of the new county shortly after its organization.

Irondale, Missouri—Irondale is a town of about 450 people in southeastern Washington County, Missouri. It was laid out in 1858, although the area was settled much earlier. In 1906, the town changed its name to Savoy so that people wouldn't confuse it with Ironton and Iron Mountain, but the name was changed back to Irondale the next year. Like many small towns in Missouri, Irondale used to have a high school but lost it to consolidation long ago.

Iron Mountain—Iron Mountain is a large mass of land in southwestern St. Francois County that resembles a small mountain and originally contained such a high concentration of iron ore that early settlers thought it was made of pure iron. The density of the iron ore was, indeed, so great that many people in the East thought that the mountain's existence was a hoax or that the purity of the iron ore had been greatly exaggerated. Millions of tons of iron ore, fifty to sixty percent of it pure iron, was mined from the area during the 1800s before the deposits began to give out during the 1880s.

Iron Mountain, Missouri--Iron Mountain is an unincorporated community in southwestern Francois County. Founded in the 1830s, it was named for the nearby geological formation of the same name.

Iron Mountain Baby—In 1902, William Helms, a 72-year-old farmer, found a five-day-old baby boy in a valise that had fallen from a passing train of the St. Louis, Iron Mountain and Southern Railway near Irondale, in Washington County, Missouri. Helms took the badly bruised baby home, and he and his wife nursed it back to health. The baby's story spread throughout the United States, and a popular folksong called "The Ballad of the Iron Mountain Baby" was written about it. Many women came forward to claim the baby was theirs, but Helms and his wife adopted the baby when he was six years old.

Iron Mountain Lake, Missouri—Iron Mountain Lake is a town of about 750 people in southwestern St. Francois County near the Iron Mountain. The town grew up around a lake by the same name that was constructed during the late 1840s.

Ironton, Missouri—Ironton is the county seat of Iron County. It was laid out and selected as the county seat at the time the county was organized in 1857. Ironton is notable as the place where General Ulysses S. Grant received his commission as a brigadier general during the Civil War. Today, Ironton has a population of about 1,500 people, and it is home to the Arcadia Valley R-2 School District.

Isabella, Missouri—Isabella is an unincorporated community in southwest Ozark County. Located near the north bank of Bull Shoals Lake, Isabella is known today mainly as a resort area, but during the late 1800s, it was a lively little hub with a school and several stores.

Izard County, Arkansas—Izard County was formed from Independence County in 1825 during Arkansas's territorial days and named for Governor George Izard. At the time, it covered most of north central Arkansas, but parts of it were later split off to form other counties. Liberty (now Norfork) in present day Baxter County was the first county seat. The seat was moved to Athens in 1830, to Mount Olive in 1836, and finally to Mill Creek (later renamed Melbourne) in 1875.

J

Jacob's Cave—Jacob's Cave is a show cave in Morgan County, Missouri, seven miles south of Versailles. Discovered in 1875, it was opened as a commercial cave in 1932.

Jacks Fork River---Part of the Ozark Scenic Riverways national park, the Jacks Fork River is a tributary of the Current River. It forms in Texas County, Missouri, flows generally eastward for 46.4 miles, and empties into the Current near Eminence in Shannon County. It is popular for canoeing and kayaking, and it and its surroundings are known for their beauty.

Jackson, Missouri—Jackson is a town of about 13,800 and the seat of Cape Girardeau County. It was laid out as the county seat in 1815 and named for Andrew Jackson. It is home to the Jackson R-2 School District and to McKendree Chapel, a log cabin chapel that dates from 1819 and is known as the oldest Protestant church west of the Mississippi.

Jackson, Claiborne F.—Claiborne F. Jackson was the governor of Missouri at the start of the Civil War. A Southern sympathizer, Jackson and his government were driven out of Jefferson City to the southwest part of the state in June of 1861 by Federal forces under General Nathaniel Lyon, and Jackson led the Confederate-allied Missouri State Guard at the Battle of Carthage in early July.

Jackson, Roscoe "Red"—Roscoe "Red" Jackson killed a traveling salesman in Taney County, Missouri, in 1934, and, in a change of venue, was convicted of murder in Stone County Circuit Court. His execution at Galena in 1937 was a public spectacle, and it was the last legal hanging in the state of Missouri.

Jackson County, Arkansas—Jackson County is located in the northeastern part of the state on the southeastern fringes of the Ozarks. Only the western portion of the county can rightfully be considered part of the Ozarks. Jackson County was formed in 1829 from territory taken from Independence County and named after the newly elected U.S. p resident, Andrew Jackson. The first county seat was located at the home of an early pioneer and then moved to Litchfield a couple of years later. The county seat later moved to Elizabeth (or

Elizabethtown), then to Augusta, and then to Jacksonport before finally settling at Newport in the 1890s.

Jacksonport, Arkansas—Jacksonport is a town of about 240 people in Jackson County at the southeast edge of the Ozarks. Located where the Black River empties into the White River, Jacksonport was an important river port for steamboats during the 1800s. It was named the seat of Jackson County in 1854. During the Civil War, the town was occupied by both Union and Confederate forces because of its strategic position, and it was the site of skirmish in April of 1864. The town dwindled in importance after the railroad bypassed it in the 1880s, and the county seat was subsequently moved to Newport.

Jacksonport State Park—Located at Jacksonport on Arkansas Highway 69 about three miles north of Newport, Jacksonport State Park commemorates Jacksonport's early history and provides educational and recreational opportunities for visitors.

Jacob Wolf House—The Jacob Wolf House is a two-story log cabin at the junction of the White and North Fork rivers in present-day Norfork, Arkansas. It was built in 1829 by Jacob Wolf, an early day Indian trader and later a state representative, to serve as the first permanent county seat of Izard County. It was placed on the National Register of Historic Places in 1973 and currently serves as a museum.

Jaeger, Hermann—Hermann Jaeger was a grape grower and winemaker who saved the European wine industry from the phylloxera root louse pest during the late 1800s. Born in Switzerland, he immigrated to the United States immediately after the Civil War and settled east of Neosho, Missouri, where he started a vineyard. When the louse pest ravaged the vineyards of France, Portugal, and Spain in the 1870s, he exported vines resistant to the pest, which he had already developed.

James, Frank and Jesse—Frank and Jesse James were infamous Missouri outlaw brothers during the post-Civil War era. Most of their deeds that can be documented took place outside the Ozarks, but legends abound of their supposed activities in southwest Missouri and northwest Arkansas. The Gad's Hill train robbery in January 1874 is one of the few known exploits of the James gang that occurred in the Ozarks. Also, Jesse James was involved in a shooting scrape near Galena, Kansas, at the edge of the Ozarks in November of 1879.

James River—The James River is a 130-mile tributary of the White River in southwest Missouri. It forms in Webster County and flows briefly northwest before turning southwest and flowing through Greene and Christian counties and into Stone County, where it becomes an arm of Table Rock Lake, a reservoir of the White River.

James River near Springfield, Mo. *Courtesy Wikimedia.*

Jamestown, Arkansas—Today, little remains of Jamestown, a small community southwest of Batesville that thrived in the late 1800s.
Jamestown, Missouri—See Galena, Missouri.
Jamesville, Missouri—Jamesville is a historic community located on the James River in Stone County, Missouri. It is not to be confused with Jamestown, which was located farther up the river.
Jam Up Cave—Jam Up Cave is a scenic cave (actually a natural tunnel) on the Jacks Fork River in western Shannon County, Missouri. It cannot be reached by automobile.
Jane, Missouri—Jane is a village in southern McDonald County near the Arkansas state line. The community was originally called White Rock Prairie, but when a post office was established in 1882, it was named Jane after the postmaster's daughter. Jane was an unincorporated community for many years but incorporated in 2005 and shortly afterwards expanded its boundaries to include several businesses along U.S. 71 (now I-49). It is home to White Rock Elementary School, part of the McDonald County School District.

Jasper, Arkansas—Jasper is the county seat of Newton County. It was founded as a village along the Little Buffalo River about 1840 and became the county seat in 1843 after Newton County had been formed the previous year. Jasper prospered during the timber industry boom of the late 1800s and early 1900s. Today, it has a population of about 465 people and is home to the Jasper School District.

Jasper, Missouri—Jasper is a town of about 930 people in northern Jasper County. It was laid out in 1868 and named Midway, taking the place of a previous Midway about a mile to the north in Barton County. Both towns were so named because they were about halfway between Carthage and Lamar. In 1876, a post office was established and named Jasper in order to utilize the post office equipment of a defunct town named Jasper that had been located southeast of Carthage. Jasper hosts a festival called Jasper Appreciation Days each September, and the town is home to the Jasper R-5 Schools.

Jasper County, Missouri—Jasper County was formed in 1841 from territory taken from Barry County, and it was named after Revolutionary War hero Sergeant William Jasper. The following year, Carthage was named the seat of the new county.

Jay, Oklahoma—Jay is a town of about 2,450 people and the seat of Delaware County. It was laid out as the county seat in 1908 shortly after the county was established, and it was named in honor of Jay Washbourne, who donated ten acres for the town site. Jay is home to several Cherokee tribal offices, and almost forty percent of the town's population is Native American. Jay holds a Huckleberry Festival each Fourth of July weekend, and the town is sometimes called the Huckleberry Capital of the World. Former heavyweight champion Tommy Morrison grew up in Jay. The town is home to the Jay Public Schools.

Jayhawkers—"Jayhawkers" was a name given to Kansans who raided across the border into Missouri during the Civil War in much the same fashion that Missouri guerrillas raided into Kansas. Both groups waged irregular warfare and were occasionally guilty of atrocities. Jayhawkers were usually affiliated at least loosely with the regular Union army, whereas Missouri guerrillas were only sometimes affiliated with regular Confederate forces.

Jayne, Mitch—Mitch Jayne was an author, storyteller, and musician from Eminence, Missouri. As a young teacher in Dent County, he documented his students' use of forgotten Elizabethan words and phrases. After teaching, he wrote bluegrass songs and became the bass player and emcee of the bluegrass band The Dillards, featured several times on *The Andy Griffith Show*. He also penned several novels, wrote a weekly column for the local Eminence newspaper, and hosted a radio show at Salem.

Jefferson City, Missouri—Jefferson City is the state capital and the seat of Cole County. Although it is south of the Missouri River, it is not considered part of the Ozarks for the purposes of this book and is mentioned here only to note the exclusion of most people, places, and events associated with the town.

Jenkins, Missouri—Jenkins is an unincorporated community in eastern Barry County

Jefferson County, Missouri—Located at the northeast edge of the Ozarks just south of St. Louis, Jefferson County was organized in 1818 prior to statehood. The first county seat was Herculaneum. However, no courthouse was ever built there, and the county seat was moved to Hillsboro, then called Monticello, in the late 1830s. By most definitions, at least part of Jefferson County, although not necessarily all of it, is considered to be in the Ozarks.

Jennison, Charles "Doc"—Charles R. "Doc" Jennison was a Union colonel during the Civil War. His unit, the Seventh Kansas Cavalry, was also known as Jennison's Jayhawkers because of the irregular warfare he and his men often waged along the Kansas-Missouri border early in the war. Later, the unit participated in several significant battles, including the Second Battle of Newtonia.

Jerico Springs, Missouri—Jerico Springs is a village in southwest Cedar County with a population of about 230. It was founded during the mineral water boom of the 1880s and thrived as a health resort for several years. Its name was derived from a combination of the ancient city of Jericho and a man named Carico, who was an early owner of the town site. A small part of the village is divided from Jerico proper by a narrow stream. In jest, residents started calling the small section of the town Jerusalem and referring to the stream that separates Jerico and Jerusalem as the Jordan, and the names have become a whimsical bit of local lore.

Jerome, Missouri—Jerome is an unincorporated community in western Phelps County. It was laid out along the railroad in the early

1870s. The plat was declared vacated in 1874, but a small community grew up at the site nonetheless.

John Brown University—John Brown University is a private, interdenominational, Christian liberal arts college in Siloam Springs, Arkansas. Founded in 1919, it also has branches in Rogers, Little Rock, and Fort Smith.

John Brown University. *Courtesy Wikimedia.*

Johnson, Arkansas—Johnson is a town of about 3,355 people in Washington County, Arkansas, between Fayetteville and Springdale. It is reported to have the highest per capita income of any town in Arkansas. Johnson's history dates back to the 1800s, but nowadays, as part of the Fayetteville-Springdale metropolitan area, the town is virtually indistinguishable to passersby from the larger towns that surround it.

Johnson County, Arkansas—Located at the southern edge of the Ozarks bordering the Arkansas River, Johnson County was formed in 1833 from Pope County and named after territorial judge Benjamin Johnson. The county seat was moved from Spadra to Clarksville in 1837.

Johnson, Don—Don Johnson is an American actor best known for his roles in the TV series *Miami Vice* and *Nash Bridges*. He was born near Galena, Missouri, and attended high school for two years at Crane.

Johnson, Waldo P.—Waldo P. Johnson was a politician from Osceola, Missouri, who served in the U.S. Senate from March 1861 until January 1862, when he was expelled for disloyalty. He became an officer in the Confederate army and later a Confederate States senator.

Johnson Shut-Ins State Park—The Johnson Shut-Ins State Park is an 8,550-acre Missouri state park in Reynolds County on the East Fork Black River. The term "shut-ins" refers to an area of the river where its breath is limited by hard rock that is resistant to erosion and the water cascades through a narrow gorge in rivulets over and around the bedrocks. A section of the Ozark Trail cuts across the state park, which is popular for camping and hiking. The park was established in 1955 through the donation of St. Louis civic leader and conservationist Joseph Desloge. There are a number of other noted shut-ins in the same general vicinity, such as the Stout Creek Shut-In near Ironton.

Jolly Mill—See Capps Creek.

Jones, Harvey—Harvey Jones was a businessman who started Jones Truck Lines in 1918 in Springdale, Arkansas, and grew it into the largest privately-owned trucking company in the United States before selling it in 1980. Prominent civic leaders and benefactors, Jones and his wife, Bernice, are also remembered for establishing Har-Ber Village near Grove, Oklahoma.

Jones, Douglas Clyde—Douglas Clyde Jones was an American author noted for his historical fiction, particularly his alternative history fiction. For example, one of his famous books is *The Court-Martial of George Armstrong Custer*, which is based on the premise that Custer survived the Battle of the Little Big Horn. Jones was born in Winslow, Arkansas, and died in Fayetteville in 1998.

Jones, E. Fay—E. Fay Jones was an American architect and designer. He was an apprentice of Frank Lloyd Wright, and in 1990 he received the AIA Gold Medal, the highest honor awarded by the American Institute of Architects. Fay is best known in the Ozarks for his design of Thorncrown Chapel in Eureka Springs. Jones served as the dean of the University of Arkansas's School of Architecture, and he died at Fayetteville in 2004.

Joplin, Missouri—Joplin is a city in Jasper County near the Kansas and Oklahoma borders. It was founded in the early 1870s as a lead-mining camp and grew rapidly during the late 1800s. Although it is not the county seat, Joplin is the largest town in Jasper County. It has a population of about 50,000 and is home to the Northpark Mall, Joplin R-8 School District, and Missouri Southern State University. Poet Langston Hughes, who has a street in Joplin named after him, is among the well-known people born there.

Joplin Tornado—The Joplin tornado was a catastrophic EF5 tornado that struck Joplin, Missouri, on May 22, 2011. The seventh deadliest tornado in U.S. history, it killed over 160 people. In terms of raw dollars, it destroyed more property than any other tornado in U.S. history, and it ranks among the top two or three most destructive when the figures are adjusted for inflation. President Barack Obama visited Joplin shortly after the tornado and again one year later to deliver the commencement address at Joplin High School's 2012 graduation.

Jordanaires—See Foggy River Boys

Jordan Creek—Jordan Creek is a tributary of Wilson Creek that flows through Springfield, Missouri.

Juanita K. Hammons Hall—Named in honor of the wife of property developer John Q. Hammons, Juanita K. Hammons Hall is a performing arts center on the Missouri State University campus in Springfield.

K

KAFT—Part of the Arkansas Educational Television Network, KAFT 13 is a PBS television station in Fayetteville.

Kahl, Gordon, shooting of—See Smithville, Arkansas.

Kansas, Oklahoma—Kansas is a town of about 700 people in Delaware County at the western edge of the Ozarks. Legend holds that the town got its name from a diminutive traveling salesman from Kansas City who camped in the area when the region was Indian Territory. Native Americans called him Little Kansas City, which was shortened to Little Kansas and eventually just Kansas. Kansas is home to the Kansas Public Schools.

Kansas City, Fort Scott and Memphis Railroad—Consolidating the Kansas City, Fort Scott and Springfield and the Kansas City, Springfield and Memphis railroads, the Kansas City, Fort Scott and

Gulf operated a line from Kansas City to Memphis by way of Fort Scott and Springfield until 1901 when it consolidated with the Frisco.

Kansas City Southern Railway—Founded in 1887, the Kansas City Southern Railway is a railroad company headquartered in Kansas City, Missouri. One of its main tracks runs from Kansas City to the Gulf of Mexico by way of the Missouri-Kansas border area and the Arkansas-Oklahoma border area.

Kansas, Oklahoma and Gulf Railway—The Kansas, Oklahoma and Gulf Railway operated from 1919 to 1964. Its main line ran south from Baxter Springs, Kansas, through the western edge of the Ozarks.

Karst Topography—Karst topography refers to natural features produced on a land surface by chemical weathering or the gradual dissolving of limestone and other minerals. Features of karst topography include caves, springs, dry valleys, and sinkholes. The Ozarks region is well known for its karst topography.

Keith, Abraham Wendall—Abraham Wendell Keith was a physician from St. Francois County, Missouri, who is best remembered as the ghostwriter/author of an autobiography by Confederate guerrilla Sam Hildebrand.

Kelso, John R.—John R. Kelso was a teacher, Union officer, and politician from southwest Missouri. During the middle part of the Civil War, he became notorious among Southern sympathizers as a zealous guerrilla fighter. In 1864, he was elected to the U.S. House of Representatives, and later he established Kelso Academy at Springfield.

KEMV—Part of the Arkansas Educational Television Network, KEMV-TV 6 is a PBS television station in Mountain View.

Kenwood, Oklahoma—Kenwood is an unincorporated community in western Delaware County. It sprang up as a lumber town in the 1910s when the National Hardwood Company began operations in the area. The town's name derived by combining the company name with the name of William Kennedy (an associate of the company). The place boomed for about ten years, gaining a post office, a school, and a population of approximately 1,000 people, before rapidly declining after the supply of timber was virtually exhausted.

Ketchel, Stanley—Stanley Ketchel was champion middleweight boxer who was shot to death at a ranch near Niangua, Webster County, Missouri, in October of 1910. In a sensational trial the following

January, Walter Dipley and his common-law wife, Goldie Smith, were convicted of murder, although Goldie's conviction was later over-turned by the Missouri Supreme Court.

Middleweight champion Stanley Ketchel. *Author's collection.*

Ketchum, Oklahoma—Ketchum is a town of about 285 people located at the western edge of the Ozarks near Grand Lake in the extreme southeast corner of Craig County. It was founded in 1899 and named for Methodist minister and Delaware Indian James Ketchum. Originally located in northeast Mayes County, it was moved about a mile away to its present location in 1912 when a railroad came through the area.

KFJX—Launched in 2003, KFJX is a Fox-affiliate television station serving the Joplin, Missouri, market. It is a sister station to CBS affiliate KOAM.

Kickapoo Trace—The Kickapoo Trace was an early Indian trail that ran southwesterly from the St. Louis area through the Ozarks. Later roads, including the Wire Road and Route 66, followed roughly the same route, as does present-day I-44.

KGBX—KGBX is a radio station in Springfield, Missouri. Although its format has changed over the years, it has been broadcasting in Springfield since 1932.

KHOG—Based in Fayetteville, KHOG-TV is a satellite of ABC-affiliate KHBS-TV in Fort Smith, Arkansas. Launched in 1971, KHOG serves northwest Arkansas, northeast Oklahoma, and extreme southwest Missouri.

Kickapoo Prairie Conservation Area—Kickapoo Prairie Conservation Area preserves 160 acres of native prairie near Miller, Missouri.

Killian, Jake—Jake Killian was one of several notorious outlaws who came out of Granby, Missouri, during the post-Civil War era. In 1869, he killed circus owner William Lake at Granby, and he himself was killed at Galena, Kansas, in 1878.

Grave of Jake Killian at Granby, Mo. *Photo by the author.*

Kimberling City, Missouri—Kimberling City is a resort town of about 2,400 people in southern Stone County on Table Rock Lake. Its forerunner, called Radical, was established in the late 1800s as a camp or stopover where the Wilderness Road of the Ozarks, which ran from northern Arkansas to Springfield, Missouri, crossed the White River.

Kimbrough, Wilson Whitaker, Jr.—Wilson Whitaker Kimbrough, Jr. was a psychology professor at the University of Arkansas from the 1950s until the 1980s and a pioneer in police and criminal psychology in the United States.

Kinderhook County—Kinderhook County was the original name of Camden County, Missouri. It was named for Kinderhook, New York, the home of President Martin Van Buren.

Kinderpost, Missouri—Kinderpost is a community in northern Texas County. It was established about 1910 with the idea of getting children out of the cities onto small tracts of land in a rural area, but the project never took hold and Kinderpost was never more than a post office and small village.

Kings River—The Kings River is a tributary of the White River. Approximately ninety miles long, it forms in Madison County, Arkansas, and flows in a northerly direction through Carroll County into Missouri, where it joins the White as an arm of Table Rock Lake.

Kingston, Arkansas—Kingston is an unincorporated community in Madison County. It is home to Kingston Elementary School and Kingston High School, which are part of the Jasper School District. It was also home to the historic Kingston School, a mission of the Presbyterian Church.

Kinney, Nat—Nat Kinney was the leader of the vigilante Bald Knobbers of Taney County, Missouri, during the mid-1880s. He killed Anti-Bald Knobber Andrew Coggburn in 1886 and was, in turn, killed by Billy Miles, another Anti-Bald Knobber, in 1888.

Kirbyville, Missouri—Kirbyville is an unincorporated community in Taney County, east of Branson on Highway 76. It is home to the Kirbyville R-6 Schools, a K-8 district.

Kleinsasser, Lois—Writing as Cait London and Cait Logan, Lois Kleinsasser is a best-selling author of romance novels. She lives in Hollister, Missouri.

Knight's Cove, Skirmish at—The Skirmish at Knight's Cove was a minor Civil War action in Stone County, Arkansas, on June 19, 1862.

KNWA—KNWA-TV is an NBC-affiliate television station serving northwest Arkansas. It is a sister station of KFTA-TV in Fort Smith, and the two stations share a studio in Fayetteville. KNWA also has a satellite studio in Rogers, its city of license.

KOAM—Launched in 1953, KOAM TV is a CBS affiliate television station serving the Joplin, Missouri, market. The call letters stand for Kansas, Oklahoma, Arkansas, and Missouri, and the station's viewing area includes parts of all four states. The studio is located south of Pittsburg, Kansas.

KODE—Launched in 1954 as KSWM, KODE-TV is an ABC-affiliate television station serving the Joplin, Missouri, market. Its studio is located in the same building as its sister station, NBC-affiliate KSNF.

KOLR—Founded in 1953 as KTTS-TV, KOLR 10 is a CBS-affiliate television station in Springfield, Missouri. It serves much of the Ozarks, and its website is called OzarksFirst.com.

Koshkonong, Missouri—Koshkonong is a town of about 210 people in western Oregon County. Founded in 1882 along the Frisco Railroad, it was named after Lake Koshkonong, Wisconsin, where one of the railroad men had often fished. Koshkonong is home to the Oregon-Howell County R-3 School District.

KOZK-KOZJ—KOZK is a PBS television station in Springfield, Missouri. It has a satellite station, KOZJ, in Joplin, and together the two stations serve the Ozarks region as Ozarks Public Television.

KOZL—KOZL Channel 27 is a television station that serves the Springfield, Missouri, market and identifies itself as Ozarks Local. Formerly a Fox network affiliate, it is now an independent station and shares offices with CBS-affiliate KOLR.

KPOB—Located at Poplar Bluff, Missouri, KPOB-TV 15 is a satellite station of ABC-affiliate WSIL-TV licensed to Harrisburg, Illinois.

KRBK—Launched in 2009, KRBK is a Fox-affiliate television station serving the Springfield, Missouri, market.

Kruse Gold Mine—The Kruse Gold Mine was a mine started by William Henry Kruse on his father's farm in Rogers, Arkansas, during the early 1900s. Prompted only by visualizations and psychic revelations that the farm contained rich deposits of gold, Kruse began official mining operations in 1905 with the goal of sharing the supposed wealth buried on the farm and relieving world poverty. The operation stalled about 1912 but did not halt altogether until Kruse's death in 1925.

KSPR—KSPR 33 is an ABC-affiliate television station serving Springfield and the Ozarks. It launched in 1983 and is a sister station to KY3.

KTTS—KTTS is a radio station in Springfield, Missouri, that began broadcasting in 1942 but traces its roots to 1922. It has been known over the years for such popular programs as the "Radio Ranch."

Ku Klux Klan—The Ku Klux Klan originally organized in Tennessee shortly after the end of the Civil War. The group's formation was somewhat a reaction to the South having lost the war, and the organization has historically opposed equality for blacks. The original Klan officially disbanded just a few years after it formed, but sporadic Klan activity has continued to the present day. The Klan was particularly active in the Ozarks during the 1910s and 1920s in opposing unionism and "cleaning up" local communities by trying to impose Victorian moral standards. Another resurgence of Klan activity occurred during the school desegregation movement of the 1950s. Isolated groups of the Klan and other white supremacist or Neo-Nazi organizations still exist in the Ozarks today.

KUOA—KUOA is a radio station in Siloam Springs. Begun in the 1920s at Fayetteville as the first radio station in the Ozarks, it was moved to Siloam Springs during the mid-1930s.

KWOG—An affiliate of the Daystar Television Network, KWOG is a television station in Springdale, Arkansas, which broadcasts religious programming.

KWTO—Begun in 1933, KWTO is a long-running and well-known AM radio station in Springfield, Missouri. For many years, the station used the slogan "Keep Watching the Ozarks," to match its call letters. See Ralph Foster.

KXNW—KXNW-TV 34 is a MyNetworkTV-affiliate television station serving the Fayetteville-Fort Smith market. Licensed to Eureka Springs, it operates out a studio in Fort Smith.

KY3—Launched in 1953 as KYTV, KY3 is an NBC-affiliate television station in Springfield, Missouri, that serves much of the Ozarks.

L

Laclede County, Missouri—Laclede County was organized in 1849 from territory previously belonging to Camden, Pulaski, and Wright counties. It was named in honor of Pierre Laclede, the founder of St. Louis, and Lebanon was laid out as the county seat shortly afterwards.

Lacrosse, Arkansas—Located in northeast Izard County, Lacrosse was a bustling community in the 1880s and home to the Lacrosse Collegiate Institute, but little of the town survives today.

Lake Charles State Park—Lake Charles State Park is a 140-acre Arkansas state park along the Black River in Lawrence County that was opened after construction of adjacent Lake Charles in the 1960s. The park offers outdoor activities like fishing and camping.

Lake Hudson—Lake Hudson is a 12,000-acre manmade reservoir in Mayes County, Oklahoma, two miles north of Locust Grove. Snowdale State Park provides access to the lake.

Lake of the Ozarks—Located mainly in Camden County, Missouri, the Lake of the Ozarks is the largest man-made lake in the Midwest.

Lake of the Ozarks. *Courtesy Wikimedia.*

Created on the Osage River in 1931 by the completion of Bagnell Dam, the Lake of the Ozarks covers about 55,000 acres and has over 1,000 miles of shoreline. During construction, it was known as Osage Reservoir or Lake Osage, and the Missouri Legislature officially named it Lake Benton after former United States senator Thomas Hart Benton. However, because of its location, it came to be known popularly as the Lake of the Ozarks, and the name stuck.

Lake of the Ozarks State Park—Lake of the Ozarks State Park is located on the Grand Glaize arm of the Lake of the Ozarks straddling the Camden-Miller county line. At 17,441 acres, it is the largest park in the Missouri state park system. Built by the National Park Service in the 1930s, it was donated to the state after World War II. It offers boating and other outdoor activities, and one of its notable spots is Party Cove, a rowdy gathering place that has been featured on the Playboy Channel and other news media.

Lake Ozark, Missouri—Lake Ozark is a resort town of about 1,600 people on the shore of Lake of the Ozarks at the Camden-Miller county line.

Lakeside, Missouri—Lakeside is a village in western Miller County on U.S. Highway 54 near Lake of the Ozarks. It was established in 1929 as a "construction town" for workers building Bagnell Dam. Part of the village today lies along the Highway 54 "Bagnell Dam Strip," and it has a population of about 200.

Lake Springfield—Located at the south edge of Springfield, Missouri, Lake Springfield is a 318-acre cooling water supply lake for the adjacent James River power plant. The lake and surrounding grounds are popular for fishing, picnicking, and other outdoor activities.

Lake Taneycomo—Lake Taneycomo is a man-made lake that covers over 2,000 acres in Taney County, Missouri. Created in 1913 when the Powersite Dam was completed by the Ozark Power and Water Company on White River near Forsyth, the lake gets its name from the county and state where it is located. Originally a warm water lake, it became a cool water lake when adjacent Table Rock Lake was completed in 1958, and it has since been very popular for trout fishing.

Lakeview, Arkansas—Lakeview is a resort town of about 900 people in Baxter County on the southeastern shore of Bull Shoals Lake.

Lake Wappapello—Lying mostly in southeastern Wayne County, Missouri, Lake Wappapello is a 45,000-acre reservoir formed in 1941 by the damming of the St. Francis River.

Lake Wappapello. *Courtesy Wikimedia.*

Lake Wappapello State Park—Lake Wappapello State Park is a 1,850-acre Missouri state park bordering Lake Wappapello in Wayne County, which offers outdoor activities like hiking and motor biking.

Lamar, Missouri—Located at the western edge of the Ozarks, Lamar is the seat of Barton County in the southwest part of the state. Lamar served as a Union post during much of the Civil War and was twice attacked by Confederate guerrillas under William Quantrill and another time was burned by guerrillas under Henry Taylor. Wyatt Earp served briefly as a constable in Lamar as a young man. However, the town is perhaps best known as the birthplace of President Harry S Truman, and the house where he was born is maintained as a state historic site. The town is also noted for its annual fair, often billed as Missouri's largest free fair. Current population of Lamar is approximately 5,000, and it is home to the Lamar R-1 School District.

Lampe, Missouri—Lampe is an unincorporated community located on State Highway 13 in southern Stone County. A post office called Baxter was established in the immediate vicinity in the mid-1880s. After several moves, the post office was relocated to its present site in 1939, where a community called Lampe had begun to spring up, and the post office was renamed Lampe as well the following year. Lampe is home to the Black Oak Amphitheater.

Lanagan, Missouri—Lanagan is a town of about 420 people in western McDonald County. A post office was established at the site in 1891. Like many small towns in the Ozarks, Lanagan had its own high school at one time, but Lanagan is now served by the McDonald County R-1 School District.

Lane, James H.—James H. Lane was a U.S. senator from Kansas who organized Kansas troops during the Civil War and conducted several raids into Missouri, notably the raid on Osceola in September of 1861.

Lane, Rose Wilder—Rose Wilder Lane was an American journalist and author who was one of the highest paid female magazine writers in the country during the late 1920s. The daughter of Laura Ingalls Wilder and Almanzo Wilder, she grew up partly on their Mansfield, Missouri farm. She was known for ghostwriting for others as well as for her own work, and the extent of her role in helping her mother with the famous *Little House* series is a matter of debate.

Langley, Oklahoma—Langley is a town of about 820 people in northeast Mayes County on the banks of Grand Lake. It was established in 1935 when construction on the lake began, and it was named for J. Howard Langley, a prominent attorney in the county

Laquey, Missouri—Laquey in an unincorporated community in southwestern Pulaski County. It was established about 1901 and named for local resident Joseph J. Laquey. Home to the Laquey R-5 School District, the community has experienced considerable growth in recent years because of its proximity to Fort Leonard Wood.

La Russell, Missouri—La Russell is a town of about 115 people in eastern Jasper County. It sprang up in the very early 1900s as a station on the Missouri Pacific Railroad and was named for railroad executive Russell Harding.

Latham, Missouri—Latham is an unincorporated community in southern Moniteau County at the north edge of the Ozarks.

Laurie, Missouri—Laurie is a village of about 950 people in southern Morgan County. It began in the 1930s as a store operated by the Laurie brothers along Highway 5.

Lawrence County, Arkansas—Located in the northeast part of the state, Lawrence County was formed in January of 1815 as part of

Missouri Territory. Nicknamed the "Mother of Counties," it included at the time almost all of present-day north Arkansas. It was named for War of 1812 hero Captain James Lawrence. The county had a succession of different seats until Walnut Ridge became a co-county seat in 1870 and was named the sole county seat in 1963.

Lawrence County, Missouri—Located in southwest Missouri, Lawrence County was formed in early 1845 from Barry and Dade counties, and Mount Vernon was named the county seat in May. On July 4, a barn dance, an outdoor dance with a bed of bran used as the dance floor, was held at Mount Vernon in celebration of Independence Day and the new county.

Layton, Bob—Bob Layton was one of several notorious outlaws to come out of Granby, Missouri, in the years after the Civil War. He and three other Granby men killed a man named William "Tiger Bill" St. Clair at Galena, Kansas, in June of 1877, and Layton himself was killed in Batesville, Arkansas, in November of 1879 while resisting arrest.

L.D. Keller and the Promenaders—L.D. Keller and the Promenaders were a popular square dance group in the Ozarks from the early 1950s to the mid-1970s. They brought national attention to square dancing through their appearances on shows like the *Ozark Jubilee.*

Leach, Oklahoma—Leach is a small community, population about 220, in southwest Delaware County. A post office was founded at the site in 1897 and named after the first postmaster, John R. Leach.

Lead Hill, Arkansas—Lead Hill is a town of about 270 people in northeast Boone County. It began as a lead mining community shortly after the Civil War and prospered until the Depression era. During the late 1940s and early 1950s, the town was moved to nearby higher ground, and the original town site was then submerged by the waters of Bull Shoals Lake. South Lead Hill was established a mile south of Lead Hill at about the same time. Lead Hill is home to the Lead Hill School District.

Lead mining—Lead mining was prominent in the eastern Missouri Ozarks' "Old Lead Belt" around St. Francois County beginning in the 1700s. Lead mining still occurs in southeast Missouri but is centered farther west around Viburnum in the "New Lead Belt." During the late 1800s and early 1900s, there was also a lead mining boom in the

Tri-State District around Joplin in southwest Missouri. Lead mining was prevalent to a lesser extent in north central Arkansas around Marion County and central Missouri around Camden County during the same time frame.

Leadwood, Missouri—Leadwood is a town of about 1,300 people in central St. Francois County. It was founded in the early 1900s by the St. Joseph Lead Company as a company town and originally called Owl Creek.

Leasburg, Missouri—Leasburg is a village of about 340 people in Crawford County. It is the site of Onondaga Cave State Park.

Lebanon, Missouri—Lebanon is a town of about 14,500 people and the seat of Laclede County. Originally called Wycota, it was renamed after Lebanon, Tennessee, which was the hometown of a respected local minister. Several notable people have lived in Lebanon at one time or another, including author Harold Bell Wright, congressman Richard Parks, Missouri governor Phil Donnelly, and Missouri senator Claire McCaskill. In the late 1800s, investors built the Gasconade Hotel, a large resort hotel, in Lebanon beside a well that purportedly had magnetic water, and people flocked to the place to use the supposed healing water. Lebanon is known today as a hub for boat manufacturing, and it has several other manufacturing companies, including Independent Stave Company. It is home to the Lebanon R-3 Schools.

Ledbetter, Suzann—Suzann Ledbetter is an author of mystery, romance, and historical novels. She was born in Joplin, Missouri, and lives in Nixa.

Lederer, Katherine—Katherine Lederer was a professor of English at Missouri State University in Springfield for forty-two years until her retirement in 2004`. She was especially noted for her research on African Americans in the Ozarks, and her extensive collection on the subject is held by the university library.

Lee, Burwell—Burwell Lee was a Methodist preacher who organized the Methodist Society at Batesville in 1835 and is considered one of the fathers of the Methodist Church in Arkansas.

Lee Creek—Lee Creek is a river that runs from near West Fork in Washington County, Arkansas, south to the Arkansas River, passing through Crawford County, Arkansas, and Sequoyah County,

Oklahoma. The small community of Lee Creek in Crawford County takes its name from the stream.

Leeper, Missouri—Leeper is an unincorporated community in southwest Wayne County. It was named after Union captain W.T. Leeper, who persuaded the Iron Mountain Railway to build a road through his property in 1871, and within a few years, the community of Leeper had grown up at the site as a booming lumber town.

Lemke, Walter John—Walter John Lemke founded the Department of Journalism at the University of Arkansas in 1928 and served as head of the department for over thirty years. He also helped found several historical organizations, including the Washington County Historical Society.

Leslie, Arkansas—Leslie is a town of about 440 people in southeast Searcy County. Originally called Wiley's Cove, it was renamed Leslie in the 1880s after either Sam Leslie or his brother Jack, both of whom were prominent early settlers. The Missouri and North Arkansas Railroad reached Leslie in 1903, turning it into a booming lumber town during the early part of the twentieth century. Leslie is home to the Ozark Heritage Arts Center and Museum and to the Leslie Intermediate School, which is part of the Searcy County School District.

Leslie, Missouri—Leslie is a village of about 170 people in western Franklin County.

Lesterville, Missouri—Lesterville is an unincorporated community in eastern Reynolds County. It served as the county seat until the courthouse burned during the Civil War, after which the seat was moved to Centerville. Lesterville is home to the Lesterville R-1 School District, one of the smallest K-12 school districts in Missouri.

Letona, Arkansas—Letona is a town of about 200 people in northern White County. Public school students in the area attend either the Pangburn or the Searcy schools.

Licking, Missouri—Licking is a town of about 3,125 people in northeast Texas County. It was established just prior to the Civil War and named for a nearby salt lick, which had been used by buffalo and deer in the very early days of white settlement in the area. The town was officially incorporated in 1878. Licking is home to the Licking R-8 Schools.

Limestone Valley—Limestone Valley is a solution valley in southern Newton County, Arkansas, and the site of a former community by the same name. During the Civil War, three Union soldiers were hanged in Limestone Valley by Confederates or Confederate sympathizers.

Lincoln, Arkansas—Lincoln is a town of about 1,755 people in western Washington County. A settlement grew up in the vicinity during the late 1800s, but the town was not officially established until the early 1900s when a railroad reached the area. Lincoln was incorporated in 1907 and prospered during the early 1900s as the area's apple-growing industry flourished. Lincoln is home to the annual Arkansas Apple Festival and to the Lincoln Public Schools.

Lincoln, Missouri—Lincoln is a town on U.S. Highway 65 in northern Benton County at the northwest edge of the Ozarks. It was established shortly after the Civil War and named for President Lincoln. It has a population of slightly over 1,000 and is home to the Lincoln R-2 School District.

Linden (aka Lindenlure), Missouri—Linden is an unincorporated community in northern Christian County. Originally known as Kenton, it was established during the 1870s. The Finley River is dammed nearby, forming a small lake, called Lindenlure, that has served as a popular swimming hole for many years.

Linn, Missouri—Linn is the county seat of Osage County. It is home to the Linn State Technical School and the Osage County R-2 School District. Its population is about 1,500.

Linn Creek, Missouri—The first Linn Creek was the county seat of Camden County from the town's formation in 1855 until it was abandoned in the early 1930s to make way for Lake of the Ozarks. At the same time, Camdenton was established as the new county seat, and a new Linn Creek was also built a couple of miles from the old town. The new Linn Creek is located a few miles east of Camdenton on U.S. Highway 54. It has a population of about 300 and is home to the Camden County Museum.

Lithium, Missouri—A village of about 90 people in northern Perry County, Lithium was founded as a health resort in 1882 at the site of two springs, one of which contained lithium salts.

Little Black River—The Little Black River is a tributary of the Black River that forms in northeast Ripley County, Missouri, and flows in a generally southward direction into Arkansas, where it joins the Black near Pocahontas.

Little Niangua River—The Little Niangua River is a tributary of the Niangua River that forms in Dallas County, Missouri, and flows north through Hickory County and into Camden County, where it joins the Niangua as an arm of the Lake of the Ozarks. It is a popular river for fishing. The Little Niangua and its tributaries are known habitats for the Niangua Darter, a small fish on the U. S. Fish and Wildlife Service's Endangered Species List.

Little Piney Creek—The Little Piney Creek is a seventeen-mile tributary of the Gasconade River located in Phelps County, Missouri. It is popular for fishing and floating.

Little Red River—The Little Red River is a tributary of the White River in north-central Arkansas. It forms as three different forks in the Ozarks Mountains west and north of Heber Springs, and the forks merge at Greers Ferry Lake, where the river is dammed. Below the dam, the river flows for about forty miles in a generally southeast direction and empties into the White near Georgetown in White County. Several skirmishes occurred on the Little Red River in White County during the Civil War.

Little Sugar Creek—Little Sugar Creek forms near Bentonville, Arkansas, and flows north into McDonald County, Missouri, where it converges near Pineville with Big Sugar Creek to form the Elk River.

Little Sugar Creek, Action at—Also called the Battle of Dunagin's Farm, the Action at Little Sugar Creek was a Civil War engagement southeast of Pea Ridge, Arkansas, fought on February 17, 1862, between Confederate forces under Colonel Louis Hebert and the advance guard of Union general Samuel R. Curtis's Army of the Southwest. Losses were approximately twenty killed or wounded on each side, although exact casualties are unknown. The first battle of the Civil War fought entirely in Arkansas, the Action at Little Sugar Creek was a precursor to the Battle of Pea Ridge three weeks later.

Little York, Missouri—Little York was a village founded prior to the Civil War in western Greene County. The village dissolved in the early 1870s after the railroad bypassed it and a new community, Brookline, was founded nearby.

Livestock Farming and Ranching—Early settlers in the Ozarks sometimes kept a few head of beef cattle, but they were often allowed to run at large and were not purebred. The beef cattle industry did not arise until the late 1800s, as fenced lots and stall feeding became more common. The Missouri Land and Livestock Company, which bought 350,000 acres in southwest Missouri near Neosho and began importing purebred Angus and Hereford, was a big impetus to the industry. Since the mid-twentieth century, the Ozarks has become increasingly a cow-calf region, meaning that feeder calves are raised until they are seven to ten months old and then sold and shipped to big feed lots elsewhere for fattening out, whereas in the past they were raised to maturity before being sold. Other types of livestock, such as hogs and horses, have also been raised in the Ozarks to a lesser extent than beef cattle.

Livingston, Thomas R.—Thomas R. Livingston was a Southern partisan leader from Jasper County, Missouri, during the Civil War. Although loosely affiliated with the regular Confederate army, he was considered a guerrilla by Union officials and even by some Confederate leaders. His most notorious action was the killing of approximately twenty black Federal soldiers at the northwest edge of present-day Joplin in May of 1863. He himself was killed by Union militia at Stockton less than two months later.

Lockwood, Missouri—Lockwood is a town of about 950 people in western Dade County. Three rival towns were laid out in the same vicinity when the Kansas City, Fort Scott and Gulf Railroad was constructed through the area in 1881, but they soon merged as Lockwood, which was named after a railroad official. Lockwood is home to the Lockwood R-1 School District.

Locust Grove, Oklahoma—Locust Grove is a town of about 1,425 people at the western edge of the Ozarks in Mayes County. Locust Grove post office was established in 1873 and named after a Civil War battle that had been fought nearby at a grove of locust trees. The current town was established a short distance away in 1912. In the Battle of Locust Grove fought on July 3, 1862, a detachment of about 250 Union soldiers surprised a similar-sized party of Confederates, killing about 100 and capturing about 100 others, while sustaining few losses of their own. Locust Grove is home to the Locust Grove Public Schools.

Lohman, Missouri—Lohman is a town of about 1,550 people in western Cole County.

Long, Billy—Billy Long is an auctioneer and politician from Springfield, Missouri. Elected in 2010, he is the current representative to the U.S. House of Representatives from southwest Missouri.

U.S. representative Billy Long. *Courtesy Wikipedia.*

Long, Isaac Jasper—Isaac Jasper Long was a Presbyterian minister who helped found Arkansas College (now Lyon College) in Batesville in 1872 and served as its first president.

Long Lane, Missouri—Long Lane is an unincorporated community in Dallas County. It is home to the Long Lane Elementary School, which is part of the Dallas County R-1 School District headquartered at Buffalo.

Longley, Alcander—Alcander Longley was a social reformer who established several communities in the Missouri Ozarks during the late 1800s and early 1900s on the principle of what he called "practical communism," meaning that he was more interested in establishing a communal life for himself and his followers than in promoting communism as a political movement.

Longtown, Missouri—Longtown is a village of about 100 people in southern Perry County.

Lost Valley State Park—Lost Valley State Park is an Arkansas state park acquired in 1975 by the National Park Service as part of the Buffalo National River. It is located in western Newton County near Ponca in an area bounded by steep bluffs and known as the Lost Valley, and it features a campground and a popular hiking trail.

Louisburg, Missouri—Louisburg is a village of about 120 people in western Dallas County. It was originally known as Round Prairie but changed its name around the 1880s.

Lovely County Arkansas—Lovely County existed for only one year, from 1827 to 1828. Created and abolished because of treaties involving Cherokee Indians, Osage Indians, and whites, it included most of present-day Benton and Washington counties and part of present-day Crawford County in Arkansas, and it also extended into present-day Oklahoma.

Lowell, Arkansas—Lowell is a town of about 7,330 people in Benton County. Located between Rogers and Springdale, it is part of the Fayetteville/Springdale/Rogers/Bentonville metropolitan area. The place was settled in the 1840s as Robinson's Cross Roads but was renamed Bloomington when the post office reopened after a period of closure. As a stop on the Butterfield Overland Stage line, it came to be known as Mudtown because stages would often get stuck in the mud nearby. In 1881, Bloomington was moved about a mile so it would be closer to a new railroad and was renamed Lowell. Lowell is home to the Lowell Elementary School, which is part of the Rogers School District.

Lowry City, Missouri—Lowry City is a town of about 750 people on U. S. Highway 13 in St. Clair County. Lakeland R-3 School District, between Lowry City and Deepwater, serves both communities. Lowry City is located at the northwest edge of the Ozarks approximately where the Great Plains begin.

Lum and Abner—*Lum and Abner* was a popular comedy radio program that was nationally broadcast from 1931 to 1954. Chester

Lauck (aka Lum) and Findley Norris Goff (aka Abner) grew up in Mena, Arkansas, in the Ouachita Mountains south of the Ozarks. However, they attended the University of Arkansas at Fayetteville, and their depiction of rural, hillbilly life in the fictional Arkansas town of Pine Ridge was connected in the American consciousness to Arkansas and the Ozarks in general.

Lumber Industry—A huge lumber industry arose in the Ozarks in the 1880s, especially in south-central Missouri around Carter County. Lumber companies like the Missouri Lumber and Mining Company and the Ozark Land and Lumber Company purchased land and built large sawmills and lumberyards. Railroads were built to serve the industry, and booming lumber towns like Ellsinore, Fremont, Grandin, and Hunter sprang up almost overnight. Farther west, the Christian County town of Chadwick was also a booming lumber town. The industry declined dramatically in the 1920s and soon died out almost completely, after most of the good timberland had been exploited. However, the lumber industry has returned to the Ozarks in recent decades, not only in the form of sawmills but also stave mills and especially wood chip mills.

Lunatic Asylum—Lunatic Asylum or Insane Asylum was the name originally given to Missouri's state hospitals for mental illness, such as the one at Farmington.

Lunenburg, Arkansas—Lunenburg is an unincorporated community about four miles south of the Izard County seat of Melbourne. A settlement, sometimes called Rocky Bayou, was established at the site prior to the Civil War, and it was a flourishing little community during the 1840s and 1850s. During the war, a small skirmish occurred at Lunenburg between a Union detachment under Captain Taylor Baxter and a Confederate cavalry force under Colonel Thomas Freeman. A post office and a school were established at Lunenburg after the war, but the town gradually declined when no railroad and no major road was built to the community.

Lutesville, Missouri—See Marble Hill.

Lutie, Missouri—Lutie is an unincorporated community in south-west Ozark County. A post office was established at the site in 1893. Lutie is home to the Lutie R-6 School District.

Lynchburg, Missouri—Lynchburg is an unincorporated community of about 400 people in southeast Laclede County. A post office was established at the site in 1899, and it was named for brothers David and R.D. Lynch.

Lynching Era—During America's lynching era from the late 1800s to the early 1900s, the South, in particular, saw a spike in extra-legal executions, especially of black people. The Ozarks, at the fringes of the upper South, also experienced increased lynchings. Notable among them were the notorious murders of three black men at Pierce City, Missouri, in August 1901; the execution at Joplin in April 1903 of a black man accused of killing a cop; and the hanging of three black men on the Springfield square during Easter weekend of 1906.

Lyon College—Lyon College is a four-year, coeducational, liberal arts college affiliated with the Presbyterian Church. Located in Batesville, it was founded as Arkansas College in 1872 and is the state's oldest independent college still operating under its original charter.

Lyon, Nathaniel—Nathaniel Lyon was a Union general who led the Federal forces at the Battle of Wilson's Creek in August of 1861. Lyon was killed during the action, becoming the first Union general to be killed during the Civil War. A monument to Lyon is located in the National Cemetery at Springfield.

Sketch of General Nathaniel Lyon at the Battle of Wilson's Creek. *From Harper's Weekly.*

M

Macks Creek, Missouri—Macks Creek is an unincorporated community on U.S. Highway 54 in southwest Camden County. A post office was established at the site in 1869, and the place was named after the stream it was located on. Macks Creek was incorporated until 2012, when residents voted to dissolve the city after it experienced major financial problems. Macks Creek is home to the Macks Creek R-5 Schools.

Madison County, Arkansas—Located in the northwest part of the state, Madison County was formed in 1836 from parts of Carroll, Newton, and Washington counties. Both Huntsville, which became the county seat, and the county were named by settlers who had migrated from the Huntsville area of Madison County, Alabama.

Madison County, Missouri—Madison County is located in eastern Missouri at the edge of the Ozarks. It was organized in 1818 and named for former President James Madison. Fredericktown was laid out as the county seat the following year. Madison County was reduced to its present limits when part of its territory was taken to form Iron County in 1857.

Magness, Arkansas—Magness is a town of about 190 people in Independence County. It was named after a member of the Magness family, which was prominent in the area before the Civil War.

Maguiretown, Arkansas—Maguiretown, or Maguire's Store, was a historic community in Washington County, Arkansas, near present-day Elkins. The place was named for Owen Maguire, who settled at the location in the 1830s. The log home his family built at the time is still standing and is on the National Register of Historic Places. In the mid-1800s, Maguiretown was an important stop on the road from Fayetteville to Huntsville, but the community declined after the railroad bypassed it in the 1880s.

Mahnkey, Mary Elizabeth—Mary Elizabeth Mahnkey was a writer and poet from Taney County, Missouri. She was a rural correspondent to various newspapers and wrote a column in the Springfield papers called "In the Hills" during the 1930s and 1940s. She published several volumes of poetry and was named Poet Laureate of the Ozarks.

Mammoth Spring, Arkansas—Mammoth Spring is a town of about 975 people in northeastern Fulton County at the Missouri state line. It is the site of Mammoth Spring, the largest spring in Arkansas. The town began in 1883 as a stop on the Springfield to Memphis railroad. It is home to the Mammoth Spring School District and is the hometown of actress Tess Harper.

Mammoth Spring National Fish Hatchery—Mammoth Spring National Fish Hatchery was established at Mammoth Spring in 1903. The site was selected because of the availability of cool water flowing from the nation's tenth largest spring.

Mammoth Spring State Park—Encompassing 62.5 acres, Mammoth Spring State Park is located at Mammoth Spring, Arkansas, surrounding Mammoth Spring. The spring, the second largest in the Ozarks, is a National Natural Landmark.

Manganese Mining—The mining of manganese ore, used primarily in the production of steel, was an important economic activity in Arkansas from 1849 to 1959. The mining was centered in northwestern Independence County, southeastern Izard County, and northeastern Stone County. Manganese has also been mined in certain areas of south central Missouri.

Mankiller, Wilma Pearl—Wilma Mankiller was the first woman chief of the Cherokee Nation, serving from 1985 to 1995. She was born and grew up near Tahlequah, Oklahoma, and died in Adair County, Oklahoma, in 2010.

Mansfield, Missouri--Mansfield is a town of about 1,300 population in southern Wright County. A post office was established at Mansfield in 1881, and the town was platted the following year and named for Francis M. Mansfield, one of the men who laid it out and sold the lots. Famous author Laura Ingalls Wilder lived at Mansfield for many years from the late 1800s until the mid-1900s. Mansfield is home to the Mansfield R-4 School District.

Mantle, Mickey—Mickey Mantle was a famous Major League Baseball player for the New York Yankees during the 1950s and 1960s. He grew up in Commerce, Oklahoma, and was known early in his career as the Commerce Comet.

Maramec Spring—Maramec Spring is located on the Meramec River near St. James in Phelps County, Missouri. It is the fifth-largest spring in the state with a daily discharge of about 100 million gallons of water. The spring and its surroundings are maintained by the nonprofit James Foundation as Maramec Spring Park, which is open to the public. The site includes the ruins of the historic Maramec Iron Works, which produced iron from the 1820s to the 1890s and was the first commercially viable iron works west of the Mississippi. The park also includes a trout hatchery and fishery run by the Missouri Department of Conservation.

Marble, Arkansas—Marble is an unincorporated community in Madison County.

Marble City, Oklahoma—Marble City (often called just Marble) is a town of about 265 people in northern Sequoyah County. Although several early post offices existed in the area, including one called Marble Salt Works, the present community of Marble City was not established until 1895 when a railroad came through the area and the post office was moved close to the tracks near a marble quarry. Marble City is home to the Marble City Schools.

Marble Falls, Arkansas—Marble Falls is an unincorporated community in Newton County. Originally known as Marble City, it became Willcockson in 1883 and was renamed Marble Falls in 1934 after the nearby waterfall. The post office assumed the name Dogpatch in the mid-1960s to promote the nearby theme park but reverted to Marble Falls after the park closed.

Marble Hill, Missouri—Laid out in 1851 and originally called Dallas, Marble Hill is a town of about 1,500 people and the seat of Bollinger County. A previous settlement on the site, New California, was absorbed by Dallas. The town was raided during the Civil War by Confederate colonel S.D. Kitchen. The name of Dallas was changed to Marble Hill in 1868 to avoid confusion with Dallas County. The name came from the belief that the hill on which the town sat was made of marble or a marble-like material. In 1869, a rival town, Lutesville, was laid out nearby, and the railroad came to Lutesville instead of Marble Hill. In 1985, over a century later, Lutesville became part of Marble Hill. Will Mayfield College, which ceased operations in 1934, formerly operated in Marble Hill, and the grounds are now the site of the Bollinger County Museum of Natural History. Marble Hill is home to the Woodland R-4 Schools.

Marbut, Curtis F.—Born and reared in Barry County, Missouri, Curtis F. Marbut was a geographer and geologist who served as director of the U.S. Soil Survey Division from 1913 until his death. He developed the country's first formal soil classification scheme.

Maries County, Missouri—Located in central Missouri, Maries County was formed in 1855 from parts of Osage and Pulaski counties, and it was named for the Big Maries and Little Maries rivers. The area of Maries County was first settled mainly by people from the South or from other parts of Missouri, but there was a large influx of German immigrants during the 1850s. Vienna became the county seat in 1856.

Maries River—The Maries River is a tributary of the Osage River. It starts near Vienna in Maries County, Missouri, flows northward through Osage County, and empties into the Osage River southeast of Jefferson City.

Marine Corps Legacy Museum—The Marine Corps Legacy Museum is a museum dedicated to preserving Marine Corps history located on the square in Harrison, Arkansas.

Marinoni, Rosa Zagnoni—Rosa Zagnoni Marinoni was poet laureate of Arkansas from 1953 until her death in 1970. Born in Italy, she came to the United States as a child and lived most of her life at Fayetteville, where her husband was on the faculty of the University of Arkansas. Marinoni was not only a prolific poet herself, but she also worked to promote a greater appreciation of poetry and helped establish a Poetry Day in Arkansas. From 1956 to 1967, she published a series of works about the Ozarks, including *The Ozarks and Some of Its People*.

Marion County, Arkansas—Located in north central Arkansas bordering Missouri, Marion County was established in 1835 from territory taken from Izard County. The new county was immediately renamed Searcy, but the name reverted to Marion in 1836. Yellville was shortly afterwards named the county seat. The county was named after Francis Marion, the "Swamp Fox" of the Revolutionary War.

Marionville, Missouri—Marionville is a town in eastern Lawrence County, Missouri, founded prior to the Civil War. It was the site of the Marionville Collegiate Institute during the late 1800s and early 1900s, but it is probably most famous as the home of white squirrels, one of only a handful of places in the United States where relatively large colonies of the albino creatures exist. Marionville is also known as an apple "capital" of southwest Missouri because of the several apple orchards located in the area. Marionville is home to the

Marionville R-9 School District and has a current population of about 2,200.

A white squirrel at Marionvillle, Mo. *Photo by the author.*

Mark Twain National Forest—Known for its rivers and trails, the Mark Twain National Forest consists of 1.5 million acres of forest land in Missouri. Although one small section of the forest is located in central Missouri near Columbia, the large majority of it is located in the Missouri Ozarks. It was established in 1938 under the 1911 Weeks Act, which allowed the federal government to purchase land for conservation.

Marmaduke, John S.—John S. Marmaduke was a Confederate general during the Civil War. He commanded a brigade at the Battle of Prairie Grove in December 1862, led two raids into Missouri during 1863, and commanded a division during Sterling Price's invasion of Missouri in 1864. He was elected governor of Missouri in 1884.

Marmaros, Missouri—Marmaros was a small town that was founded with the opening of the Marble Cave Mining and Manufacturing Company in 1884 near present-day Marvel Cave inside Silver Dollar City. It became a ghost town after the company closed within a few years.

Marquand, Missouri—Marquand is a town of about 200 people in eastern Madison County. The area was originally called Whitener

Settlement, and the town was laid out in 1869 on land owned by Henry Whitener and given the name Marquand, after railroad administrator Henry G. Marquand. The town is home to the Marquand Elementary School.

Marshall, Arkansas—Marshall is a town of about 1,360 people and the county seat of Searcy County. It was founded as the county seat in 1857 and named Burrowsville, but the name was changed in 1867 in honor of Chief Justice John Marshall of the Supreme Court. Marshall was the site of a popular strawberry festival for many years, and since the early 1990s it has hosted an annual north Arkansas genealogy fair. It is home to the Searcy County School District.

Marshfield, Missouri—Marshfield is the county seat of Webster County. It was settled about 1830 but not organized until 1856, after the county was formed and Marshfield was named the county seat. President Truman visited Marshfield in 1948, and President George H.W. Bush visited in 1991 during the town's annual Fourth of July celebration, the oldest such celebration west of the Mississippi. Marshfield's annual Cherry Blossom Festival is another popular celebration, and the town is also known for being the birthplace of famous astronomer Edwin Hubble. Marshfield has a population of about 6,700, and it is home to the Marshfield R-1 Schools.

Scale model of Hubble telescope on courthouse grounds at Marshfield. *Courtesy Wikimedia.*

Marshfield Tornado—The Marshfield tornado was a devastating F4 tornado that struck Marshfield, Missouri, on April 18, 1880. It killed over ninety people and destroyed or heavily damaged almost the whole business district of the town. The event inspired a popular song by ragtime composer and musician John William "Blind" Boone entitled "The Marshfield Tornado."

Martial Law—Martial law was proclaimed in Missouri by General John C. Fremont in late August of 1861, declaring that civilians in arms would be subject to court martial and execution, that the property of anyone aiding the secessionists would be confiscated, and that the slaves of Southern sympathizers were emancipated. Fearing the proclamation would prompt Missouri to support the Southern cause, President Lincoln revoked the edict and relieved Fremont of his command two months later.

Martinville, Arkansas—Martinville is a small community in northern Faulkner County at the southern edge of the Ozarks. It was founded in the mid-1880s by Christadelphian leader James Daniel Martin. It was the site of Christadelphian meetings for many years, and a Christadelphia Bible school was established there in 1923.

Martin, Mark—Mark Martin is a former professional stock car driver on the NASCAR circuit. He was born and grew up in Batesville, Arkansas, where he owns an automobile dealership and has a museum that houses some of his past cars, many of his trophies, and other memorabilia of his racing career.

Martin, William Franklin "Billy"—Billy Martin was a young man from Laclede County, Missouri, whose romantic story made headlines across the country in the early 1880s. Acquitted of a manslaughter charge in 1879, he was arrested less than a year later on a charge of killing his uncle. He was convicted and sentenced to death, but the sheriff's niece helped him escape while he was in the county jail awaiting execution. The couple fled together and married while on the run. Later, Martin was arrested in Tennessee and brought back to Missouri, but he was granted a new trial and found not guilty in the death of his uncle.

Marvel Cave—Marvel Cave is a large cave located on the grounds of Silver Dollar City west of Branson, Missouri. The first known exploration of the cave occurred in 1869. The explorers reported deposits of marble inside the cave, and it was named Marble Cave.

The "marble" turned out to be limestone, but during the 1880s, guano was commercially mined from the cave. Owners of the cave began offering tours during the 1890s, and the cave's name was changed about 1927 to Marvel Cave. The cave prospered as a tourist destination during the mid-twentieth century, and Silver Dollar City grew up around it.

Mary's Home, Missouri—Mary's Home is a small community in northeast Miller County. The area was settled mostly by German immigrants, and the community grew up around the Catholic Church they attended. The place was at first going to be called Morgan after a protestant saloonkeeper until the priest objected and insisted on naming it Mary's Home.

Massey, Ellen Gray—Ellen Gray Massey was a teacher, speaker, and author whose work, both fiction and nonfiction, focused on the Ozarks. Among the publications for which she was noted is *Bittersweet, the Ozarks Quarterly*, a student-written magazine that she produced and edited while teaching at Lebanon (Missouri) High School. Massey died in 2014.

Ellen Gray Massey outside her Lebanon, Missouri, home. *From www.ellengraymassey.com.*

Matthews-Payton Feud—The Matthews-Payton feud was a disagreement between the L.T. Matthews family and the Alex Payton family of southern Christian County, Missouri, during the 1880s. The feud started as a property dispute and ultimately resulted in the serious wounding (and possible death) of one child, the killing of a second child, the killing of a man, one murder conviction, and two other murder trials. This feud occurred in the same general area as the Meadows-Bilyeu feud ten years later. (See entry on page 188.) Bud Meadows of the latter feud was implicated in this one as well.

Max Hunter Song Collection—Held at Missouri State University, the Max Hunter Song Collection is an archive of about 1,600 Ozark Mountain folk songs recorded by Springfield traveling salesman Max Hunter between 1956 and 1976. In addition to the songs, the collection also includes stories and voices of the people who shared their songs and recollections.

Mayes County, Oklahoma—Mayes County is located at the western edge of the Ozarks, and only the eastern part is in the Ozarks. The county was formed shortly before Oklahoma statehood in 1907 and named in honor of Cherokee chief Samuel H. Mayes. Pryor or Pryor Creek became the county seat.

Maynard, Arkansas—Maynard is a community of about 425 people in northern Randolph County approximately six miles south of the Missouri state line. It was founded shortly after the Civil War. From the 1890s to the 1920s, Maynard was the home of the Maynard Baptist Academy. Today it is home to the Maynard Pioneer Museum and to the Maynard School District.

McAfee, Charles B.—Charles B. McAfee was a Union officer during the Civil War, serving primarily in southwest Missouri, and a prominent Springfield lawyer after the war.

McCann, Gordon—Gordon McCann is a Springfield, Missouri, businessman known for his large collection of Ozarks fiddle tune recordings and other Ozarks folklore. The collection is housed at Missouri State University. McCann is also associated with *OzarksWatch Video Magazine.*

McCaskill, Claire—Claire McCaskill is Missouri's senior U.S. senator. She was born in Rolla and spent much of her childhood in Houston and Lebanon.

McClurg, Joseph W.—Joseph W. McClurg was an army officer and politician from the area of Camden and Laclede counties, Missouri. During the Civil War, he was a colonel of Missouri State Militia. After the war, he was elected three times to the U.S. House of Representatives and later served one term, 1869-1871, as governor of Missouri. He died at Lebanon in 1900.

McCord, May Kennedy—May Kennedy McCord was an Ozarks folklorist, storyteller, singer, and writer. During the 1930s and early 1940s, she had a column called "Hillbilly Heartbeats" in Springfield, Missouri, newspapers, and during the 1940s she began a radio program by the same name on Springfield's KWTO. Called the Queen of the Hillbillies or the First Lady of the Ozarks, she entertained listeners by singing and telling stories about the Ozarks.

McCormick, James R.—James R. McCormick was a physician, military officer, and politician from southeast Missouri during the Civil War era. During the war, he served as a brigadier general in charge of Enrolled Missouri Militia for twenty-two counties in southeast Missouri, and after the war he served as a U. S. congressman from 1866 to 1873. He died at Farmington and is buried there.

McCracken, Missouri—McCracken is an unincorporated community east of Ozark in Christian County. It was founded about 1900.

McCulloch, Benjamin—Benjamin McCulloch was a Confederate brigadier general during the Civil War. He led the Confederate forces at the Battle of Wilson's Creek in August of 1861, and he was killed at the Battle of Pea Ridge in March of 1862.

McDonald, Andrew—Andrew McDonald was a longtime basketball coach and chairman of the physical education department at Missouri State University, and McDonald Hall and Arena on the campus is named after him.

McGinnis, Jumbo—Jumbo McGinnis was a Major League Baseball pitcher of the 1880s who was born at Alton, Missouri, in 1854.

McMurray, Jamie—Jamie McMurray is a professional race car driver in the NASCAR Sprint Cup Series who was born and grew up in Joplin, Missouri. He was the winner of the 2010 Daytona 500.

McNeil, John—John McNeil was a Union general during the Civil War. Perhaps best known in Missouri for his role in the Palmyra Massacre, he commanded the District of Southwest Missouri during the summer and fall of 1863 and briefly commanded the District of Rolla in 1864.

McNeil, W. K. (William Kinneth)—W. K. McNeil was a prominent author and historian of Ozarks folklore, including the folksongs, speech, and legends of the region. From 1976 until his death in 2005, McNeil held the position of folklorist at the Ozark Folk Center in Mountain View, Arkansas.

Meadows-Bilyeu Feud—The Meadows-Bilyeu Feud was a long-standing disagreement between neighbors Bud Meadows and Steve Bilyeu that erupted into violence on November 28, 1898, south of Ozark, Missouri, near the Christian-Taney county line. The incident left three Bilyeus dead and Meadows and three of his cohorts indicted for murder.

Melbourne, Arkansas—Melbourne is a town of about 1,850 people and the county seat of Izard County. In 1875, the county seat was moved from Mount Olive to Mill Creek, and the following year the name of Mill Creek was changed to Melbourne. The town was incorporated in 1878. Melbourne is home to Ozarka College and to the Melbourne Public Schools.

Meramec Caverns—Located near Stanton, Missouri, in Franklin County, Meramec Caverns is the largest and most-visited commercial cave in Missouri. It was discovered in the early 1700s by a French explorer. During the Civil War era, it was used for mining saltpeter, and later it was used as a social gathering place. It was opened as a commercial cave in 1935.

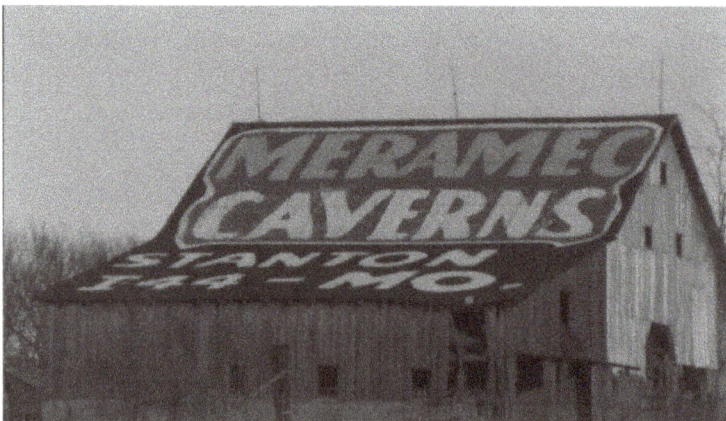

Barn sign along Interstate 44 advertising Meramec Caverns. *Photo by the author.*

Meramec River—The Meramec River forms in Dent County, Missouri, and flows in a generally northeast direction for over 200 miles until it empties into the Mississippi about twenty miles south of St. Louis. It is one of the longer rivers in the state.

Meramec State Park—Meramec State Park, located along the Meramec River southeast of Sullivan, is a Missouri state park covering almost 7,000 acres and offering outdoor activities like fishing and canoeing.

Meta, Missouri—Meta is a town of about 230 people in southwest Osage County. It grew up along the line of the Chicago, Rock Island, and Pacific Railroad in the early 1900s.

Miami, Oklahoma—Located at the western edge of the Ozarks, Miami is a town of about 14,000 people and the seat of Ottawa County. It was established in 1891 and named the county seat of Ottawa County at the time of Oklahoma statehood in 1907. Former Heisman trophy winner and NFL player Steve Owens grew up in Miami, and one of the main streets in the town is named for him. Famous ballerina Moscelyne Larkin was born in Miami. The town is the home of the Miami Public Schools and Northeast Oklahoma A & M College, a two-year, state-funded institution. It is also home to the Miami, Modoc, Ottawa, Peoria, Seneca-Cayuga, and Shawnee Indian tribes.

Historic Coleman Theater in Miami, Okla. *Photo by the author.*

Midway—There are two or three current communities in the Ozarks named Midway, and there were a couple of historic communities in the region by that name. Perhaps the most noteworthy of the current communities is the Midway in northwest Baxter County near Bull Shoals Lake. It has a population of about 1,100 people and is home to the Baxter County Regional Airport and the Baxter County Industrial Park.

Military Road—The Military Road was a federal road built in the early 1830s that entered Missouri near Cape Girardeau, angled through southeast Missouri, crossed the Current River into Arkansas at Pitman's Ferry, and continued south to Pocahontas and beyond. The Military Road generally followed the route of the earlier Natchitoches Trace, and part of it followed the Southwest Trail. A second Military Road approximate to the Ozarks ran south from Fort Scott, Kansas, along the western edge of the region to Fort Gibson in Indian Territory (Oklahoma).

Militia Springs, Missouri—Militia Springs was a Union encampment in central Douglas County during the Civil War. A post office continued there after the war but was vacated when Ava was laid out nearby and named the county seat in 1871.

Miller, Harry Lewis—Harry Lewis Miller was a photographer from Batesville, Arkansas, around the turn of the twentieth century. His work was generally unattributed until years after his death, when it was researched and exhibited. His landscape scenes and scenes of daily life in north central Arkansas form an important aesthetic and social-history record of the region.

Miller, Missouri—Miller is a town of about 700 people in northern Lawrence County. It was laid out in 1890 along the railroad and named for a railroad man. It was incorporated as a village in 1896 and as a city in 1915. Miller is home to the Miller R-2 Schools.

Miller, Nick—Nick Miller was a stone carver in northwest Arkansas during the late 1800s. He was known for the artistry of his tombstones, which can still be found throughout the region.

Miller, William Read—William Read Miller was the twelfth governor of Arkansas, serving from 1877 to 1881. The first native of the state to hold the office, Miller was born at Batesville in 1823.

Miller County, Missouri—Located in central Missouri, Miller County was formed in 1837 from territory taken from Cole County, and the county seat was soon afterwards located at what later became Tuscumbia. The county was named for John Miller, former governor of the state.

Mills, Wilbur—Wilbur Mills was a U.S. congressman from Arkansas from 1939 to 1977 and the chairman of the powerful House Ways and Means Committee for many years. He represented the state's Second District, the upper reaches of which include part of the Ozarks. The end of Mills's career was hastened after he became involved in an infamous scandal involving stripper Fanne Foxe in 1974.

Mill Spring, Missouri—Mill Spring is a village of about 200 people located in western Wayne County near the Black River. It was laid out in 1871 by the Iron Mountain Railroad Company and was given its name because a mill there was run by a large spring.

Millstream Gardens Conservation Area—Millstream Gardens Conservation Area is a 916-acre tract of Missouri Department of Conservation land in Madison County about eight miles west of Fredericktown. The Tiemann Shut-Ins on the St. Francis River are located within the area.

Mina Sauk Falls—See Taum Sauk Mountain.

Mineral Area—Mineral Area is a term used to indicate a broad section of southeast Missouri that encompasses the Old Lead Belt centered in St. Francois County but also includes areas where iron and other minerals are or have been mined.

Mineral Point, Missouri—Mineral Point is a village of about 350 people in Washington County about three and a half miles east of Potosi. Mineral Point was laid out in 1858.

Mining—Among the minerals that have been mined in the Ozarks are barite, coal, iron, lead, lime, manganese, salt, saltpeter, tripoli, and zinc. Certain areas of the region, such as the Old Lead Belt of southeast Missouri and the Tri-State Mining District around Joplin, Missouri, developed largely because of mining.

Mingo National Wildlife Refuge—Mingo National Wildlife Refuge is a 21,676-acre national wildlife refuge located on the Wayne-Stoddard county line at the southeast edge of the Ozarks.

Missouri and North Arkansas Railway—The Missouri and North Arkansas Railway was a regional railroad that operated from 1906 to 1946 and at its peak connected Joplin, Missouri, to Helena, Arkansas. It started in the early 1880s as a connection of the Frisco Railroad between Seligman, Missouri, and Eureka Springs, Arkansas, but was reorganized as the M&NA in 1906. This historic railroad is not to be confused with the still-operating Missouri and North Arkansas Railroad that is headquartered in Carthage, Missouri.

Missouri Lumber and Mining Company   See lumber industry.

Missouri Mines State Historic Site—See St. Joe State Park.

Missouri Pacific Railroad—Originally called the Pacific Railroad, the Missouri Pacific Railroad was one of the first railroads west of the Mississippi. It began in St. Louis in 1851, and a line was completed to Kansas City in 1865. Through growth and mergers, it became one of the largest railways in the country, and it had several lines and trains that served the Ozarks, including a train called the Ozarker that ran between St. Louis and Little Rock.

Missouri Southern Railroad—The Missouri Southern Railroad was a railroad during the late 1800s and early 1900s that primarily served the timber industry in the Reynolds County area.

Missouri Southern State University—Missouri Southern State University is a public institution of higher learning located in Joplin, Missouri. Founded in 1937 as Joplin Junior College, the school became a four-year institution named Missouri Southern State College in 1968. It was renamed Missouri Southern State University-Joplin in 2003, and two years later the school dropped Joplin from its name. It has an undergraduate enrollment of about 5,500 students.

Missouri Sports Hall of Fame—Started by John Q. Hammons in 1994, the Missouri Sports Hall of Fame is located in Springfield, Missouri. It recognizes outstanding sports figures who have some connection to Missouri and displays memorabilia and exhibits pertaining to Missouri sports.

Missouri State Guard—The Missouri State Guard was a military force organized in Missouri by pro-Southern governor Claiborne F. Jackson at the start of the Civil War to protect the state and to resist an "invasion" by Federal forces. Although not officially part of the Confederacy, the State Guard fought alongside Confederate forces at early battles like Wilson's Creek, and many members of the State Guard eventually joined the Confederacy when the former organization began to disintegrate.

Missouri State Militia—The Missouri State Militia was a Union military force during the Civil War that was equipped and financed by the Federal government but under the control of the state of Missouri. Authorized in late 1861 and organized in early 1862, the Missouri State Militia was primarily a cavalry force that was not subject to service outside Missouri except to counter a direct threat to the state. Its mission was to eradicate Confederate guerrillas and to oppose raids into the state by regular Southern forces

Missouri State University—Missouri State University is an institution of higher learning located at Springfield. Begun in 1905 as the Fourth District Normal School, it became Southwest Missouri State Teachers College in 1919, Southwest Missouri State College in 1945, Southwest Missouri State University in 1972, and Missouri State University in 2005. In addition to the main campus at Springfield, the university has three satellite campuses and an overall student population of about 23,000, making it the second largest university in the state. Prominent alumni include actors John Goodman and Kathleen Turner and businessman David Glass.

Missouri University of Science and Technology—Originally named the Missouri School of Mines and Metallurgy and later known as the

Rolla Building at Mo. Univ. of Science & Technology. *Courtesy Wikipedia.*

the University of Missouri-Rolla, the Missouri University of Science and Technology is a four-year institution of higher learning located at Rolla, Missouri. It is a branch of the University of Missouri System headquartered at Columbia. The Rolla school has a student body of about 7,500. It is known primarily as an engineering school, but it also offers many other fields of study.

Molloy, Emma—Emma Molloy was a nationally known temperance revivalist who was involved in a notorious murder case in Greene County, Missouri during the mid 1880s. George Graham, who was bigamously married to Molloy's foster daughter Cora Lee and was staying on the Molloy farm west of Springfield, killed his first wife, Sarah Graham, and stuffed her body in an abandoned well on the farm in the fall of 1885. When the body was discovered early the next year, Graham was arrested for murder, and both Molloy and Lee were held as accessories. Graham was lynched by a mob before he came to trial, while Cora Lee was found not guilty and the charges against Emma Molloy were eventually dropped

Sketch of Emma Molloy. *Author's collection.*

Monday Hollow, Battle of—The Battle of Monday Hollow (aka Dutch Hollow) was a Civil War action that occurred on October 13,

1861, northwest of present-day Richland, Missouri, between Union forces under the command of Colonel John B. Wyman and Missouri State Guard forces under Lieutenant-Colonel William W. Summers. Approximately 60 State Guardsmen were reportedly killed in the action, while the Union lost only one man killed.

Monegaw Springs, Missouri—Monegaw Springs is a small village in St. Clair County. Established prior to the Civil War, it was burned by Kansas jayhawkers during the war but flourished as a mineral-water resort town after the war. Today, easy access to Monegaw Springs has been cut off by lakes that virtually surround it, and the once thriving little town barely survives.

Monett, Missouri—Monett is a town of about 8,875 people located primarily in Barry County on the Barry-Lawrence county line. Originally called Billings, the settlement changed its name to Plymouth in 1871 and came to be known as Plymouth Station when a railroad was constructed through the community about the same time. The railroad vacated Plymouth in the mid-1870s, and an adjacent town, Monett, was platted during the 1880s. It eventually engulfed old Plymouth, and the entire place became known as Monett. The town is home to the Monett R-1 Schools.

Moniteau County, Missouri—Moniteau County is located in central Missouri on the northern fringes of the Ozarks. It was formed in 1845 from parts of Cole and Morgan counties and named after Moniteau Creek. California was named the county seat soon after the county was formed.

Monkey Run, Arkansas—Monkey Run is a small community in western Baxter County. Founded in the 1870s as Pilgrim's Rest, the community changed its name shortly afterwards. The name change reportedly came about either because a storekeeper chased some boys away from his store and remarked, "Look at those monkeys run" or because the storekeeper himself was referred to as a monkey. Monkey Run thrived during the 1920s and 1930s as a zinc mining center, but it declined rapidly thereafter. Today little remains of the community.

Monks, William—A resident of Howell County, Missouri, William Monks was captain in the Union Army who made a name for himself during the Civil War for his aggressive campaign against guerrillas in south central Missouri and north central Arkansas. After the war he became even more notorious (at least in the eyes of many) fighting outlaws and bushwhacker holdouts in the same region as an officer in the Missouri state militia.

Montauk, Missouri—Montauk is a small community in southwest Dent County. It was founded near the beginning of the Civil War and named after the Montaukett Indians.

Montauk State Park—Montauk State Park is located at the headwaters of the Current River in southwest Dent County near the small community of Montauk. It is well known as a trout-fishing destination.

Monte Ne, Arkansas—Featuring the world's largest log hotels, Monte Ne was a resort town developed in 1900 in Benton County by William Hope "Coin" Harvey. The community began as Silver Springs, but Harvey changed its name to Monte Ne (meaning "mountain water") after he bought 320 acres that included the area of Silver Springs. The place was popular as a resort until the early 1920s, when it began to decline. In 1964, much of what remained of the town was submerged by water when Beaver Lake was formed by the construction of Beaver Dam, although remnants of the town are still visible, especially during periods of low water.

Partially submerged ruins of amphitheater at Monte Ne. *Courtesy Wikimedia.*

Monte Ne Railway—Monte Ne Railway was a five-mile railroad that Monte Ne resort developed built in 1902 to connect his resort to the Frisco line at Lowell, Arkansas.

Montreal, Missouri—Montreal is an unincorporated community in eastern Camden County. Originally called Buffalo Prairie, it became Montreal when a post office was established during the 1890s.

Moody, Missouri—Moody is an unincorporated community in southern Howell County near the Arkansas border. It was a prosperous little place during the early 1900s but has since declined.

Moondog—Louis T. "Moondog" Hardin, Jr. was an iconoclastic musician and composer admired in jazz, classical, and rock circles. He grew up partly in Hurley, Missouri, and lived as a young man in Moorefield, Arkansas. During the mid-1900s, he lived in New York and was often seen on the streets of Manhattan dressed as a Viking and banging a drum.

Moorefield, Arkansas—Moorefield is a town of about 160 people in Independence County. It was named after Jesse A. Moore, who owned the land where the town was platted.

Moreau River—The Moreau River is a tributary of the Missouri that meanders south of Jefferson City at the northern edge of the Ozarks.

Morgan, Missouri—Morgan is an unincorporated community in southern Laclede County. A post office was established at the site in 1879, and the place was named after Asa Morgan, a Confederate officer who settled in the area after the war.

Morgan, Charles Henry—Charles Henry Morgan was a lawyer and politician from Lamar, Missouri and later Joplin, Missouri. He served five terms in the U. S. Congress between 1875 and 1911.

Morgan, Tom Perkins—Tom Perkins Morgan was writer from Rogers, Arkansas. His humorous stories about the Ozarks region and its people appeared regularly in the *Kansas City Star* and in national publications like *Life* and *Ladies Home Journal* during the late 1800s and early 1900s. He also owned and operated a bookstore in Rogers.

Morgan County, Missouri—Morgan County was established in 1833 from territory taken from Cooper County and named after General Daniel Morgan of Revolutionary War fame. Versailles was laid out in 1835 as the county seat.

Morgan's Mill, Skirmish at—The Skirmish at Morgan's Mill, also known as the Battle of Martin's Creek, was a minor Civil War action in northern Sharp County, Arkansas, on February 8, 1864, near the confluence of Martin's Creek and Spring River.

Morrisville, Missouri—Morrisville is a town of about 390 people in southern Polk County. The area was originally called Pleasant Prairie and then Mount Pleasant. Morrisville was formed about 1870 when Morris Mitchell donated land for a Methodist college at the site. During Morrisville's early days, it was sometimes informally called Shave Tail. Morrisville College was a forerunner of the Scarritt-Morrisville College that formed in 1909 from a merger of Ebenezer College and Scarritt College of Neosho. Morrisville is home to the Marion C. Early R-5 Schools.

Morrow, Lynn—Lynn Morrow is the former director of the local records section of the Missouri State Archives and the author or editor of numerous books and articles about the Ozarks.

Mountain Crest Academy—Located in northern Franklin County, Arkansas, near the Madison County line, the Mountain Crest Academy was one of a large number of schools founded during the early 1900s as a mission of the Presbyterian Church to serve the "backward" youth of the rural mountain South, especially Appalachia. The Mountain Crest Academy existed from about 1916 until 1931.

Mountain Grove, Missouri—Mountain Grove is town of about 5,000 people located in southeastern Wright County. Mountain Grove was established as a village in 1882, although communities named Fyan, Hickory Springs, and Mountain Store existed in the same immediate vicinity prior to Mountain Grove's organization. Mountain Grove got its name from the fact that it was located on a tree-lined ridge. The town is home to the Mountain Grove R-3 Schools.

Mountain Grove Campus-Missouri State University—MSU Mountain Grove is a 190-acre campus of Missouri State University located at Mountain Grove that consists primarily of the State Fruit Experimentation Station operated by the university's agriculture department. Faculty at the campus primarily teach through the university's plant science master's degree program, but courses are also offered leading to an associate degree in viticulture or enology.

Mountain Home, Arkansas—Mountain Home is a town of about 12,500 people and the seat of Baxter County. It was established prior to the Civil War and called Rapp's Barren or Talbert's Barren, but when a post office was established in 1857, it took the name Mountain Home. In the late 1850s, the Male and Female Academy was established at Mountain Home, and the town essentially grew up around the school, which drew students from throughout the region. The town was the site of a minor Civil War skirmish in October of 1862, and it was sacked by jayhawkers and the academy was burned in April of 1864. The town was quickly rebuilt after the war and was named the county seat in 1873 when Baxter County was formed. From 1892 to 1933, the town was home to the Mountain Home College, also known as the Mountain Home Baptist College. Today, it is home to Arkansas State University—Mountain Home, a branch campus of ASU, and to the Mountain Home Public Schools. Since construction of the nearby Norfork and Bull Shoals lakes in the 1940s and 1950s, Mountain Home has become increasingly popular as a recreation and retirement area.

Mountain Meadows Massacre—The Mountain Meadows Massacre was the mass slaughter in September 1857 at Mountain Meadows, Utah, of approximately 120 settlers from northern Arkansas on their way to California. The massacre was carried out by Mormon militia disguised as Indians, aided by a few Paiute Indians. A historic marker is located at Caravan Spring, about four miles south of Harrison, Arkansas, from where the wagon train carrying the settlers started in April of 1857.

Mountain View, Arkansas—Mountain View is a town of about 2,750 people and the seat of Stone County. When Stone County was formed in 1873, Mountain View was laid out as the seat of the new county. Mountain View is home to the Ozark Folk Center State Park and to the annual Arkansas Folk Festival, and the town sometimes promotes itself as the "Folk Music Capital of the World." It is also home to the Mountain View School District.

Mountain View, Missouri—Mountain View is a town of about 2,720 people in northeast Howell County. The first store was located at the site in the years after the Civil War, and the town got its first post office in 1878 or 1879. It was named Mountain View at that time because the store was located on a small elevation. The town was formally platted in the late 1880s after a railroad reached the community. Former Walmart CEO and current Kansas City Royals owner David Glass grew up in Mountain View. The town is home to the Mountain View Birch Tree R-3 School District.

Mount Pleasant, Arkansas—Mount Pleasant is a town of about 400 people in southeast Izard County. It was established shortly after the close of the Civil War as Barren Fork. In 1878, the Mount Pleasant Academy was established at Barren Fork. In 1905 the school's building burned, and the academy closed. Barren Fork was renamed Mount Pleasant a few years later in honor of the former academy. Mount Pleasant is home to the Mount Pleasant Elementary School, which is part of the Melbourne School District.

Mount Sterling, Missouri—Mount Sterling is an unincorporated community in western Gasconade County in the northern Ozarks. Originally called Shockley's Bluff, it was an early county seat of Gasconade.

Mount Vernon, Missouri—Mount Vernon is a town of about 4,600 people and the seat of Lawrence County. It was laid out as the seat shortly after the county was formed in 1845. A post office by the same name existed in the vicinity a couple of years prior to the town's formation. A popular festival called Apple Butter Makin' Days is held in Mount Vernon each October. The town is home to the Mount Vernon R-5 Schools and the Mount Vernon Missouri Veterans Home.

Mulberry River—The Mulberry River is a 70-mile tributary of the Arkansas River that forms in northern Johnson County, Arkansas. It flows generally west at first and then turns south and joins the Arkansas near the Franklin-Crawford county line about three miles south of the town of Mulberry. Popular for fishing, boating, and other outdoor activities, the river was supposedly named for the many mulberry trees that grew in its vicinity.

Mullin, Markwayne—Markwayne Mullin is businessman and politician from Adair County, Oklahoma, who has represented northeast Oklahoma in the U.S. Congress since January of 2013.

Mullins, Johnny—Johnny Mullins was a songwriter from Springfield, Missouri, who wrote such songs as Porter Wagoner's "Company Comin'" and Emmylou Harris's "Blue Kentucky Girl."

Murder Rocks—The Murder Rocks are large limestone boulders on Highway JJ in southern Taney County, Missouri, which Civil War bushwhacker Alf Bolin reportedly used as his base of operations.

Murphy Movement—The Murphy Movement was a temperance movement that started in Pittsburg, Pennsylvania, in 1876. In early 1878, it swept across the Ozarks, and thousands of people flocked to churches throughout the region to hear sermons by representatives of the movement. Hundreds of converts pledged not to drink alcoholic beverages, and they sported blue ribbons as tokens of their vow.

Murphy, Isaac—Isaac Murphy was the eighth governor of Arkansas, serving from 1864 to 1868. An avowed Unionist, he was named provisional governor after the Union army gained control of most of the Confederate state of Arkansas, and he became governor after a new constitution was adopted overriding the Confederate constitution passed at the beginning of the Civil War. Murphy lived and died in Huntsville.

Murrell Home—Maintained as an Oklahoma historic site, the Murrell Home was built at Park Hill in 1845 by George M. Murrell, the nephew by marriage of Cherokee chief John Ross.

Mussel Industry—The harvesting of freshwater mussels from the White River of Arkansas thrived during the first half of the twentieth century. The mussel shells were polished and used as buttons, but the mussel industry declined when plastic buttons began to be mass produced.

Mystic Caverns and Crystal Dome Caverns—Mystic Caverns and Crystal Dome Caverns are dual, commercial caves located on the same property about eight miles south of Harrison, Arkansas, on Scenic Highway 7 near the former Dogpatch theme park. Although the entrances to the two caves are located only about 100 feet apart, Crystal Dome was discovered about 100 years after Mystic Caverns.

Inside Mystic Caverns. From www.mysticcaverns.com.

N

Narrows, The—Located between the Eleven Point River and Frederick Creek in Oregon County, Missouri, the Narrows is a narrow strip of land that is hedged in by high bluffs on either side and noted for its scenic beauty. There is also a place called the Narrows in Crawford County, Arkansas, that is a gap between high hills.

Natchidoches Trace—See Military Road.

Nathan Boone Homestead—The Nathan Boone Homestead is a state historic site near Ash Grove, Missouri, where pioneer explorer and surveyor Nathan Boone lived for about the last twenty years of his life. The family cabin and cemetery are preserved at the site.

Nation, Carrie—Carrie Nation was a militant temperance crusader during the late 1800s and early 1900s who would sometimes enter saloons and smash up the fixtures and whiskey bottles with a hatchet. Most of her crusading activities occurred while she lived in Kansas, but she lived the last few years of her life in Eureka Springs, Arkansas, in a home called Hatchet Hall, which still stands today.

National Cemetery, Fayetteville—The Fayetteville National Cemetery was established in 1867 as a burial place for Union soldiers killed during the Civil War. The first burials were re-interments of soldiers who had initially been buried elsewhere. Many of them had been killed at nearby battles like Pea Ridge and Prairie Grove and buried on the spot. Fayetteville National Cemetery is now open to veterans of any war.

National Cemetery, Springfield—The Springfield National Cemetery was, like the one at Fayetteville, established in 1867, and many of the first interments were soldiers who had been killed during the Civil War at nearby battles like Wilson's Creek and initially buried where they died. An adjacent Confederate Cemetery later became a part of the National Cemetery. Veterans of subsequent wars are also buried at the cemetery.

Natural Bridge—The Natural Bridge of Arkansas is a large slab of stone, about 120 feet long, across a small ravine or waterway, just off U.S. Highway 65 a few miles north of Clinton, Arkansas.

Natural Dam, Arkansas—Natural Dam is a small community in Crawford County, named after a rock dam across Mountain Fork Creek at its confluence with Lee Creek. Lee Creek Bridge, which is on the National Register of Historic Places, carries Highway 59 across Lee Creek at Natural Dam. Another historic Lee Creek Bridge, along Highway 220 a few miles away, is also on the register.

Natural Falls State Park—Located six miles west of West Siloam Springs, Natural Falls State Park is an Oklahoma state park featuring a 77-foot water falls on Dripping Springs Branch.

Naylor, Missouri—Naylor is a town of about 650 people in southeastern Ripley County. It was established along the Doniphan branch of the Iron Mountain Railroad in the late 1800s. Originally called Barfield, the town was sometimes confused with Barfield, Arkansas; so it was renamed Naylor after William A. Naylor, a land surveyor in the region. Naylor is home to the Naylor R-2 School District.

Neelyville, Missouri—Neelyville is a town of about 500 people in southwestern Butler County near the Arkansas border. It was established in the early 1870s along the line of the railroad and named for local landowner Obadiah Neely.

Neill, Robert—Robert Neill was a soldier, lawyer, and politician from Batesville, Arkansas. He served as an officer in the Confederate Army and was a member of the U.S. House of Representatives from 1893 to 1897.

Neosho, Missouri—Neosho is a town of about 11,850 people and the county seat of Newton County. It was settled during the 1830s, became the permanent county seat in the early 1840s, and was incorporated in 1847. The word "Neosho" is thought to derive from a Native American term meaning "clear, cold water" that was given to the location by early Indians because of its numerous springs. Neosho has been variously known as the City of Springs, the Gateway to the Ozarks, and the Flower Box City (because of the numerous flower boxes placed in the city as a beautification project that began in the 1950s). Neosho is home to the Neosho R-5 School District.

Neosho National Fish Hatchery—The Neosho National Fish Hatchery at Neosho, Missouri, is one of seventy fish hatcheries operated by the U.S. Fish and Wildlife Service. Founded in 1888, it is the oldest operating federal fish hatchery in the country.

Neosho Legislature—Neosho, Missouri, served briefly during the fall of 1861 as the Confederate capital of Missouri. After the duly elected governor, Claiborne F. Jackson, and his followers in the legislature were ousted from the state capital at Jefferson City, they fled to southwest Missouri, where they met in exile at Neosho in late October and passed an ordinance of secession, which theoretically took the state out of the Union, and the Confederacy recognized Missouri as a Confederate state. However, critics have argued that the ordinance was invalid because the session lacked a quorum (which may or may not have been true) and because a state convention, previously vested with the power to decide the issue of secession, had already met and replaced the ousted state government with a new provisional one.

Neosho Male and Female Seminary--Founded in 1878 at Neosho, Missouri, the Neosho Male and Female Seminary was an academy originally established for the training of Methodist missionaries. In 1880, its name changed to the Neosho Collegiate Institute, and in 1887 it was reconstituted as the Scarritt Collegiate Institute. Later it operated as Scarritt College, and in 1909 it merged with Ebenezer College and moved to Morrisville, Missouri, as the Morrisville-Scarritt College. In 1924, Central Methodist College at Fayette, Missouri, absorbed the Morrisville school, and Scarritt College reopened at Nashville, Tennessee.

Neosho, Skirmishes at—Neosho, Missouri, was the site of several skirmishes during the Civil War, but three of them were perhaps more noted than the others. On May 31, 1862, a combined force of Stand Watie's Cherokee Mounted Rifles and John T. Coffee's partisans attacked and scattered a force of Missouri State Militia under Colonel John M. Richardson. On September 3, 1862, the Third Indian Home Guard drove a body of Southern forces out of Neosho during the preliminary maneuvering that led to the First Battle of Newtonia. On September 4, 1863, Colonel Jo Shelby and his Missouri Brigade attacked the Federal forces at Neosho and took temporary possession of the town near the beginning of Shelby's noted invasion of Missouri.

Newark, Arkansas—Newark is a town of about 1,200 in Independence County. It is home to the Cedar Ridge School District.

Newburg, Missouri—Newburg is a town of about 470 people in Phelps County approximately three miles south of I-44. It was laid out in 1883 as a division point on the Frisco Railroad. The town is home to the Newburg R-2 Schools.

New Haven, Missouri—New Haven is a town of about 2,010 in northwest Franklin County on the Missouri River. Settled in the 1830s as Miller's Landing and laid out as New Haven when the railroad came through in 1856, it is home to the New Haven Public Schools.

New Madrid Earthquakes—The New Madrid earthquakes were a series of earthquakes in late 1811 and early 1812 measuring about 7.0 on the Richter scale, which were centered around New Madrid in the boot heel area of Missouri but strongly felt for many miles around, including much of the Ozarks.

Newport, Arkansas—Newport is a town of about 7,880 people and the seat of Jackson County. It is located at the southeastern edge of the Ozarks, where the region's foothills change to Delta flatland.

Newth, Rebecca—Rebecca Newth is a writer from Fayetteville, Arkansas, whose work includes award-winning poetry, a memoir, and a collection of children's books. She also is the founder of Will Hall Books and an advocate for the arts in northwest Arkansas.

Newton County, Arkansas—Newton County was formed in 1842 from territory taken from Carroll County, and Jasper was named the county seat the following year. However, neither the county nor its seat are reportedly named after the often-paired Revolutionary War heroes Sergeant John Newton and Sergeant William Jasper. Instead Newton County was supposedly named for U.S. marshal Thomas W. Newton, later a U.S. congressman from Arkansas, while several legends purport to explain how Jasper got its name.

Newton County, Missouri—Located in southwest Missouri, Newton County was formed in 1838 from Barry County and named after Revolutionary hero Sergeant John Newton. The first court met shortly afterwards near the present site of Neosho, which became the county seat. In the early days, the area of Newton County was called Six Bulls, a colloquialization of "six boils," which referred to the six large streams that flowed through the region.

Newtonia, Missouri—Newtonia is a village of about 200 people in eastern Newton County. It was founded prior to the Civil War and was the site of two fairly significant battles during the war.

Newtonia, First Battle of—The First Battle of Newtonia was a Civil War engagement fought at Newtonia, Missouri, on September 30,

1862, between Confederate forces under Brigadier General Douglas
Cooper and Union forces under Brigadier General Frederick
Salomon. The engagement was a Confederate victory, but the
Southern forces were driven out of Newtonia and forced to retire to
Arkansas a few days later.

Newtonia, Second Battle of—The Second Battle of Newtonia was a
Civil War engagement fought at Newtonia, Missouri, on October 28,
1864, between Confederate forces under Brigadier General Joseph O.
Shelby and Union forces under Major General James G. Blunt. The
battle, occurring at the tail end of Confederate general Sterling Price's
failed invasion of Missouri, was a Union victory, but Shelby
accomplished his mission of stalling the Union pursuit and covering
Price's retreat.

Nez Perce—The Nez Perce are a Native American tribe from the
Pacific Northwest. As a result of the Nez Perce War of 1877, they
were driven out of their home territory and exiled to Ottawa County,
Oklahoma. Placed under the jurisdiction of the Quapaw agency, they
suffered great hardship and privation during their eleven-month stay
from 1878 to 1879.

Niangua, Missouri—Niangua is a town of about 405 people in
northern Webster County. It was laid out in 1870 as a station along
what was then the South Pacific Railroad. Niangua is home to the
Niangua R-5 School District.

Niangua River—The Niangua River is a tributary of the Osage River
in south central Missouri. It forms in Webster County, flows generally
northward through Dallas, Laclede, and Camden counties for
approximately 125 miles, and joins the Osage as an arm of the Lake
of the Ozarks.

Niangua River, Little—The Little Niangua River is a sixty-four-mile
tributary of the Niangua River. It forms in Dallas County, flows in a
generally north direction through Hickory and Camden counties, and
joins the Niangua River as an arm of the Lake of the Ozarks, which
was formed by the damming of the Osage River.

Nixa, Missouri—Nixa is a town of about 20,000 in northern Christian
County. It began in the mid-1800s as a crossroads stopover point for
teamsters and other travelers between Springfield and northern
Arkansas. When the first post office was established about 1878, the
place was named Nixa, reportedly after local landowner Nicholas A.

Inman. The beginning of his first name was combined with his middle initial to get Nixa. Nixa was incorporated as a village in 1902 and later as a city. Nixa has hosted Sucker Day, a popular annual festival during which sucker fish are fried and served, since 1957. One of the fastest growing towns in Missouri during recent years, Nixa is home to the Nixa R-2 Schools.

Nixon, Jeremiah "Jay"—A lifelong resident of DeSoto, Missouri, and one-time mayor of the city, Jay Nixon has been governor of Missouri since 2009.

Noel, Missouri—Noel is a town of about 1,850 people in southwest McDonald County. A post office was established at the site in 1886, and the place was named Noel after a pioneer family of the area. Noel is one of several Christmas cities in the United States. Each year during the Christmas season, thousands of cards and letters are sent from throughout the country to the Noel post office for postmarking. Noel is also known for its steep bluffs that overhang the highway leading into town. Noel is home to the Noel Elementary School, which is part of the McDonald County School District.

Bluffs overhanging highway near Noel, Mo. *Photo by the author.*

Noland, Charles Fenton Mercer—Charles Fenton Mercer "Fent" Noland was politician, soldier, and author from Batesville, Arkansas, known nationally for his humorous writings about Arkansas and the frontier during pre-Civil War days.

Norfork, Arkansas—Located at the confluence of the White River and North Fork River, Norfork is a town of about 550 people in Baxter County. Originally called Liberty, the town is home to the historic Jacob Wolf House, which served as the seat of justice for Izard County during Arkansas's territorial days. Today, the area is popular for fishing and other outdoor activities, and the town is home to the Norfork School District.

Norfork Dam and Lake—Norfork Lake is a lake in Baxter County, Arkansas, formed by the damming of the North Fork River. Construction of the dam was begun in 1941 and completed in 1944. President Harry S Truman visited the dam for a dedication ceremony on July 2, 1952, and dedicated Bull Shoals Dam later the same day. Norfork Lake covers about 22,000 acres and has about 550 miles of shore line. It is very popular for fishing, boating, water skiing, and other outdoor activities.

Norfork Dam. *Courtesy Wikimedia.*

Norfork National Fish Hatchery—One of the U.S. Fish and Wildlife's largest-producing fish hatcheries in the country, the Norfork National Fish Hatchery is located near Norfork Dam in Baxter County, Arkansas.

North Arkansas College—North Arkansas College is a two-year public college at Harrison, Arkansas, offering associate's degrees and other certificates or programs of study. It was established in 1974 and has a current student population of about 2,400. A branch campus at Berryville opened in 2008.

North Fork River (aka North Fork of the White River)—The North Fork River is a tributary of the White River in Baxter County, Arkansas. It is only five miles long between the Norfork Dam and the White River but was considerably longer before the dam turned the upper waters into a lake. The North Fork River is very popular for fishing.

North Miami, Oklahoma—North Miami is a town in Ottawa County at the northern edge of Miami. Established in 1915 during northeast Oklahoma's lead and zinc mining boom, it has a current population of about 450.

North Springfield, Missouri—North Springfield was a community that sprang up about a mile and a half north of the Springfield public square after the area's first train depot was located there in 1870. The town was jokingly nicknamed Moon City, because a St. Louis newspaper had once said that a railroad was just as likely to be built to the moon as to Springfield. The two towns were strong rivals for several years, but North Springfield later consolidated with Spring-field.

Northwest Arkansas Community College—Northwest Arkansas Community College is a two-year public institution of higher learning headquartered at Bentonville, Arkansas. Established in 1990, it had a student population of about 8,300 in 2013 and is one of the largest and fastest-growing junior colleges in Arkansas. In addition to the main branch in Bentonville, it also has five satellite facilities in the region.

Northwest Arkansas Naturals—The Northwest Arkansas Naturals are a Double-A minor-league baseball affiliate of the Kansas City Royals. The team is based in Springdale and plays its games at Arvest Ballpark.

Home field of the Northwest Arkansas Naturals. *Courtesy Wikimedia.*

Northview, Missouri—Northview is an unincorporated community in western Webster County near Interstate 44. Originally called Bunker Hill, the town changed its name in the early 1870s after a railroad was constructed through the area and passing trainmen claimed the location offered a "good north view." Northview had a population over 200 at one time but little survives to suggest its earlier prosperity.

Norwood, Missouri—Norwood is a town of about 665 people in southern Wright County. The area was settled during the 1850s, but the town was not laid out until 1882 when a railroad came through the region. The town's name was taken from the title of a book by Henry Ward Beecher. Norwood is home to the Norwood R-1 School District.

O

Oak Grove, Arkansas—Oak Grove is a town of about 375 people in Carroll County. There are a number of other communities in Arkansas that also have the name Oak Grove.

Oak Grove Village, Missouri—Oak Grove Village is a village of about 510 people in southern Franklin County, located along I-44 at the northeast edge of Sullivan.

Oak Ridge, Missouri—Oak Ridge is a village of about 245 people in northern Cape Girardeau County. Organized in 1852, it is home to the Oak Ridge R-6 Schools.

Oaks, Oklahoma—Oaks is a community of about 410 people in southern Delaware County near the Cherokee County border. The Moravian Church established New Springdale Indian Mission near the site shortly after the Cherokee people were removed to Indian Territory in the late 1830s. A post office was established at the future site of Oaks in 1881, and the town was platted in 1906 and given the name Oaks, probably because of the many oak trees nearby. Mission programs similar to the New Springdale Indian Mission have continued to serve Native Americans at Oaks, with a few interruptions, to the current day, and Oaks is presently home to the Oaks Indian Mission, an outreach of the Evangelical Lutheran Church of America. The town is also home to the Oaks-Mission Public Schools.

Oil Trough, Arkansas—Oil Trough is a town of about 220 people in southern Independence County. It is thought to have gotten its name from a trough used to render bear fat during the early nineteenth century. A Civil War skirmish occurred on March 25, 1864, in the Oil Trough Bottoms, the area where the town is located.

Oklahoma Girl Scout Murders—The Oklahoma Girl Scout murders is an unresolved crime that occurred on June 12, 1977, at Camp Scott in rural Mayes County at the western edge of the Ozarks. On the morning of the 13th, the bodies of three girls, aged eight to ten, were found in the woods near their tent, having been raped and murdered. The case was considered solved when jail escapee and convicted rapist Gene Leroy Hart was arrested and tried for the murders, but he was acquitted.

Old Appleton, Missouri—Old Appleton (aka Appleton) is a village of about 85 people on the Cape Girardeau-Perry county line. Originally called Apple Creek after the nearby stream of the same name, the community was settled in 1824.

Oldfield, Missouri—Oldfield is an unincorporated community located on Highway 125 in Christian County. It is the home of the

Oldfield Opry, an informal, weekly country music show that operates on a donation-only basis.

Oldfield, William A.—Born in Izard County, Arkansas, William A. Oldfield practiced law at Batesville and served in the U.S. House of Representatives from 1909 until his death in 1929. He was succeeded by his wife, Pearl Peden Oldfield, who was elected in a special election and served until 1931.

Old Fort Wayne, Battle of—The Battle of Old Fort Wayne was a Civil War action fought on October 22, 1862, between Union forces under Brigadier General James G. Blunt and Confederates under Colonel Douglas Cooper across the Arkansas line from Maysville in present-day Adair County, Oklahoma. The action was a clear Union victory, as Cooper was routed and some of his arms and equipment captured.

Old Mines, Missouri—Old Mines is an unincorporated community in Washington County about six miles north of Potosi. Considered the oldest community in Missouri, the area was first settled as a mining operation by the French during the 1720s. The town got its name in 1836 when original land grants claimed by thirty-one early settlers were granted as the "Old Mines Concession."

Old Sacramento—Old Sacramento or Old Sac was a name given to at least two different artillery pieces captured by U. S. forces at the Battle of Sacramento during the Mexican War. One of them was later used by Missouri State Guard captain Hiram Bledsoe at the Battle of Carthage, where the big gun's effective firing and distinctive sound reportedly stood out.

Old Salt Road—The Old Salt Road was a historic road used in the 1800s for freighting salt and other goods from Norfork, Arkansas, northwest along the White River to Branson, Missouri, and then north to Springfield.

Old Spanish Treasure Cave—The Old Spanish Treasure Cave is a commercial cave located about two miles north of Gravette, Arkansas. According to legend, Spanish conquistadors hid a treasure in the cave hundreds of years ago, and the treasure is still there.

Olean, Missouri—Olean is a village in northern Miller County with a population of about 130 people. It was laid out in 1882 as a railroad town and first called Proctor Station after local landowner James G.

Proctor. However, the post office was known as Cove, and another Proctor already existed. So, the name was changed to Olean.

Oliver, M.E.—M.E. (aka Marvin Elmer) Oliver was a farmer, civil servant, and artist, who, in 1955, produced a book called *Strange Scenes in the Ozarks*. It described backwoods life as Oliver remembered it from his youth but primarily drew notice because of its unusual artistic qualities. A native of Madison County, Arkansas, Oliver later published another book entitled *Old Mills of the Ozarks*, which contained sketches and descriptions of water-powered mills in the Ozarks.

Olyphant Train Robbery—The Olyphant train robbery was a notorious crime that took place at the Olyphant train station in Jackson County, Arkansas, in November of 1893. Eight men held up a train of the St. Louis, Iron Mountain and Southern Railway and killed the conductor. The gang was apprehended, and three of the outlaws were hanged the following spring in the only triple execution in Jackson County history.

Official Starts Process of Placing, Adjusting Nooses

Triple execution of train robbers at Newport, Arkansas, 1894. *Courtesy Jacksonport State Park.*

Omaha, Arkansas—Omaha is a town of about 155 people in northern Boone County on old U.S. Highway 65. A post office was established at the site in 1873. Omaha is home to the Omaha School District.

On a Slow Train Through Arkansaw Written by Thomas W Jackson and published in 1903, *On a Slow Train Through Arkansaw* was a bestselling joke book that perpetuated the idea that not only the trains of Arkansas but also the people themselves were "slow" or backward.

O'Neill, Rose Cecil—Rose O'Neill was a famous illustrator whose Kewpie cartoon character spawned the Kewpie doll in 1912. She lived much of her life at Bonniebrook, a mansion and farm north of Branson, Missouri, which is now preserved as a museum.

A youthful Rose O'Neill. *Courtesy Wikimedia.*

Onondaga Cave—Onondaga Cave is a tourist cave located in Onondaga Cave State Park near Leasburg in Crawford County, Missouri. After its discovery in 1886, the cave was explored for possible mining, but throughout most of its history it has been open for tours. The cave and its surrounding grounds became a state park in 1982. In addition to cave tours, the state park offers outdoor activities like camping, fishing, and picnicking.

Lily Pad Room inside Onondaga Cave. *Courtesy Wikipedia.*

Onyx Cave—Onyx Cave is a commercial cave located about six miles northeast of Eureka Springs. First opened in 1893, it is one of the oldest show caves in Arkansas. It does not contain onyx but instead contains a type of flowstone that resembles onyx.

Opening the Ozarks—Published in 2002, *Opening the Ozarks: A Historical Geography of Missouri's Ste. Genevieve District, 1766-1830* is a study by geographer Walter A. Schroeder of the settlement of the eastern Ozarks by Europeans and Americans. Published in 2005, *Opening the Ozarks: First Families in Southwest Missouri, 1835-1839* is a four-volume genealogical study by sociologist Marsha

Hoffman Rising of the first one thousand families to acquire land through the Springfield Land Office

Opera in the Ozarks—Opera in the Ozarks is a summer training program for aspiring professional singers. It is located at Inspiration Point, a scenic overlook about six miles northwest of Eureka Springs, Arkansas, on Highway 62. It was established in 1950 as a summer music camp for college, high school, and junior high school students, but the program has evolved over the years into a selective workshop for outstanding university students and university graduates from throughout the United States. Four weeks of intense rehearsals during the early part of summer are followed by a month of performances. Many alumni of the program have gone on to professional careers in opera.

Madame Butterfly performance at Opera in the Ozarks. *From www.onlyinark.com.*

Oregon, Missouri—When Kinderhook County, predecessor of Camden County, was established in 1841, Oregon, a small settlement located where Linn Creek emptied into the Osage River, was named the county seat. When the name of the county was changed to Camden in 1843, the name of the county seat was changed to Erie. However, the county seat was subsequently moved a half mile up the creek to a new town called Linn Creek, and Erie soon ceased to exist as a town.

Oregon County, Missouri—Oregon County is located in the south central part of the state, bordering Arkansas. It was founded in 1845 from territory taken from Ripley County, and Thomasville was named the county seat. Later, Alton became the county seat. Oregon County has a population today of about 11,000 people. A large section of the Mark Twain National Forest, including the Irish Wilderness, is located in Oregon County. The county is also home to numerous springs, and the Eleven Point River flows through it. Fishing, camping, canoeing, and hiking are popular outdoor activities in the county.

Oronogo, Missouri—Oronogo is a community in northern Jasper County with a population of about 2,500 people. Originally called Minersville, it was established prior to the Civil War as a mining camp. The name was changed to Oronogo, which was supposedly a contraction of "ore or no-go," several years after the war. After prospering as a mining town for many years, Oronogo fell into decline during the latter part of the twentieth century but has rebounded in recent years as a bedroom community for Joplin, Webb City, and other surrounding towns. It is home to the Harry S Truman Elementary School, part of the Webb City district.

Old bank building at Oronogo once robbed by Bonnie and Clyde. *Photo by the author.*

Oronogo Circle Mine—Covering about twelve acres and about 250 feet deep, the Oronogo Circle Mine near Oronogo, Missouri, was said to be the largest open pit lead and zinc mine in the world at the time mining was suspended at the site about 1950. It later filled in with water and became a popular swimming hole for the daring and then a commercial scuba diving site. Under the supervision of the EPA, the pit (aka Big Blue) was filled with area mine waste starting in the fall of 2012.

Orphan Train Heritage Society of America, Inc.—The Orphan Train Heritage Society of America, Inc. was an organization founded in Springdale, Arkansas, in 1986 to preserve the history of the orphan train era. From 1851 to 1929, approximately 200,000 homeless and orphaned children were shipped west from the eastern United States with the idea of finding homes for them. From 1986 until 2003, the Orphan Train Heritage Society maintained a museum and research center in Springdale, but the organization moved to Concordia, Kansas, in 2003, and it is now called the National Orphan Train Complex, Inc.

Osage Beach, Missouri—Osage Beach is a town of about 4,350 people on the banks of the Lake of the Ozarks. It grew up after the lake was formed by construction of Bagnell Dam. It is known mainly as a resort town, and it is the home of the Osage Beach Premium Outlets mall. It is located primarily in Camden County but spills over into Miller County.

Osage County, Missouri—Located at the northern edge of the Ozarks bordering the Missouri River, Osage County was formed in 1841 from Gasconade County, and Linn was shortly thereafter named the county seat. Using a strict geographic definition of the Ozarks, one might consider all of Osage County to be in the Ozarks, but probably a more popular definition would include only the southern part of the county. Certainly, many residents of Osage County, which was largely settled by German immigrants, do not consider themselves to be part of the Ozarks.

Osage Indians (aka Osage Nation)—Originally from the region of the Ohio River valley, the Osage Indians are a Native American tribe who inhabited the Ozarks beginning in the mid-1600s. At the height of its power in the early 1700s, the Osage Nation controlled almost all the land between the Missouri River and the Red River. Beginning in the early 1800s, the tribe was relocated to Kansas and Oklahoma through a series of treaties with the U.S. government. Today, the tribe is centered in Osage County, Oklahoma, but many members live throughout the country.

Osage Iron Works, Missouri—Osage Iron Works, also known as Iron Town, was a community in northern Camden County just south of the Osage River. It was founded in the 1870s as an iron mining camp, and although the mining operation soon shut down, the town continued to exist until the early 1930s when the land was purchased and the remaining buildings destroyed to make way for the Lake of the Ozarks.

Osage Orange Tree—The Osage orange tree, also called the hedge apple or the bodark, is a tree that typically grows to a height of about thirty feet and produces a round but bumpy, softball-sized fruit that is generally considered inedible. The tree is native to the Red River Valley that separates Texas and Oklahoma, but it was often planted throughout the Ozarks from the late 1800s through the Depression era as a hedge fence or windbreak. The Osage orange tree is a member of the mulberry family.

Osage River—The Osage River is a major tributary of the Missouri River. Forming in southwest Missouri northeast of Nevada near the Vernon-Bates county line with the confluence of the Marais des Cygnes and the Little Osage, the Osage flows generally east for about 275 miles through the northern part of the Ozarks and empties into the Missouri east of Jefferson City.

Osage Trail—See Wire Road.

Osage War—The Osage War was a bloodless campaign by Missouri militia in the winter of 1836-1837 to remove some Osage Indians from southwest Missouri to their allotted lands in Indian Territory.

Osceola, Missouri—Located at the northwest edge of the Ozarks, Osceola is a town of about 950 people and the county seat of St. Clair County. The town was established in the mid to late-1830s and named the county seat shortly after the county was formed in 1841. Osceola is home to the Osceola Public Schools.

Osceola, Sacking of—The Sacking of Osceola, Missouri, on September 22, 1861,was the culmination of a Civil War raid carried out by a group of irregular Union recruits, often called jayhawkers, under Kansas senator James Lane. After driving off a small Southern force under John M. Weidemeyer, Lane virtually destroyed the town and carried off over a million dollars' worth of plunder. Some of William Quantrill's guerrillas claimed that the Lawrence Massacre, which they carried out in August of 1863, was partially in retaliation for the raid on Osceola.

Ottawa County, Oklahoma—Ottawa County was established in 1907 at the time of Oklahoma statehood, and Miami was named the county seat. It is located in the northeast corner of the state.

Otterville, Missouri—Laid out in 1837, Otterville is a town of about 455 people in southwest Cooper County. It is the home of the Otterville R-6 School District, and in 1876 it was the site of a notorious train robbery by the James-Younger gang.

Ousley, Mayme—Elected mayor of St. James, Missouri, in 1921, Mayme Ousley was the first woman mayor in Missouri.

Owensville, Missouri—Owensville is a town of about 2,700 people in central Gasconade County in the northern foothills of the Ozarks. It was laid out at a well-traveled crossroads in 1886 by the Owensville Improvement Company and named for the owner of the company, Francis Owen. It grew after a railroad was built to the town in 1902 and was incorporated in 1911. Owensville is home to the Gasconade R-2 School District.

Oxford, Arkansas—Oxford is a town of about 640 people in northern Izard County. Although it was not incorporated until 1945, a settlement has existed at the site since the mid-1800s. A post office was first established in 1878 and named Crooms Mill. Four years later, the postmaster changed the name to Oxford after his hometown of Oxford, Mississippi. Oxford Schools consolidated with Violet Hill in 1985 and became part of the Izard County Consolidated School District.

Ozark, Arkansas—Ozark, one of two county seats of Franklin County, is a town of about 3,500 people located in the Arkansas River Valley and, therefore, is, ironically, not actually a part of the Ozarks.

Ozark, Missouri—Ozark is a town of about 18,000 people and the seat of Christian County. Settled during the 1830s, it was named the county seat after Christian County was formed in 1859. A historic marker on the public square marks the approximate spot where three members of the notorious Bald Knobbers were hanged in the late 1880s. The town is home to the Ozark R-6 School District.

Ozarka College—Ozarka College is a public institution of higher learning headquartered at Melbourne, Arkansas, with satellite centers at Mountain View, Ash Flat, and Mammoth Spring. It began in 1975 as Ozarka Vocational Technical School, but its name was changed to Ozarka College in 1999 to reflect its expanding range of associate degree programs.

Ozark Airlines—Ozark Airlines was an airlines that was founded in Springfield, Missouri, in 1945 and operated with its headquarters in St. Louis from 1950 until its merger with TWA in 1986.

Ozark Cavefish—The Ozark cavefish is a small, subterranean freshwater fish native to the Ozarks. Found only in caves, it has no pigmentation and receives nutrients from tree roots above the cave without photosynthesis or chemosynthesis. The Ozark cavefish is listed as an endangered species by the Missouri Department of Conservation.

Ozark Caverns—Ozark Caverns is a tour cave located at Lake of the Ozarks State Park.

Ozark County, Missouri—Ozark County was formed from Taney County in 1841. The name was changed to Decatur in 1843 and changed back to Ozark in 1845. The original boundaries of Ozark County included much of present-day Douglas and Howell counties. Gainesville replaced Rockbridge as the county seat shortly after the county was reduced in size in 1857 by the formation of Douglas and Howell.

Ozark Creative Writers—The Ozark Creative Writers, Inc. is a writers' organization that has been meeting each October in Eureka Springs, Arkansas, since the mid-1970s.

Ozark Empire Fair—The Ozark Empire Fair is an annual fair at Springfield, Missouri, usually held in early August. It began in Springfield in the early 1900s as an annual display of areas crafts and handwork, but it had no permanent home. The fair was moved to its current location on the north side of the city in the mid-1930s and became known as the Ozark Empire District Free Fair. It has since grown into the second-largest fair in Missouri, offering cattle and produce exhibits, carnival rides, sideshows, and grandstand entertainment, in addition to arts and crafts displays, but, of course, it is no longer free.

Entrance to Ozark Empire Fairgrounds. *Photo by the author.*

Ozark Folk Center State Park—The Ozark Folk Center State Park is a living history state park located in Mountain View, Arkansas, dedicated to preserving the traditional music, crafts, and folkways of the Ozarks. The state park, which opened in 1973, grew out of the success of the Arkansas Folk Festival, which had begun in 1963 under the sponsorship of the Ozark Foothills Handcraft Guild and the Rackensack Folklore Society.

Ozark Folklore Society—The Ozark Folklore Society was started in 1949 by University of Arkansas artist-in-residence John Gould Fletcher, noted folklorist Vance Randolph, and others to collect material related to the culture of the Ozarks and archive it at the university. The name of the organization was changed to the Arkansas Folklore Society in 1951. After a long period of inactivity, the society was revived and reorganized in 1978, but its work has since been taken over by the Center for Arkansas and Regional Studies, a program of the university.

Ozark Folkways—Ozarks Folkways is a heritage center just south of Winslow, Arkansas, dedicated to preserving the arts, crafts, and music of the Ozarks. It was established as the Ozark Native Craft

Association in 1969, and its name was changed to Ozarks Folkways in 1994 to reflect an increased emphasis on educating people in the traditional arts, crafts, and heritage of the region rather than simply providing a place for craftsmen and artisans to display and sell their products.

Ozark Golden Wedding Jubilee—Hosted by the Rogers, Arkansas, Chamber of Commerce, the Ozark Golden Wedding Jubilee was a commemoration on June 23, 1949, and June 16, 1950, of couples who had been married fifty years. Couples from across the country were invited to participate, and an average of nearly a hundred couples reaffirmed their vows each of the two years.

Ozark Hellbender—The Ozark hellbender, at nearly two feet long, is one of the largest salamanders in the world. Found only in the streams of the Arkansas and Missouri Ozarks, the Ozark hellbender has been on the decline in recent years and is currently the target of a concerted conservation effort.

Ozark Heritage Arts Center & Museum—Dedicated to preserving Ozarks culture and history, the Ozark Heritage Arts Center and Museum consists of a performing arts theater, an art gallery, and a museum at Leslie, Arkansas. Housed in a former school gymnasium built during the Depression by the WPA, the center opened in 1990. The theater, occupying the main part of the old gym, hosts regular bluegrass musical performances and an annual fiddle contest.

Ozark Highlands National Recreational Trail—The Ozark Highlands National Recreational Trail is a 165-mile hiking and backpacking trail across northern Arkansas, running from Crawford County to Searcy County through the Ozark National Forest, which regulates its use.

Ozark Institute—see Far West Seminary

Ozark Jubilee—The *Ozark Jubilee*, later renamed *Country Music Jubilee* and then *Jubilee USA*, was a country music show broadcast nationally on ABC television from 1954 until 1960. It originated in Springfield, Missouri, and for a while enabled Springfield to challenge Nashville as America's country music capital. Hosted by Red Foley, the show featured big-name stars like Patsy Cline and introduced new singers like Brenda Lee. This show is not to be confused with the Ozark Mountain Jubilee, a current Branson show.

Carl Perkins performs on the Ozark Jubilee. *Courtesy Wikipedia.*

Ozark Land and Lumber Company—See lumber industry.

Ozark Mountain Daredevils—The Ozark Mountain Daredevils is a country/rock band that formed in Springfield, Missouri, in 1972 and became popular shortly afterwards with hits like "Jackie Blue."

Ozark Mountains—The Ozark Mountains, also known as the Ozark Plateau or Ozark Plateaus and often called merely the "Ozarks," is a highland region of the central United States that is characterized by uplifted, level plateaus composed of Paleozoic rocks. Millions of years older than either the Appalachians or Rockies, the Ozarks are one of the oldest mountainous areas in North America. Three distinct plateaus make up the Ozarks. The Boston Plateau (aka Boston Mountains), the southernmost and highest of the plateaus, is a relatively narrow band stretching across north central and northwest Arkansas and extending into eastern Oklahoma. The Springfield Plateau, to the north of the Boston Plateau, covers a strip of northern Arkansas, parts of southwest Missouri and northeast Oklahoma, and a small corner of southeastern Kansas. It is the least hilly and most populous of the three sub-regions. The Salem Plateau to the north and east of the Springfield Plateau is the largest in area of the three plateaus, covering much of southern Missouri. The St. Francois Mountains, located within the Salem Plateau, form the geological core of the Ozarks and are often considered a separate area. The word "Ozarks" is believed to be the corruption of the French abbreviation "aux Arcs," short for "aux Arkansas" (i.e. at or of Arkansas), which referred to the Arkansas Post, a trading post near the confluence of the Arkansas and Mississippi rivers in the years before the French and Indian War. "Arkansas" seems to have been the French version of what the Illinois tribe, farther up the Mississippi, called the Quapaw Indians, who lived in the vicinity of Arkansas Post.

Ozark National Forest—The Ozark National Forest is a U.S. national forest covering about 1,200,000 acres in northern Arkansas. Created in 1908, the forest contains several wilderness areas, wildlife management areas, and hiking trails, and it features natural wonders like Falling Water Falls and Twin Falls (aka Richland Creek Falls).

Ozark National Scenic Riverways—Ozark National Scenic Riverways is a national park created in 1964 to protect the Current and Jacks Fork rivers in southern Missouri. Encompassing about 80,000 acres, the park offers recreation like canoeing and horseback riding and is home to a large amount of wildlife.

Ozark Natural Science Center—Located at Huntsville, Arkansas, the Ozark Natural Science Center is an organization founded as a non-profit in 1993 to promote an understanding and appreciation of the natural environment of the Ozarks through educational programs for students and adults.

Ozark Plateau National Wildlife Refuge—Originally known as the Oklahoma Bat Caves National Wildlife Refuge, the Ozark Plateau National Wildlife Refuge was established in 1986 to protect several species of endangered bats. It consists of several parcels of land in northeast Oklahoma that contain numerous caves.

Ozark Playgrounds Association—The Ozark Playgrounds Association was a group formed in 1919 to boost tourism in the Ozarks region. Headquartered in Joplin, Missouri, it was an influential organization for many years but disbanded in 1979.

Ozark Society—The Ozark Society is an environmental organization originally founded in the 1960s by Bentonville physician and conservationist Neil Ernest Compton to save the Buffalo River from damming. Based in northwest Arkansas, the group now has chapters in Louisiana, Missouri, and Oklahoma, as well as Arkansas.

Ozark Trail—The Ozark Trail is a hiking, backpacking, and, in some places, biking and equestrian trail that is under construction from St. Louis to Arkansas. Almost 400 miles of the trail have been completed, over 200 miles of which form a through trail. When the trail is finished, it will be over 500 miles long and will link up with the Ozark Highlands Trail in Arkansas to form about 700 miles of through trail. The Ozark Trail had its beginnings with organizational meetings in the late 1970s, and construction on the trail began in 1981. Environmental groups, governmental agencies, and one private landowner banded together to form the Ozark Trail Council to oversee construction and maintenance of the trail. The Ozark Trail Association, founded in 2002, is a volunteer group that provides resources to help build and maintain the trail.

Ozark Trails Association—Not to be confused with the present Ozark Trail Association, the Ozark Trails Association was a group organized in 1913 by Monte Ne resort developer Coin Harvey to maintain and promote the use of a system of roads known as the Ozark Trail. Traversing Missouri and Oklahoma and passing into Texas and New Mexico, the trail approximated Route 66, which was built later.

Ozark Water Mill Trail—The Ozark Water Mill Trail is a popular driving tour of historic water mills in south-central Missouri. Included among the mills are Dawt Mill, Greer Mill, Hammond Mill, Hodgson Mill, Rockbridge Mill, Topaz Mill, and Zanoni Mill.

Ozarks at Large—*Ozarks at Large* is a daily radio program on KUAF 91.3 FM in Fayetteville, Arkansas, that focuses on the people, places, and events of the Ozarks and Arkansas River Valley.

Ozarks Heritage Foundation—Ozarks Heritage Foundation is an organization based in Branson, Missouri, and dedicated to teaching, learning, and keeping alive the culture, customs, and history of the Ozarks. The group offers educational classes as a vendor of Road's Scholar, Inc. (formerly known as Elderhostel).

Ozarks Mountaineer—*The Ozarks Mountaineer* was a magazine published in the Branson, Missouri, area from 1952 until 2012. Founded by Roscoe Stewart, it emphasized the history, folklore, and culture of the Ozarks region. Other editors and/or publishers associated with the publication over the years included Clay Anderson, Barbara Wehrman, and Fred Pfister.

Ozarks Reader—*The Ozarks Reader* was a magazine published in Neosho, Missouri, from 2004 to 2012 dealing with the history and culture of the Ozarks. Its editor/publisher was Rex Jackson.

Ozarks Regional Commission—Created during the 1960s as one of President Lyndon Johnson's "Great Society" initiatives and terminated during the Reagan administration, the Ozarks Regional Commission was an economic development agency of the federal government designed to help modernize the supposedly backward and deprived Ozarks.

Ozarks Studies Institute—The Ozarks Studies Institute is a program of Missouri State University in Springfield that seeks to preserve the heritage of the Ozarks by fostering knowledge and encouraging research about the region.

Ozarks Technical Community College—Ozarks Technical Community College is a community college headquartered in Springfield, Missouri, with several branch campuses throughout the Ozarks. Founded in 1990, it offers training programs and associate degrees in technical and general education subjects.

OzarksWatch—Founded in 1987, *OzarksWatch* is a magazine put out by the Ozarks Studies Institute of Missouri State University at Springfield. There is also an *OzarksWatch Video Magazine*, hosted by Jim Baker and Dale Moore, that is a production of Ozarks Public Television. Both the print magazine and the TV program seek to preserve the heritage of the Ozarks region.

Ozarks Writers League—Founded in 1983, the Ozarks Writers League is a writers' group that meets quarterly at the Table Rock campus of Ozarks Technical College in Hollister, Missouri, after many years of meeting at the nearby College of the Ozarks.

P

Pacific, Missouri—Pacific is a town of about 7,000 people at the northeast edge of the Ozarks. It is located primarily in Franklin County but straddles the St. Louis County line. The town was laid out in 1852 as Franklin, but, when it was incorporated in 1859, the name was changed to Pacific in honor of the Pacific Railroad that was then being laid across Missouri. Pacific is home to the Meramec Valley R-3 Schools.

Pacific Railroad, Southwest Branch—The Southwest Branch of the Pacific Railroad was completed from Franklin (now Pacific) to Rolla in 1861. Progress was interrupted by the Civil War and financial difficulties, and the road was not completed to Springfield and surrounding points until several years later after the railroad had changed hands and been renamed.

Palmer, John William—John William Palmer was a U.S. congressman from 1929 to 1931. He was born near Macks Creek, Missouri, and practiced medicine and law at Climax Springs before entering politics.

Pangburn, Arkansas—Pangburn is a town of about 600 people at the southern edge of the Ozarks in northern White County. It was established prior to the Civil War as Judson and renamed in 1880 in honor of a local doctor, William David Pangburn. The town incorporated in 1911, shortly after a railroad reached the site. Pangburn is home to the Pangburn School District.

Paris, Twila—Twila Paris is a famous contemporary Christian singer and songwriter who lives in Fayetteville, Arkansas.

Park Hill, Oklahoma—Park Hill is a town of about 3,900 in southwestern Cherokee County. It was established as a headquarters for the Cherokee Indians and the home of Cherokee chief John Ross after the tribe was removed from the East to present-day Oklahoma during the 1830s. It is home to the Keys Public Schools.

Park Hills, Missouri—Park Hills is a town of about 8,760 people in central St. Francois County. It was formed in 1994 by the unprecedented merger of four distinct towns: Flat River, Elvins, Esther, and Rivermines. The new town's name was selected from entries submitted by area residents. Another community, Fairview Acres, had previously merged with Flat River in 1983. All of these communities had started in the late 1800s or early 1900s as lead mining communities. Ferlin Husky, a country singer popular during the 1950s and 1960s, was born at nearby Cantwell. Darrell Cole, Medal of Honor winner during World War II and namesake of the USS Cole, was born at Flat River and went to high school at Esther. Major League Baseball players Bill and Tom Upton were born at Esther. Park Hills is home to the Mineral Area College, formerly Flat River Junior College. It's also home to the Central R-3 School District.

Parler, Mary Celestia—Mary Celestia Parler was a professor of English and folklore at the University of Arkansas during the mid-twentieth century and the wife of noted folklorist Vance Randolph. She was responsible for implementing the most extensive folklore research project in Arkansas history, collecting thousands of stories and songs with the help of her students and assistants.

Patterson, Missouri—Patterson is an unincorporated community in western Wayne County. It was established in 1854 when a man named Isbell opened a store there. It was later named Patterson after G.R. Patterson, a dealer in farm implements. Patterson was the site of a Civil War skirmish during Confederate general John S. Marmaduke's second invasion of Missouri. See Stony Battery Skirmish.

Patterson, Roscoe—Roscoe Patterson was an attorney and politician from Springfield, Missouri. He served in the U.S. House of Representatives from 1921 to 1923 and in the U.S. Senate from 1929 to 1935.

Patton, Missouri—Patton is an unincorporated community in northern Bollinger County. It was established in 1874 and named for the Patton family, who lived in the area. Patton is home to the Meadow Heights R-2 Schools.

Pea Ridge, Arkansas—Pea Ridge is a town of about 5,000 people in northern Benton County. A post office was established at the site in 1850. Robert Carroll Foster laid out the town, and Robert H. Wallace was the first postmaster. The town's name, spelled as one word at first, came from the wild peas that grew on nearby ridges. Part of the Bentonville-Rogers metropolitan area, Pea Ridge has grown rapidly in recent years. The Pea Ridge Mule Jump, a unique competition that involves mules jumping barricades from a standstill position, is held each year at Pea Ridge. The town is home to the Pea Ridge School District.

Pea Ridge, Battle of—Also called the Battle of Elkhorn Tavern, the Battle of Pea Ridge was a Civil War battle fought on March 7 and 8, 1862, a few miles east of Pea Ridge, Arkansas. The Union forces of Major General Samuel R. Curtis, numbering slightly over 10,000 men, faced the Confederate forces of Major General Earl Van Dorn, numbering about 16,000. The result was a Union victory, with the Federals suffering about 1,400 casualties compared to the Confederate casualties of about 2,000. The outcome secured Missouri for the Union and opened up Arkansas for Union occupation.

Pea Ridge Academy—The Pea Ridge Academy, later known as the Mount Vernon Normal College (or Pea Ridge Normal College) and still later as the Mount Vernon Masonic College, was an institution of higher learning that operated in Pea Ridge, Arkansas, from 1874 to 1916

Elkhorn Tavern at Pea Ridge National Military Park. *Photo by the author.*

Pea Ridge National Military Park—Pea Ridge National Military Park is a 4,300-acre park that preserves the battlefield of the 1862 Battle of Pea Ridge. It was created by an act of Congress in 1956 and dedicated as a national park in 1963. Located about five miles east of the town of Pea Ridge, it is one of the best preserved Civil War battlefields in the nation.

Pearce, Nicholas Bartlett—Nicholas Bartlett Pearce, commonly known as N. Bart Pearce, was a brigadier general of Arkansas State troops during the early months of the Civil War. A resident of Benton County, he led his brigade at the Battle of Wilson's Creek in August of 1861. He spent most of the rest of the war as a major in the commissary department of the Confederate army.

Peel, Arkansas—Peel is an unincorporated community on Bull Shoals Lake in northern Marion County near the Missouri state line. It was originally called Needmore, but the name was changed when storekeeper Sam Peel opened a post office in the late 1860s and named it after himself. Peel is the site of the Peel Ferry, operated by the Arkansas Highway and Transportation Department, which ferries automobiles and passengers back and forth across the lake between Peel and Protem, Missouri.

Peel, Samuel W.—Samuel West Peel had a varied career as a county

Peel Mansion Museum in Bentonville, Ark. *Photo by the author*

clerk, a Confederate officer during the Civil War, a businessman, an attorney, a politician, an Indian agent, and a banker. He is perhaps best remembered as the first person born in Arkansas to be elected to the U.S. Congress. He served from 1883 until 1893. His fourteen-room mansion, built at the edge of Bentonville in 1875, is now a museum in Bentonville, and Peel is buried in the Bentonville Cemetery.

Peggs, Oklahoma—Peggs is an unincorporated community of about 100 people in northern Cherokee County. A post office was established at the site in 1899 and named for Thomas Pegg, a Cherokee chief during the Civil War. A deadly tornado hit Peggs on May 2, 1920, killing 71 people. Peggs is the site of the Peggs Public School, an elementary-only school.

Pensacola, Oklahoma—Pensacola is a town of about 125 people in Mayes County at the western edge of the Ozarks. It started in 1840 as a trading post at the Cabin Creek crossing along the Texas Road. Two battles were fought here during the Civil War, and the place was destroyed during the war. A store and post office were re-established in 1896, and the town was platted in 1912. The nearby Pensacola Dam (aka Grand Lake Dam) was built between 1938 and 1940 to create Grand Lake o' the Cherokees.

Pentecostal Church of God—The Pentecostal Church of God is a Pentecostal denomination that started in Chicago in 1919 and has had its national headquarters in Joplin, Missouri, since 1951.

Peoria, Oklahoma—Peoria is a town of about 140 people in northeast Ottawa County near the Missouri border. It began in 1891 as a lead mining camp and was named in honor of the Peoria Indian tribe.

Perry County, Missouri—Formed in 1820 from territory taken from Ste. Genevieve County, Perry County is located in southeast Missouri along the Mississippi River. Although geographers often extend the eastern boundary of the Ozarks to the Mississippi River or beyond, the people of Perry County tend not to think of themselves as residing in the Ozarks, and most people living in the heartland of the Missouri Ozarks, around Springfield, for instance, do not generally think of the Mississippi River counties as being part of the Ozarks. So, Perry County is mentioned here primarily to note the limited coverage in this encyclopedia of people, places, and events associated with the county.

Perryville, Missouri—Perryville is a town of about 8,225 people and the seat of Perry County. Laid out in 1821, it was named the county seat about the same time. The town is home to the historic St. Mary's of the Barrens Catholic Church, which once included a seminary, and to several historic homes, such as the Doerr-Brown House and the Shelby-Nicholson-Schindler House. It is also home to the Perryville School District No. 32 and to two private, parochial schools.

Pettigrew, Arkansas—A former timber boom town, Pettigrew is a small community in southern Madison County.

Pettit, Oklahoma—Pettit is a community of about 770 people in southern Cherokee County.

Pfister, Fred—Fred Pfister is a retired English professor from College of the Ozarks, a former editor of *The Ozarks Mountaineer*, and author of *Insiders' Guide to Branson and the Ozark Mountains*.

Phelps, Missouri—Phelps is an unincorporated community in Lawrence County, located on State Highway 96 (old U.S. Route 66). It was established about 1880 and was a fairly prosperous little town during the heyday of Route 66.

Phelps, John S.—John S. Phelps was a lawyer, politician, and military officer from Springfield, Missouri. He served eighteen years as a U.S. congressman prior to and during the Civil War. At the beginning of the war, while still a congressman, he raised a regiment for the Union, was commissioned a colonel, and led the regiment at the Battle of Pea Ridge. After the war, he served as governor of Missouri from 1877 to 1881.

Phelps County, Missouri—Located in central Missouri, Phelps County was formed in 1857 from parts of Crawford, Maries, and Pulaski counties. It was named after John S. Phelps, a U.S. congressman at the time, and Rolla was named the county seat in 1858.

Phillipsburg, Missouri—Phillipsburg is a village in southwest Laclede County along Interstate 44. It was named after Rufus Phillips, who came to the area before the Civil War and established a store. It got a railroad in 1869 and a post office in 1876. The town had a high school in the early 1900s but consolidated with Conway in the mid twentieth century.

Picher, Oklahoma—Picher is a virtual ghost town in Ottawa County at the edge of the Ozarks. It was a booming lead mining town during the early 1900s, but it declined during the latter half of the century after mining operations ceased. A study in 1996, showing lead poisoning in many of the children in Picher, prompted a federal buyout of the town, and residents began leaving in droves. Another study in 2006, showing the town was dangerously undermined and subject to collapse, accelerated the exodus, and an EF-4 tornado in 2008 destroyed much of what was left of the town. Picher's population fell from 1,640 in 2000 to just 20 people in 2010.

Piedmont, Missouri—Piedmont is a town of about 1,975 people in western Wayne County. A settlement called Danielsville was established at the site prior to the Civil War. In 1871, when the Iron Mountain Railroad reached the area, a town was laid out and called Piedmont (a combination of the French words for foot and mountain) because of its location near the base of Clark Mountain. Piedmont is home of the Clearwater R-1 Schools.

Pierce City, Missouri—Pierce City is a town of about 1,300 people in the southwest corner of Lawrence County. It was laid out in 1870 as a station along the new Atlantic and Pacific Railroad. The town was named after the railroad president, Andrew Peirce or Perice, and was usually spelled Peirce City in early days but has been known as Pierce City since the 1930s. From 1879 to 1905, Pierce City was home to the Pierce City Baptist College, which later became part of Southwest Baptist at Bolivar. Harold Bell Wright was briefly pastor of the Pierce City First Christian Church during the 1890s, and the old church building is now the town's museum. The most notorious event in the history of Pierce City is the 1901 lynching of three black men by a mob outraged by the murder of a young white woman. Pierce City was the hometown of noted ragtime composer Theron Bennett and the longtime residence of artist Grace Tinker. On May 4, 2003, an EF3 tornado, part of a large outbreak of tornadoes in the Ozarks on that date, destroyed most of Pierce City's business district. Pierce City is home to the Pierce City R-6 Schools.

Pike, Albert—An Arkansas lawyer at the start of the Civil War, Albert Pike was appointed a Confederate envoy to Native Americans in Indian Territory and negotiated several treaties with the tribes. Appointed a brigadier general, he helped organize and train three regiments of Indians for the Southern army. He led them at the Battle of Pea Ridge in March 1862 but received intense criticism for their alleged misconduct and shortly afterwards resigned his commission.

Pilot Grove, Missouri—Laid out in 1873, Pilot Grove is a town of about 770 people in western Cooper County. It is home to the Pilot Grove C-4 School District.

Pilot Knob, Missouri—Pilot Knob is a town of about 750 people in Iron County, located about two and a half miles north of the county seat of Ironton. The town is named after a nearby mound or hill. Pilot Knob is notable as the site of the Battle of Pilot Knob during the Civil War, and today it is home to the Fort Davidson State Historic site, which commemorates the battle.

Pilot Knob, Battle of—The Battle of Pilot Knob (aka the Battle of Fort Davidson) was the first important engagement of Confederate general Sterling Price's invasion of Missouri in the fall of 1864 during the American Civil War. Although outnumbered about eight to one, the Federal troops, entrenched in their fortifications, were able to repulse Price's army of about 12,000 men on September 27 and then slip off in the middle of the night. The Confederates took possession of the fort the next day, but the delay caused Price to abandon his goal of marching on St. Louis and contributed to the invasion's ultimate failure.

Pindall, Arkansas—Pindall is a town of about 110 people in northwest Searcy County on U.S. Highway 65. It was named for Xenophon Overton Pindall, governor of Arkansas from 1907-1909.

Piney Creek Wilderness—Designated in 1980, the Piney Creek Wilderness is an 8,178-acre area of the Mark Twain National Forest in eastern Barry County, Missouri.

Pineville, Arkansas—Pineville is a town of about 245 people in northwest Izard County. It was formed about the time of the Civil War and got its first post office in 1867. Although never a large community, it was incorporated in 1973 and today has several small businesses.

Pineville, Missouri—Pineville is a town of about 790 people and the seat of McDonald County. It was platted in the 1840s and, according to some sources, was at first called Maryville. However, the name Pineville was soon adopted, either because of a nearby pine grove or in honor of a town in Kentucky by the same name. Pineville was the site of the notorious 1883 murder of Dr. Albert Chenoweth, which ultimately led to the lynching of Garland Mann, who was suspected of the crime. In 1938, the movie *Jesse James* was filmed in Pineville, and the town still holds an annual Jesse James Days festival each year. Pineville is home to the Pineville Elementary School (K-8), which is part of the McDonald County School System.

Pioneer Forest—See Leo Drey

Pitman Ferry—See Current View, Missouri.

Pitt, Brad—Brad Pitt is a famous movie actor who grew up in Springfield, Missouri, and graduated from Kickapoo High School there in 1982.

Actor and Springfield native Brad Pitt. *Courtesy Wikimedia.*

Pittsburg, Missouri—Pittsburg is an unincorporated community in southeastern Hickory County. It was settled prior to the Civil War and named for the Pitts family, who lived in the area.

Plaster, Robert W.—Robert W. Plaster was a well-known businessman and philanthropist in the Ozarks. Born in Neosho, Missouri, he attended Joplin Junior College. He started Empire Gas in 1963 and grew it into one of the largest LP gas distributors in the U.S. He created the Robert W. Plaster Foundation to benefit colleges and universities in the region. He died at his home near Lebanon, Missouri, in 2008.

Plato, Missouri—Plato is a town of about 1,400 people in northwest Texas County. Established in 1874, it was named for the Greek philosopher Plato by its founders, who visualized it as an ideal community such as described by Plato in his *Republic*. Based on the 2010 census, Plato was the approximate mean center of U. S. population. Plato is home to the Plato R-5 School District.

Pleasant Hope, Missouri—Pleasant Hope is a town in southeastern Polk County that predates the Civil War. It has often been called Pin Hook over the years, and many locals still refer to it by that name. Explanations for the derivation of the nickname differ. One story says that Pin Hook was an earlier name for Pleasant Hope or the name of an earlier but separate place very near where Pleasant Hope was established. However, other evidence suggests that the community was always officially known as Pleasant Hope and that Pin Hook was never anything more than a nickname. Pleasant Hope is home to the Pleasant Hope R-6 schools and has a population of about 600 people.

Pleasant Plains, Arkansas—Pleasant Plains is a town of about 265 people in southern Independence County. It is home to the Midland School District.

Pocahontas, Arkansas—Located on the Black River, Pocahontas is a town of about 6,800 people and the seat of Randolph County. It was established as the county seat about the time the county was formed in 1835 and was named for Pocahontas, the Native American of Jamestown fame. Pocahontas is home to the Randolph County Heritage Museum, the Eddie Mae Herron Museum (a one-room, African-American schoolhouse on the National Register of Historic Places), the Black River Technical College, and the Pocahontas School District.

Pocahontas, Missouri—Settled in 1856, Pocahontas is a village of about 115 people in northern Cape Girardeau County.

Point Lookout, Missouri—Point Lookout is an unincorporated community in Taney County just south of Branson. It is the home of the College of the Ozarks.

Polk County, Missouri—Located in the southwest part of the state, Polk County was formed in 1835 from territory taken from Greene County. It was named for Tennessee congressman and future president James K. Polk. Polk County was reduced to its present limits during the 1840s.

Pomona, Missouri—Pomona is an unincorporated community in Howell County on Highway 63 midway between West Plains and Willow Springs. It was established in 1895 and named for Pomona, the Roman goddess of fruit, because it was situated in a major apple-growing area.

Pomme de Terre Lake—Pomme de Terre Lake is a man-made reservoir covering about 7,820 acres in Hickory County, Missouri, which was formed by the damming of the Pomme de Terre River. The dam was completed in 1961 by the U.S. Army Corps of Engineers.

Pomme de Terre River—The Pomme de Terre River is a 130-mile tributary of the Osage River that flows through southwest Missouri. It forms in Webster County and flows in a north and northwest direction through Greene, Dallas, Polk, Hickory, and Benton counties. It is dammed in Hickory County to form the Pomme de Terre Lake, and it joins the Osage in Benton County as an arm of Truman Lake.

Ponca Elk Education Center—The Ponca Elk Education Center was established in 2002 to serve visitors coming to Newton County, Arkansas, to view elk. It is housed in a log building in the village of Ponca in western Newton County. It offers displays and information about elk and other wildlife, plus tips and directions for viewing them.

Ponce de Leon, Missouri—Ponce de Leon is an unincorporated community in northeast Stone County. It was established in the early 1880s as a health resort and named for Juan Ponce de Leon, who sought the fountain of youth. The town boomed for a while but had already started to decline by 1885. Today the community, usually called "Poncie" by locals, is little more than a wide place in the road

Ponder's Mill, Skirmish at—The Skirmish at Ponder's Mill was an engagement between a detachment of Confederate soldiers under Jo

Shelby's command and a detachment of Federals at Ponder's Mill (aka Power's Mill) on the Little Black River at the western edge of Butler County, Missouri, on September 20, 1864. It was the opening action of General Sterling Price's noted invasion of Missouri.

Pope County, Arkansas—Formed from Crawford County in 1829 and named for territorial governor John Pope, Pope County is located along the Arkansas River. Only the northern portion is in the Ozarks.

Poplar Bluff, Missouri—Poplar Bluff is a town of about 17,000 people in Butler County at the eastern edge of the Ozarks. It was established and named the county seat shortly after the county was organized in 1849. Situated on the Black River, Poplar Bluff got its name from the tulip trees, often called poplars, which originally covered a bluff where the town was laid out. Sometimes called the Gateway to the Ozarks, Poplar Bluff is home to the Poplar Bluff R-1 School District and to Three Rivers Community College. NBA basketball player Tyler Hansbrough grew up in Poplar Bluff.

Poplar Bluff Tornado—A tornado hit Poplar Bluff, Missouri, on May 9, 1927, leveling much of the downtown and killing 98 people. It is among the top twenty deadliest tornados in U.S. history.

Portia, Arkansas—Incorporated in 1886, Portia is a town of about 440 people located west of Walnut Ridge in northern Lawrence County. It thrived during the late nineteenth century and much of the twentieth but has declined in recent years.

Potosi, Missouri—Potosi is the county seat of Washington County. It was founded by the French during the mid to late 1700s as a lead mining camp and called Mine au Breton. Moses Austin, father of Texas pioneer Stephen F. Austin, arrived in 1798, started large-scale mining operations in the area, and was instrumental in building a new town adjacent to Mine au Breton. The new town was named Potosi after the silver mining town of Potosi, Bolivia, and it eventually engulfed the old town of Mine au Breton. The foundation of Austin's home, Durham Hall, can still be seen. Potosi has a population of about 2,700, and it is the home of the Potosi R-3 School District.

Potosi, Skirmish at—The so-called First Battle of Potosi occurred on August 10, 1861, when a Union home guard unit was attacked by about 120 Rebels under Benjamin Talbot and a Captain White of Fredericktown. The Southerners were repelled with a loss of about five men killed or wounded on each side. Another "Battle of Potosi" took place on September 27, 1864, when Confederates under General Jo Shelby overran the town during Price's invasion of Missouri.

Pottersville, Missouri—Pottersville is an unincorporated community in eastern Howell County. The place was settled before the Civil War by Josiah Carrico and Joel M. Potter and was named after Mr. Potter when a post office was established shortly after the war.

Potts Hill, Action at—The Action at Potts Hill, also known as the Skirmish at Big Sugar Creek, was a running fight between cavalry detachments of General Samuel R. Curtis's Union army and General Sterling Price's Confederate-allied army that occurred on February 16, 1862, north of Pea Ridge, Arkansas, just south of the Missouri border. A Union victory, the skirmish was the first clash between Union and Confederate armies in Arkansas during the Civil War. It was a precursor to the Battle of Pea Ridge fought three weeks later.

Poultry Industry—Early Ozarks farmers often kept a few chickens or turkeys for their own use, but the poultry industry did not emerge until the 1890s when Millard Berry of Springdale, Arkansas, started raising chickens on a large scale and helped form the Arkansas Poultry Breeders. A century later, Tyson Foods, based in Springdale, had become one of the largest agribusinesses in the U.S., and today Tyson and other large poultry firms play an important economic role in northwest Arkansas and southwest Missouri.

Powder Mill Ferry—Powder Mill Ferry was a historic ferry that operated on the Current River east of Eminence, Missouri, from the early 1920s until about 1970, when a bridge across the river was built. The site is now part of the Ozark National Scenic Riverways.

Powell, Dick—Born at Mountain View, Arkansas, Dick Powell was a famous actor and musician from the 1930s to the 1960s.

Powell, Missouri—Powell is an unincorporated community in eastern McDonald County. A post office was established at the site in 1871, and it was a thriving community at one time. During the mid-1900s, it was perhaps best known as the home of gospel composer Alfred E. Brumley. It is home to the historic Powell Bridge, which is on the National Register of Historic Places.

Powhatan, Arkansas—Powhatan is a town of about 70 people in northern Lawrence County. Founded in the early 1800s on the Black River, it was a hub of economic activity prior to the Civil War and had a population of about 500 when it was incorporated in 1853. Although slowed by the war, the town recovered afterwards and was named the Lawrence County seat in 1869. The town's decline began after it was bypassed by the railroad in the early 1800s and Walnut Ridge became a second seat of county government in 1887. The decline continued in the twentieth century when U.S. Highway 63 routed traffic away from the town. In 1963 the county seat was consolidated at Walnut Ridge, and Powhatan would scarcely exist today if it were not for Powhatan Historic State Park, consisting primarily of the old courthouse, at the site.

Prairie Creek, Arkansas—Prairie Creek began in the mid-1800s as a farming community of just a few families in eastern Benton County. When Beaver Lake was completed in the 1960s, Prairie Creek was developed as a planned community on the banks of the lake, and today it has a population of about 2,065.

Prairie Grove, Arkansas—Prairie Grove is a town of about 2,550 people in Washington County about twelve miles southwest of Fayetteville. A post office was established at the site in 1840 and originally called Sweet Home. It was later renamed Ada and still later Prairie Grove, supposedly after the parents of a girl who had passed away requested that she be buried "in the grove of trees on the prairie." Prairie Grove gained notoriety during the Civil War because of the battle fought there in December 1862, but the community was not platted until 1877 and not incorporated until 1888. Prairie Grove is home to the Prairie Grove Schools.

Prairie Grove, Battle of—The Battle of Prairie Grove was a Civil War battle fought near Prairie Grove, Arkansas, on December 7, 1862, between Confederate general Thomas Hindman's First Corps, Trans Mississippi Army and Union general James G. Blunt's Army of the Frontier. Total forces engaged were about 11,000 Confederates and 9,000 Federals, and losses in killed, wounded, or missing were about equal on each side (about 1,200 to 1,300). Although the battle was a tactical stalemate, the result enabled the Federals to hold northwest Arkansas. Thus, it is considered a strategic victory for the Union.

Prairie Grove Battlefield State Park—The Prairie Grove Battlefield State Park is a state park near Prairie Grove, Arkansas, that preserves the history of the Civil War battle fought there in 1862. It offers both walking and driving tours of the battlefield, and it hosts a reenactment of the battle every other year.

Prairie Home, Missouri—Home to the Prairie Home R-5 Schools, Prairie Home is a town of about 280 people in eastern Cooper County.

Praying Hands Statue—The Praying Hands Statue is a 32-foot-tall structure sculpted by artist Jack Dawson during the early 1970s in King Jack Park at Webb City, Missouri. It has become an attraction and a source of inspiration for travelers along old Route 66.

Precious Moments Chapel—Precious Moments Chapel is a chapel opened near Carthage, Missouri, in 1989 by artist Sam Butcher featuring murals painted by Butcher, a gift shop with numerous Precious Moments figurines, and other attractions. Free tours of the chapel are available every day except Easter Sunday, Thanksgiving, Christmas, and New Year's Day.

Precipitation Extremes—The most rain ever recorded during a single day at the Springfield, Missouri, weather station was 6.27 inches on November 24, 1987. The rainiest month ever in Springfield was July 1958 with 18.75 inches. The driest month is shared by January 1986, September 2004, and February 2006, which each recorded only .1 inches of precipitation. Notable periods of drought in the Ozarks occurred during the Dust Bowl years, especially 1934 to 1936, and during the mid-1950s from 1953 to 1956.

Presleys—The Presleys are a family musical group that has been performing in Branson since the 1960s and lays rightful claim to having the first theater on the Branson Strip (aka West Highway 76).

Preston, Missouri—Preston is a community in Hickory County near the junction of U.S. Highway 65 and U.S. Highway 54. Originally known as Black Oak or Black Oak Point, it was established during the 1850s. It was virtually destroyed during the Civil War but was rebuilt and thrived as a small village until approximately the 1950s, when it lost its school through consolidation. It is now, at least metaphorically, a mere wide place in the road. There is also a Preston in Jasper County.

Price, Sterling—Sterling Price was the governor of Missouri from 1853 to 1857. At the outbreak of the Civil War, he was appointed commanding general of the Missouri State Guard, which he led at the Battle of Wilson's Creek in August 1861 and the Battle of Pea Ridge in March of 1862. After Pea Ridge, he joined the Confederate army, and in the fall of 1864, he led an unsuccessful invasion of Missouri.

General Sterling Price. *Courtesy Library of Congress.*

Price's 1864 Raid—General Sterling Price led a Confederate invasion of Missouri in the fall of 1864 that started from Pocahontas, Arkansas, in late September. The first major battle of the campaign happened in the eastern Ozarks on September 27 at Fort Davidson (i.e. Pilot Knob). Repelled at Fort Davidson, the Confederates veered northwest and threatened the state capital at Jefferson City, then continued west and were again defeated at the Battle of Westport on October 23. Retreating down the Missouri-Kansas border, Price's forces fought two more battles, at Mine Creek on October 25 and at Newtonia on October 28, as they made their way back to Arkansas.

Principia Community—Principia was a short-lived utopian community established near Halfway, Missouri, in the early 1880s, by Alcander Longley, who founded several experimental communities throughout Missouri during the late 1800s and early 1900s on the principles of what he called "practical communism."

Proctor, Oklahoma—Proctor is a community of about 230 people on U.S. Highway 62 in western Adair County. It was named after Ezekiel "Zeke" Proctor, the central figure in the so-called Goingsnake Massacre.

Protem, Missouri—Protem is an unincorporated community of about 150 people in southeast Taney County near the Arkansas border. When the post office was established in 1870, the postmaster was told he could use any name he wanted "pro tem" (a Latin term meaning "for the time being") until a permanent one was chosen, and the name stuck.

Provisional Enrolled Missouri Militia—The Provisional Enrolled Missouri Militia was a full-time state militia force created in 1863 by Missouri's Union governor. The force was created because the earlier, part-time Enrolled Missouri Militia was not considered an effective force and the loyalty of many its members was considered dubious. When the PEMM formed, the EMM was disbanded, and its more reliable members were recruited for the new organization. The PEMM was paid by the state but outfitted and supplied by the federal government. Its primary roles were to fight guerrillas within the state and to serve as local garrisons.

Pryor, Mark—Mark Pryor was a U.S. senator from Arkansas from 2003 to 2015. The son of former Arkansas governor and U.S. senator David Pryor, Mark Pryor was born in Fayetteville and graduated from the University of Arkansas there.

Pulaski County, Missouri—The Missouri Territorial Legislature created a county named Pulaski in 1818 at the same time that several of the other very earliest counties were formed. However, this county was never fully organized nor its boundaries completely defined. The current Pulaski County was formed in 1833 out of territory taken from Crawford County and named for Count Pulaski, the Polish patriot who was a general in the Continental Army during the American Revolution. Court was held mostly at private residences during Pulaski County's early years, until Waynesville was laid out and named the permanent county seat in 1843. Pulaski County was reduced to its current size when parts of its territory were taken to form several later counties.

Pulaskifield, Missouri—Pulaskifield is an unincorporated community in northwest Barry County. It was originally called Bricefield, but the name was changed after a group of Polish immigrants settled in the area in the late 1800s.

Purcell, Missouri—Purcell is a town of about 410 people in central Jasper County. It was founded in 1903 and named for Jasper County sheriff James Purcell.

Purdy, Missouri—Purdy is a town of about 1,100 people in northern Barry County. It was laid out along the railroad about 1880, and two movements, one to name the town Winslow after a railroad executive and another to name it Purdy after a real estate agent for the railroad, arose almost simultaneously. The name Purdy eventually won out. Purdy is home to the Purdy R-2 School District.

Pyatt, Arkansas—Pyatt is a town of about 220 people in western Marion County. It was laid out in the early 1900s when a railroad was built to the area and named after a construction engineer who was helping oversee the project, although two previous settlements in the same vicinity, Stringtown and Powell, were precursors to Pyatt. Pyatt was a thriving little town during the early and mid-1900s. In 1973, Pyatt's school district consolidated with Bruno, and a new school was built at Eros, located between the two towns. The Bruno-Pyatt School is now part of the Ozark Mountain School District.

Pyles, Lida Wilson—Lida Wilson Pyles was an author, who, from the 1950s to the 1970s, wrote newspaper columns and magazine articles about the Ozarks. She also wrote several books, including *Tall Tales from the Hills* and *It Happened in the Ozarks*. Born in Barry County, Missouri, she lived much of her life at Carthage. She was a founding member of both the Ozark Writers-Artists Guild and the Ozark Creative Writers and was also noted for her appearance on Johnny Carson's *Tonight Show* during which she played the jawbone of a horse (widely reported as an ass) as a rhythm and percussion instrument.

Q

Quantrill, William C.—William Quantrill was a noted Confederate guerrilla leader during the Civil War, infamous for his sacking of Lawrence, Kansas. Although most of his activity was confined to the Jackson County area of Missouri, he also made several forays through the Ozarks, including a raid through Cedar County, Missouri, and a battle/massacre at Baxter Springs, Kansas, both in 1863. His men fought at the Battle of Prairie Grove in late 1862 and the Battle of Springfield in early 1863, but Quantrill himself was not present.

Guerrilla leader William Quantrill. *Author's collection.*

Quapaw Indians—The Quapaw people are a tribe of Native Americans who, when first encountered by white explorers in 1673, occupied an area near the confluence of the Arkansas and Mississippi rivers in present-day Arkansas. The state is named for the Quapaw tribe, whom Europeans first knew as the Arkansas. In the early 1800s, the Quapaw were forced to cede their Arkansas lands and were removed to a reservation in present-day northeast Oklahoma. Today their tribal headquarters is located at Quapaw, Oklahoma, and tribal members number about 3,240. The tribe owns two casinos, the Quapaw Casino and Downstream Casino.

Quapaw, Oklahoma—Quapaw is a town of about 900 people in northeast Ottawa County near the borders of Kansas and Missouri. It was established in the early 1890s when a Kansas settler and his family started a store and other businesses at the site and Quapaw chief John Quapaw donated land for a school. A new town to the east of the old one was platted in 1917, and the town prospered during the next thirty years or so as lead and zinc mining boomed in the area. Quapaw is home to the Quapaw Public Schools, and the Quapaw Indian tribe.

Quincy, Missouri—Quincy is an unincorporated community in northwest Hickory County. The first settler at the site came in the late 1830s or early 1840s, and the place was called Judy's Gap. The town was platted about 1848 and named Quincy, reportedly after former president John Quincy Adams.

Quinine Brigade—The so-called "Quinine Brigade" was a makeshift military force comprised largely of convalescent soldiers recruited from the local military hospital that helped defend the town of Springfield, Missouri, during the Battle of Springfield in January of 1863.

R

Racial Cleansing—Racial cleansing was a phenomenon that occurred in the Ozarks in the late 1800s and early 1900s during which blacks were driven out of many communities by the white majority. Pierce City, Missouri, where three black men were lynched in 1901, and Harrison, Arkansas, which drove many of its black residents out of town in 1905, were examples of what came to be known as "sundown towns," so called because blacks were told, under threat of lynching, not to let the sun go down on them while they were in those towns. See, for example, Kimberly Harper's *White Man's Heaven: The Lynching and Expulsion of Blacks in the Southern Ozarks*.

Rackensack Folklore Society—The Rackensack Folklore Society is an organization that was founded during the 1960s for the purpose of preserving the traditional folk music of Arkansas, particularly in the mountainous north-central part of the state. The society was centered in Stone County, although a branch later opened in Little Rock.

Rafferty, Milton D.—Milton D. Rafferty is a professor emeritus of geography and geology at Missouri State University. He helped establish the Center for Ozarks Studies in 1976 and is the author of several books about the Ozarks, including *The Ozarks, Land and Life*.

Rains, James S.—James S. Rains was a politician from Sarcoxie, Missouri, who served as a state representative and state senator prior to the Civil War. At the outset of the war, he was appointed a brigadier general commanding the Eighth Division of the Missouri State Guard, which encompassed the southwest part of the state. He served in that capacity during 1861 and 1862 but clashed with Confederate generals and balked at joining their army.

Railroads, coming of—The mid to late nineteenth century was a time of great activity in the building of railroads throughout the Ozarks in order to provide a means of transporting goods and people more efficiently. Begun during the decade before the Civil War, construction was interrupted by the war but resumed afterwards at an even more feverish pace. Many new communities sprang up along the lines of the railroads during the post-Civil War era. The building slowed somewhat during the very late 1800s and ground to a gradual halt during the early 1900s, when highways and motor vehicles began to compete with railroads as a means of transportation.

Rainfall—See precipitation extremes.

Ralph Foster Museum--In the 1960s, broadcasting pioneer Ralph Foster donated his large collection of Native American and Western artifacts to the School of the Ozarks at Point Lookout, Missouri, and the Ralph Foster Museum was established on campus in 1969. Today the museum's focus is the history and culture of the Ozarks.

Rand, Sally—see Helen Gould Beck

Randolph County, Arkansas—Located in the northeast part of the state, Randolph County was established in 1835 from territory taken from Lawrence County, and Pocahontas was named the county seat.

Randolph, Vance—Vance Randolph was a writer and folklorist known for his many books and magazine articles on Ozarks folklore and other topics. In 1949, he co-founded the Ozark Folklore Society. His *Pissing in the Snow and Other Ozark Folktales* (1976) was a national bestseller. Born in Pittsburg, Kansas, he lived much of his adult life in McDonald County, Missouri, and he died in Fayetteville, Arkansas, in 1980.

Vance Randolph, relaxing. Mary C. Parler papers, Special Collections, *University of Arkansas Library.*

Raney, John Henry—John Henry Raney was a lawyer and politician from Wayne County, Missouri. He served in the U. S. House of Representatives from 1895 to 1897.

Ranger Boats—Started in Flippin, Arkansas, in 1968 by Forrest Lee Wood and his wife, Nina, Ranger Boats is the largest maker of bass boats in the United States.

Ravenden, Arkansas—Ravenden is a town of about 500 people in northwest Lawrence County.

Ravenden Springs, Arkansas—Ravenden Springs is a town of about 135 people in western Randolph County.

Rawls, Wilson—See Scraper, Oklahoma

Rayburn, Otto Ernest—Otto Ernest Rayburn was a writer, magazine publisher, promoter of the Ozarks, and collector of Ozarks folklore. He started his first magazine, *Ozark Life: The Mirror of the Ozarks*, in 1925 at Kingston, Arkansas. Perhaps his most successful book,

Ozark Country, came out in 1941, and his autobiography, *Forty Years in the Ozarks*, was published in 1957. He died in Fayetteville in 1960.

Raymondville, Missouri—Raymondville is a village of about 365 people in eastern Texas County. A post office was established at Raymondville in 1876. The community is home to the Raymondville Public School District, a K-8 district. High school students in the area attend Houston Public Schools.

Razorbacks—Razorbacks are wild or feral pigs that inhabit the Ozarks and elsewhere, and the razorback is the mascot of the University of Arkansas athletic teams.

Read, Lessie Stringfellow—Lessie Stringfellow Read was a longtime editor of the Fayetteville Democrat during the early twentieth century, a writer for national periodicals, and a champion of women's rights.

Rebel's Bluff, Legend of—Rebel's Bluff is a high bluff overlooking

Rebel's Bluff west of Mt. Vernon, Mo. *Photo by the author.*

Highway V about three miles west of Mt. Vernon, Missouri. Legend holds that during the Civil War a small body of troops, being chased by a detachment of the enemy, plunged over the bluff to their deaths because they were not familiar with the territory.

Red Oak II—Inspired by artist Lowell Davis's memories of growing up in the now-defunct Missouri community of Red Oak, Red Oak II is the re-creation of an early nineteenth century rural village located about two miles northeast of Carthage. Davis is known for his figurines and oil paintings depicting rural scenes.

Artist Lowell Davis outside his Red Oak II home, ca. 1995. *Photo by the author.*

Reeds, Missouri—Reeds is a town in eastern Jasper County. It began in 1896 as a station on the railroad and was named for W.T. Reed, who owned the land where the station was built.

Reeds Spring, Missouri—Reeds Spring is a town of about 915 people in central Stone County. The area became known as "Reed's Spring" during the post-Civil War era because a nearby spring was used by the Reed brothers, cattlemen from Texas, as a stopover point for their herds as they drove them to markets in central Missouri. In the early 1880s, the community of Stultz (aka Stutts), now known as Reed's Spring Junction, was established a couple of miles northeast of the spring. When a railroad came through the area southwest of Stultz near the spring in the early 1900s, some of the residents of Stultz moved to be nearer the railroad, and the community of Reeds Spring grew up around the railroad. Reeds Spring is home to the Reeds Spring R-4 Schools.

Reeves, Timothy—Timothy Reeves was a Baptist minister from Ripley County, Missouri, and a Confederate officer during the Civil War, commanding the Fifteenth Missouri Cavalry. (See Christmas Day Massacre for additional information.)

Regulators—The Regulators was a vigilante group that formed in Greene County, Missouri, in 1866 to combat a perceived outbreak of lawlessness in the area around Walnut Grove. After shooting one accused lawbreaker to death, hanging three others, and briefly occupying Springfield in the process, the Regulators disbanded as quickly as they had formed, because, some said, the group had done its job so well that its services were no longer needed. There was also a vigilante group called the Regulators formed in the vicinity of St. Charles, Missouri, during Missouri's territorial days to combat an outbreak of counterfeiting.

Reno, Missouri—Located in southwest Christian County, Reno was one of many towns that sprang up in the Ozarks almost overnight during the medicinal water craze of the 1880s. The place boomed briefly, but today nothing remains even to suggest its whereabouts other than nearby Reno Spring, after which the town took its name.

Republic, Missouri—Republic is a town of about 14,750 people in southwest Greene County at the Christian County line. It was platted in 1879, and the town began prospering not long afterwards when a depot was built at the site along the line of the Frisco Railroad.

Republic hosts a fall festival and a Pumpkin Daze celebration each year, and it is home to the Republic R-3 Schools. Harry Young killed a night watchman at Republic a few years prior to the Young brothers' infamous 1932 shootout with law officers at nearby Brookline.

Reunion Community—The Reunion Community was one of several utopian communities started by Alcander Longley in the Ozarks during the late nineteenth century based on what he called "practical communism." Located in Jasper County near present-day Oronogo, it was founded in 1868 and disbanded three years later.

Reyno, Arkansas—Reyno is a town of about 460 people at the edge of the Ozarks in eastern Randolph County. The town was named after William Reyno, an early settler in the area. Public school students formerly attended the Biggers-Reyno District, but Biggers-Reyno consolidated with Corning about 2006.

Reynolds County, Missouri—Located in southeast Missouri, Reynolds County was formed in 1845 from Shannon County. The first county seat was Lesterville, but it was changed to Centerville, the current county seat, after the courthouse at Lesterville was burned during the Civil War.

Rice, Theron Moses—Theron Moses Rice was lawyer and politician from Moniteau County, Missouri, who served in the U.S. House of Representatives from 1881 to 1883.

Richards, Dusty—Dusty Richards is a nationally known writer of western fiction from Springdale, Arkansas. Active in several regional writers' groups, he is also known as a mentor of other writers.

Richardson, John M.—A citizen of Springfield, John M. Richardson served as the Missouri secretary of state prior to the Civil War, and during the war he was a colonel in the Missouri State Militia Cavalry.

Richardson, Nolan—Nolan Richardson was a longtime head coach of men's basketball at the University of Arkansas, and he led the team to the national championship in 1994.

Richland, Missouri—Richland is a town of about 1,865 people located mainly in western Pulaski County but straddling the county lines of Camden and Laclede. It was laid out in 1869 along the line of the Atlantic and Pacific Railroad and named for G. W. Rich, an official of the railroad. Richland is home to the Richland R-4 Schools.

Richland Creek, Skirmish at—The Skirmish at Richland Creek was a Civil War action that occurred on May 3, 1864, in the Richland

Creek area of Searcy County, Arkansas, involving a Federal foraging detail under Lieutenant Andrew J. Garner and Confederate recruits under Colonel Sidney D. Jackman. Between thirty-six and forty-two Federals were killed in the action with no Confederate casualties. Two days later a Federal force under Colonel John E. Phelps came back to the same area and scattered the Confederates in another skirmish that resulted in few casualties on either side.

Richmond, Ted—Ted Richmond was the founder of the Wilderness Library at Mount Sherman in Newton County, Arkansas. The library provided free reading material to residents of northwest Arkansas for twenty-five years during the mid-twentieth century.

Richwoods, Arkansas—Richwoods is a narrow basin or valley in the Boston Mountains south of Mountain View in Stone County. The area is home to two communities known respectively as East Richwoods and West Richwoods.

Richwoods, Missouri—Founded about 1830, Richwoods is an unincorporated community in northeast Washington County. It is home to the Richwoods R-7 School District, a K-8 district. After completing eighth grade, students may choose one of several area high schools for further education.

Riddle, Almeda James—Almeda James Riddle, from Greers Ferry, Arkansas, was a prominent figure in the folk music revival of the 1950s and 1960s. Heralded for the breadth of her repertoire of traditional ballads, hymns, and children's songs, she was "discovered" in the early 1950s when she was over fifty years old, and she continued to record and perform into the 1980s. She received the National Heritage Award from the National Endowment for the Arts for her contributions to preserving the folksong traditions of the Ozarks.

Ridge, Major—Major Ridge was a Cherokee Indian leader who, along with his son (John Ridge) and nephew (Elias Boudinot), was killed in the Indian Nation on June 22, 1839, by the anti-treaty faction of the tribe because of his support of the Treaty of New Echota, which effected the tribe's removal from the southeastern United States. (See Cherokee Indians)

Ripley County, Missouri—Located in the southeast part of Missouri bordering Arkansas, Ripley County was organized in 1833 out of territory taken from Wayne County and named for Eleazer W. Ripley, an American general during the War of 1812. When it was first formed, Ripley County comprised almost one-fifth of the entire state of Missouri, but it was gradually reduced as new counties were formed from its territory. The first county seat of Ripley was Van Buren, but the seat was moved to Doniphan when Carter County was formed.

Risenhoover, Theodore M.—Theodore M. Risenhoover was a newspaperman and politician from Tahlequah, Oklahoma. He represented northeast Oklahoma in the U.S. House of Representatives from 1975-1979.

Ritchey, Missouri—Ritchey is a small village on Shoal Creek in northeast Newton County that was laid out by and named for Matthew Ritchey, a prominent Newton County citizen, shortly after the Civil War. It has a population of fewer than 100 people.

Ritchey Mansion—The Ritchey Mansion is a two-story, Civil War-era home at Newtonia, Missouri. Built by Matthew Ritchey around 1852, the home served as a headquarters and a hospital during the two battles of Newtonia, which occurred in September 1862 and October 1864. Today, the mansion is maintained by the Newtonia Battlefields Protection Association and is available for tours during special events or by appointment.

Ritchey Mansion at Newtonia, Mo. *Photo by the author.*

Riverdale, Missouri—Riverdale is a historic mill town that was located on the Finley River in Christian County.

R. M. Ruthven Bridge (aka Cotter Bridge)--The R. M. Ruthven Bridge spans the White River on old U.S. Highway 62 just west of Cotter, Arkansas, and connects Baxter and Marion counties. When it was completed in 1930, it was the first bridge across the White for many miles, and it opened up parts of the Ozarks to motorists who previously were loath to cross the river because of the unreliable ferry system. Originally called the Cotter Bridge, it was officially renamed in 1976 after former Baxter County judge R.M. Ruthven, who had pushed for its authorization. It was dedicated as a National Historic Civil Engineering Landmark in 1986 and placed on the National Register of Historic Places in 1990.

R. M. Ruthven Bridge (aka Cotter Bridge) across the White River. *Courtesy Wikipedia.*

Roach, Sidney C.—Sidney C. Roach was a lawyer and politician from Camden County, Missouri, who served in the U.S. House of Representatives from 1921 to 1925.

Roaring River—Roaring River is an approximately fifteen-mile tributary of the White River in Barry County, Missouri. Forming at Roaring River Spring in Roaring River State Park, it flows eastward to Eagle Rock, where the White River is an arm of Table Rock Lake.

Roaring River State Park—Roaring River State Park is a Missouri state park covering approximately 4,093 acres in southern Barry County, Missouri. Established in 1928, it is home to a Missouri Department of Conservation trout hatchery, and Roaring River, which flows through the park, is popular for trout fishing. The park also offers other activities like camping and hiking, and it is home to the Ozark Chinquapin Nature Center.

Robert E. Talbot Conservation Area—Maintained by the Missouri Department of Conservation, the Robert E. Talbot Conservation Area preserves about 4,400 acres of land, containing woodland, grassland, and other geographic features, in Lawrence County. It offers fishing and other outdoor activities.

Rockaway Beach, Missouri—Rockaway Beach is a resort community of about 500 permanent residents located in Taney County on Lake Taneycomo. Founded in 1917 and originally called Taneycomo, it was a very popular destination during the mid-twentieth century, not only for vacationing families but also for area young people.

Rock Balls—See Weaubleau-Osceola Structure

Rockbridge, Missouri—Rockbridge is an unincorporated community in northern Ozark County. It was a thriving village in the late 1800s and served as the county seat until near the time of the Civil War.

Rocky Comfort, Missouri—Rocky Comfort is an unincorporated community in northeast McDonald County. The area was settled before the Civil War. One story holds that it was named after Rocky Comfort, Arkansas, while another version says it was so named because of the area's rocky hillsides and its beautiful valley suggesting comfort. A post office was established in 1866. The community thrived into the mid-1900s but has declined since it lost its high school to consolidation in the late 1960s.

Rocky Ford State Park—Rocky Ford State Park is an Oklahoma state park located in northern Cherokee County about four miles south of Leach.

Rocky Mount, Missouri—Rocky Mount is an unincorporated community in southeastern Morgan County. It predates the Civil War and was a thriving little community for a short while after the war.

Rodeo of the Ozarks—Held annually in Springdale, Arkansas, since its founding in 1945, Rodeo of the Ozarks has been ranked several times as one of the top five outdoor rodeos in the United States.

Rodger's Crossing, Skirmish at—The Skirmish at Rodger's Crossing was a minor Civil War action on the White River near Huntsville, Arkansas, on September 14, 1864.

Roe, Preacher—Elwin Charles Roe, known as Preacher Roe, was a Major League Baseball player for the St. Louis Cardinals, Pittsburgh Pirates, and Brooklyn Dodgers. Born in 1916 in Ash Flat, Arkansas, he grew up in Viola, Arkansas, and lived much of his adult life in West Plains, Missouri, where one of the main streets is named for him.

Roger Pryor Pioneer Backcountry—The Roger Pryor Pioneer Backcountry is a 60,000-acre undeveloped area in eastern Shannon County. Privately owned, it is managed by the Missouri State Parks.

Rogers, Arkansas—Rogers is a city of about 57,500 people in Benton County. It has recently been one of the fastest growing towns in Arkansas. Rogers was established in 1881 with the coming of the Frisco Railroad and was named after Charles W. Rogers, general manager of the railroad. During the late 1800s and early 1900s, the town developed as a shipping point for the area's apple industry. In 1962, Sam Walton opened the first Wal-Mart store in Rogers. Today the town has numerous businesses and industries, such as Daisy Products and the Pinnacle Hills shopping center. From the late 1800s to the early 1900s, Rogers was home to the Rogers Academy, and today it is home to the Rogers Public Schools. It is also home to the Rogers Historical Museum, the largest museum in Benton County.

Rogersville, Missouri—Rogersville is a town of about 3,075 people located in southwest Webster County at the Greene County line. It was laid out in 1882 when the Kansas City and Memphis Railroad came through the area, and it was named for Dr. Isaac Rogers. Rogersville is home to the Logan-Rogersville R-8 School District.

Rolla, Missouri—Rolla is a town of about 20,000 people and the seat of Phelps County. After plans for a railroad through the area were announced in the mid-1850s and the county was formed in 1857, Rolla was established as the county seat in 1858 along the route of the proposed railroad. One version of how the town got its name holds that it was named after Raleigh, North Carolina, but with a vernacular spelling of the word. Rolla was an important Union army post during the Civil War. The town is home to the Missouri University of Science and Technology and to the Rolla Public Schools. Olympic gold medal gymnast Shannon Miller was born in Rolla.

Rolling Prairie, Skirmish at—The Skirmish at Rolling Prairie was a Civil War action on January 23, 1864, in Boone County, Arkansas.

Rome, Missouri—Rome is unincorporated community in southwest Douglas County. The post office was established prior to the Civil War, and Rome served briefly as the county seat during the war. Rome thrived for many years during the late 1800s and early 1900s, but very little remains today of the once-flourishing community.

Roper, Jesse B.—Jesse Roper gained notoriety in June 1892 when he killed Baxter County, Arkansas, sheriff Abraham Byler, who was trying to arrest him at the time. Authorities sought the desperado for several years afterwards, and several false sightings were reported. However, he was never captured.

Rosebud, Missouri—Rosebud is a town of about 400 people in eastern Gasconade County.

Rosati, Missouri—Rosati is an unincorporated community near Interstate 44 in eastern Phelps County. It was established before the Civil War as Knobview, but its name was changed to Rosati in the 1890s after an influx of Italian immigrants arrived in the area. Located in Missouri's grape growing region, Rosati is known for its vineyards and wine industry.

Roscoe, Missouri—Roscoe is a village of slightly over 100 people on Highway 82 in southern St. Clair County. It is perhaps best known for the shootout between Pinkerton agents and the Younger brothers that happened near the village in 1874.

Ross, John—See Park Hill, Oklahoma.

Rossiter-Modeland, Phyllis—Phyllis Rossiter-Modeland was an author from Flippin, Arkansas, perhaps best known for her book, *A Living History of the Ozarks*. She died in 2007.

Roubidoux Creek—Named after French fur trader Joseph Robidoux, Roubidoux Creek is a tributary of the Gasconade River in south central Missouri. Approximately fifty-seven miles long, it rises in Texas County and flows northward into Pulaski County, where it joins the Gasconade just north of Waynesville. The Roubidoux Conservation Area is located near the confluence of the two streams.

Round Spring Cave—Part of the Ozark National Scenic Riverways, Round Spring Cave is a cave about ten miles southeast of Van Buren, Missouri. It, with the surrounding campground, was a Missouri state park from 1932 to 1964, when it was donated to the National Park Service. During the summer, the cave is open for tours, which are led by park rangers.

Route 66—Route 66 was one of the original highways of the United States Highway System. Established in 1926, it ran from Chicago, Illinois, to Santa Monica, California. It passed through the Ozarks as it crossed Missouri from St. Louis to Joplin, and Springfield, Missouri, is considered its birthplace. The fabled highway, sometimes called the Mother Road or Main Street of America, was memorialized by a pop song and a TV series. Use of Route 66 in the Ozarks faded after Interstate 44, which approximates the route of the old highway, was built in the 1960s. However, recent years have seen an increase in traffic among nostalgia buffs and other travelers who prefer to get off the beaten path and see the country at yesteryear's slower pace.

Royal Gorge—Royal Gorge is a scenic shut-in that can be accessed by road about four miles southwest of Arcadia, Missouri.

Ruddells, Arkansas—Located in the southwest corner of Izard County, Ruddells thrived as a lime mining town for about twenty-five years during the early 1900s, but now about all that remains of the community are the abandoned mines and a cemetery.

Rudolph, William "the Missouri Kid"—William Rudolph was a notorious outlaw who robbed a bank at Union, Missouri, in December of 1902 and the next spring killed a Pinkerton agent who was investigating the case. Given the nickname "the Missouri Kid" by a sensationalist newspaperman, Rudolph was convicted of killing the agent and hanged at Union in 1905.

Rural Free Mail Delivery—Rural Free Delivery of U.S. mail began in the Ozarks on a limited basis in the 1890s and developed more fully in the early 1900s coincident with the development of automobiles.

Rural Electrification—Electricity came to the rural Ozarks in the mid-1900s after passage of the Rural Electrification Act in 1936. At the time the law was enacted, only about five percent of farms in the region had electricity, but by the mid-1950s the large majority did.

Rush, Arkansas—Rush is a ghost town in Marion County southeast of Yellville. It was a booming zinc mining town during the late 1800s and early 1900s, but it declined after World War I and lost its post office in the mid-1900s. It was officially declared a ghost town in 1972 when it was included in the land of the Buffalo River National Park.

Russellville, Missouri—Russellville is a town of about 810 people in western Cole County. It was founded in 1838 and named for Buckner Russell. Russellville is home to the Cole County R-1 Schools.

S

Sac River—The Sac River is a 118-mile tributary of the Osage River in southwest Missouri. Forming in Greene and Lawrence counties, the headwaters of the Sac come together near Greenfield, and the river then flows north through Dade and Cedar counties into St. Clair County, where it joins the Osage near Osceola as an arm of the Truman Reservoir. The Sac and Little Sac rivers are inundated by Stockton Lake south and southeast of Stockton.

St. Clair, Missouri—St. Clair is a town of about 4,475 people located in Franklin County along Interstate 44. Originally called Traveler's Repose, the town was founded in 1859, about the same time that the Southwest Branch of the Pacific Railroad was being built through the area, and the name was changed to St. Clair in honor of a railroad engineer by that name. St. Clair is home to the St. Clair R-13 Schools.

St. Clair County, Missouri—Located at the northwest edge of the Ozarks, St. Clair County was originally established in 1833 and named for Revolutionary general Arthur St. Clair. The county was attached to Rives County (now Henry) two years later but was re-established as a separate county in early 1841. Osceola was named the county seat in November 1841 after a bitter contest throughout the year.

St. Cloud, Missouri—St. Cloud is a small village of about 50 people located along Interstate 44 in Crawford County between Bourbon and Sullivan.

St. Elizabeth, Missouri---St. Elizabeth is a village of about 335 people in northeast Miller County, Missouri. The original St.

Elizabeth was established as a German settlement on the Osage River in 1869 but was abandoned about 1880 in favor of the current town site a couple of miles inland from the river. The new town was at first known as Charleston and did not officially change its name to St. Elizabeth until 1961. St. Elizabeth is home to the St. Elizabeth R-4 Schools.

St. Francis River—The St. Francis River is an approximately 426-mile tributary of the Mississippi River that forms in Iron County, Missouri, and flows generally south through the Ozarks until it reaches the Missouri boot heel. There it forms part of the border separating Missouri and Arkansas and then continues south to join the Mississippi near Helena, Arkansas.

St. Francois County, Missouri—Located in the eastern Ozarks, St. Francois County was established in 1821 from parts of Jefferson, Ste. Genevieve, and Washington counties. Farmington was named the county seat in 1823.

St. Francois Mountains—Located in eastern Missouri along the St. Francis River, the St. Francois Mountains derive their name from the river. Although nowhere near the center of the Ozarks, the St. Francois Mountains form the geological core of the Ozark Mountains.

St. Francois State Park—St. Francois State Park is a Missouri state park located on the Big River north of Bonne Terre. It consists of about 2,700 acres and offers canoeing, hiking, and other outdoor activities.

St. James, Missouri—St. James is a town of about 4,215 people in northeast Phelps County along I-44. It was laid off as Scioto about 1858, but its name was changed to St. James a year or so later when the railroad reached the area and the first town lots were sold. St. James is home to several wineries, including the St. James Winery. It is also home to the St. James R-1 School District and the St. James Missouri Veterans Home (originally established after the Civil War as a home for Union veterans).

St. Joe, Arkansas—St. Joe is a community of about 130 people in northwest Searcy County on U.S. Highway 65. The area was settled near the time of the Civil War, but the town was not incorporated until 1904 shortly after a railroad came through the area. According to legend, the place was originally called Monkey Run. It got its current name about 1900 when six miners from St. Joseph, Missouri, received the largest quantity of mail to come into the local post office. The town boomed during the early 1900s when lead and zinc mining flourished in the area. Today, it is home to the Ozark Mountain School District, which includes St. Joe High School and several other schools.

St. Joe State Park—Located near Park Hills, St. Joe State Park is one of only two off-road vehicle parks in the Missouri state system. The park also features an equestrian trail and a hiking and bicycle trail. The Missouri Mines State Historic Site, which preserves the area's mining heritage, is located at the edge of the park.

St. Joseph Lead Company—Founded in 1864, St. Joseph Lead Company was the dominant mining company in southeast Missouri for over a hundred years, and it became the largest producer of lead and zinc in the U.S.

St. Louis Game Park—The St. Louis Game Park was an approximately 5,000-acre game preserve and resort in south-central Taney County, Missouri, which was started by some St. Louis businessmen in the 1890s and stocked with elk and other game as a hunting resort for members of their club and other dignitaries. See Lynn Morrow's "St. Louis Game Park," *White River Valley Historical Quarterly*, Spring 1997.

St. Martins, Missouri—St. Martins is a town of about 1,150 people in northwest Cole County just west of Jefferson City.

St. Paul, Arkansas—St. Paul is a town of about 165 people in southern Madison County. A previous community, now called Old St. Paul, was established in the same vicinity prior to the Civil War. The current St. Paul was laid out in 1887 when a railroad came through the area. The town is home to the St. Paul Public Schools.

St. Robert, Missouri—St. Robert is a town in Pulaski County adjacent to Fort Leonard Wood. After the fort was constructed in the early 1940s, a Catholic church was built nearby and named St. Robert after St. Robert Bellarmine, a sixteenth century Jesuit. The town that grew up around the church was also named St. Robert.

St. Louis-San Francisco Railroad—The St. Louis-San Francisco Railroad (usually called the Frisco) was a railway that operated in the Midwest and south-central United States from 1876 to 1980. The most important railroad in the Ozarks, its main shops were located at

Springfield, Missouri, where its two principal lines (St. Louis to Tulsa and Kansas City to Memphis) intersected.

St. Louis, Iron Mountain and Southern Railroad—The St. Louis, Iron Mountain and Southern Railroad was a historic railroad that operated in Missouri and Arkansas during the 1800s and early 1900s. It ran from St. Louis through southeast Missouri and then crossed Arkansas in a southwesterly direction to Texarkana. It was originally established as the St. Louis and Iron Mountain Railroad to haul iron ore from Iron Mountain to St. Louis.

St. Thomas, Missouri—St. Thomas is a town of about 265 people in southern Cole County. It was settled prior to the Civil War but consisted of only three buildings until after the war. St. Thomas is home to the St. Thomas the Apostle Catholic School, a K-8 school.

Ste. Genevieve County, Missouri—Located in southeast Missouri along the Mississippi River, Ste. Genevieve County was formed in 1812 during territorial days. Its county seat, also named Ste. Genevieve, is the oldest white settlement west of the Mississippi and was important as a gateway for very early settlers to the eastern Ozarks. With these brief exceptions, however, people, places, and events associated with Ste. Genevieve County will scarcely be covered in this encyclopedia, as it is not popularly considered part of the Ozarks. Not only do people in the heart of the Ozarks tend to think of the Mississippi River counties as lying outside the Ozarks, but also the people of those counties themselves tend not to consider themselves residents of the Ozarks.

Salem, Arkansas—Salem is a town of about 1,590 people and the seat of Fulton County. Pilot Hill, the predecessor of Salem, was established about 1839. Both the county seat and a post office were established at the site in 1844. During the Civil War, the Action at Spring River just northeast of town (also known as the Battle of Salem) occurred on March 13, 1862. The name of the town was officially changed to Salem in 1872. Salem is home to the Salem Public Schools.

Salem, Missouri—Salem is a town of about 4,950 people and the seat of Dent County. It was laid out as the county seat shortly after the county was formed in the early 1850s. Salem was the site of a Civil War skirmish on December 3, 1861, that was made semi-famous by an artist's rendering in *Leslie's Weekly*. The courthouse at Salem was burned by rebels later in the war. The town is home to the Salem R-80 School District.

Salem Plateau—See Ozark Mountains

Salesville, Arkansas—Salesville is a town of about 450 population in central Baxter County. It was named after John Sales, who came to the area prior to 1860, but Salesville, or Sales as it was called for many years, remained an unincorporated rural community that grew very slowly until after Norfork Lake was built nearby in the 1940s, when the town experienced a boom. It was incorporated in 1968.

Salina, Oklahoma—Salina is a town of about 1,400 people in Mayes County near the western edge of the Ozarks. It was established prior to the Civil War by Cherokee Indians. The killing of county attorney Jack Burris, one of the most famous unsolved murders in Oklahoma history, occurred at Salina in 1952. Salina is home to the Salina Public Schools.

Salomon, Frederick—Frederick Salomon was a Union officer during the Civil War. He was a captain under Colonel Sigel at the Battle of Wilson's Creek. He was second in command of the "Indian Expedition" into Indian Territory in June of 1862 and took charge of the expedition after he had the commander (William Weer) arrested for drunkenness and incompetence. He was promoted to brigadier general and commanded the Union forces at the First Battle of Newtonia in the fall of 1862.

Saltpeter Mining—During the Civil War, especially the early part of the war, potassium nitrate or saltpeter, a naturally occurring mineral needed for the production of gunpowder, was mined in north-central Arkansas to aid in the Confederate effort.

Sam A. Baker State Park—Sam A. Baker State Park is a 5,323-acre Missouri state park in northern Wayne County. Named after former governor Samuel Aaron Baker, it offers camping and other outdoor activities and is the site of Mudlick Mountain Natural Area, where Mudlick Mountain is located.

Sanborn, John B.—John B. Sanborn was a Union general during the Civil War. He was commander of the Southwest District of Missouri, headquartered at Springfield, during the latter part of the war.

Sarah Bird Northup Ridge House—Dating to 1836, the Sarah Bird Northup Ridge House is the oldest house in Fayetteville, Arkansas, and it is on the National Register of Historic Places.

Saratoga Springs, Missouri—Saratoga Springs was a mineral water town that sprang up in southwest McDonald County during the medicinal water craze of the 1880s. One of many such towns across the Ozarks, it dwindled almost as fast as it had sprung up. Today, the community, now known as Saratoga, is still listed on some maps, but little of it remains.

Sarcoxie, Missouri—Sarcoxie is a town of about 1,350 people in southeastern Jasper County. It was first settled in the early 1830s and soon became known as Centerville, because it was near the center of what was then Barry County. When the town got its first post office, however, it was discovered that a Centerville, Missouri, already existed, and the name was changed to Sarcoxie in honor of a Shawnee chief who had lived in the area when white settlers first arrived. Sarcoxie claims title to the "oldest town in Jasper County." During the late 1800s and early 1900s, it was known as the "strawberry capital of the world," and it is still sometimes called the "peony capital of the world" because of the tremendous quantity of peonies grown at the Wild nurseries nearby. Sarcoxie is home to the Sarcoxie R-2 School District.

Sarcoxie War—The so-called Sarcoxie War, following close on the heels of the Osage War, was a fifteen-day campaign in 1837 by southwest Missouri militia to remove some Osage Indians from around the Sarcoxie area and drive them out of the state because of their supposed suspicious and threatening behavior. The term "Sarcoxie War" was used in jest rather than earnest, because the Indians were friendly and offered little resistance other than to protest their innocence.

Saults, Dan—Dan Saults was a longtime editor of the *Missouri Conservationist* who also wrote extensively about the Ozarks.

Scarritt Collegiate Institute—See Neosho Male and Female Academy

Schofield, John M.—John M. Schofield was a Union officer during the Civil War. He served as General Nathaniel Lyon's chief of staff at the Battle of Wilson's Creek. Promoted to general in the fall of 1861, he became commander of the newly created Missouri State Militia. In the fall of 1862, he led the Army of the Frontier during the First Battle of Newtonia and the Battle of Prairie Grove. From May 1863 until January 1864, he commanded the Department of the Missouri.

Schoolcraft, Henry Rowe—Henry Rowe Schoolcraft was a geologist and explorer whose expeditions into Missouri and Arkansas brought early notice of the Ozarks to the outside world. In 1819, he published *View of the Lead Mines of Missouri*, based on his visit to the lead mines of southeast Missouri, and *Journal of a Tour into the Interior of Missouri and Arkansaw*, published in 1821, resulted from a three-month expedition he and a companion had taken two or three years earlier through the Missouri and Arkansas Ozarks.

Schoonover, Wear Kibler—In the late 1920s, Wear Schoonover became the first Arkansas Razorback football player to be named to the All-American team. Originally from Pocahontas, Arkansas, he was elected to the College Football Hall of Fame in 1967.

Scott, James—James Scott is considered one of the three most important composers of classic ragtime music, along with Scott Joplin and Joseph Lamb. He was born in Neosho, Missouri, in 1885 and grew up in Carthage.

Scraper, Oklahoma—Scraper is a community of about 475 people in northeast Cherokee County. It was named for Civil War captain Archibald Scraper of the Indian Home Guard. Wilson Rawls, author of *Where the Red Fern Grows*, was born and grew up in Scraper.

Searcy, Arkansas—Searcy is a town of about 22,900 people and the seat of White County. It is not part of the Ozarks by strict definition, although it is sometimes thought of as being in the foothills.

Sedgewickville, Missouri—Established prior to 1874, Sedgewickville is a village of about 175 people in northeast Bollinger County.

Seligman, Missouri—Seligman is a town of about 850 people in southern Barry County near the Arkansas border. It was platted in 1880 when a railroad came through the area, and it was named for Joseph Seligman, a prominent American businessman during the nineteenth century. Seligman had its own school district until the 1950s and 1960s, when its schools were consolidated into the Southwest R-5 School District at Washburn.

Seneca, Missouri—Seneca is a town of about 2,340 people in western Newton County near the Oklahoma border. Located on Lost Creek, it was platted in 1868, and during the early days it was sometimes called Lost Creek. Its official name derives from the Seneca Indians, who were prominent in the area. The town is home to the Seneca R-7 Schools and the Eastern Shawnee Indian tribe.

Sequoyah County, Oklahoma—Located in east-central Oklahoma bordering Missouri, Sequoyah County was formed in 1907 at Oklahoma statehood. It was named after the old Sequoyah District of the Cherokee Nation, which in turn was named for Sequoyah, inventor of the Cherokee alphabet. Only the north portion of Sequoyah County is in the Ozarks.

Sequoyah State Park—See Fort Gibson Lake.

Seymour, Missouri—Seymour is a town of about 1,920 people in southeast Webster County. It was formed in 1895. During the early 1900s the area around Seymour was one of the leading apple-producing regions in Missouri, with the Thomas C. Love orchard north of town producing about ten percent of the state's entire apple crop. The Thomas C. Love House is now on the National Register of Historic Places. Nicknamed the "Land of the Big Red Apple," Seymour is home to the Seymour R-2 Schools.

Shangri-La Resort—Located near Grove, Oklahoma, Shangri-La is one of the larger and better known resorts on Grand Lake.

Shannon County, Missouri—Located in south central Missouri, Shannon County was formed in 1841 from territory taken from Crawford County and named for George F. Shannon, a member of the Lewis and Clark expedition and later U.S. attorney for Missouri. A couple of years later, the county seat was shortly afterwards located at the site of present-day Eminence.

Shannon, Henry Karr—Henry Karr Shannon was an author and newspaper columnist from Izard County, Arkansas. He was known especially for his popular daily column "Run of the News" that appeared in the *Arkansas Democrat* from 1944 to 1971. Among his books was *On a Fast Train Through Arkansas*, published in 1948 as a rebuttal to the negative stereotypes about Arkansas in the 1903 book *On a Slow Train Through Arkansas*.

Sharp County, Arkansas—Located in north-central Arkansas bordering Missouri, Sharp County was formed in 1868 from territory taken from Lawrence County and named for Ephraim Sharp, a state legislator from the area. For many years Sharp County had two seats of justice, one at Hardy and one at Evening Shade, but in the 1960s the county seat was consolidated at Ash Flat.

Shaver, Robert Glenn—Robert Glenn Shaver was a Confederate officer who raised the Seventh Arkansas Regiment (called Shaver's

Regiment) from his home territory around Lawrence County, Arkansas, at the outset of the Civil War. He held the rank of colonel throughout the war, and fought at Prairie Grove and several other battles. After the war, his Ku Klux Klan activities forced him at one point to flee the state to avoid arrest, and later he was the Arkansas commander of the United Confederate Veterans.

Shawnee—The Shawnee are a Native American tribe. During the early 1800s, a large group of them lived in the Ozarks around Yellville, Arkansas, which was called Shawneetown at the time.

Sheid, Vada Webb—Vada Webb Sheid was a politician who was born in Izard County, Arkansas, and lived much of her adult life in Baxter County. She was the first woman to serve in both houses of the Arkansas legislature, representing Baxter and surrounding counties during the late 1960s, 1970s, and early 1980s.

Shelby, Joseph O.—Joseph Orville "Jo" Shelby was a Confederate general during the Civil War whose Missouri cavalry unit was sometimes called the "Iron Brigade" because of its reputation for unyielding fighting during combat. Shelby's men saw action at virtually every significant Civil War battle in the Ozarks, including Wilson's Creek, Pea Ridge, and Prairie Grove.

Shelby's Raid—Jo Shelby's Raid into Missouri in the fall of 1863, covering a reported 1,500 miles, was the longest cavalry raid of the Civil War. Starting deep in Arkansas, Shelby and his brigade cut a swath through the western Ozarks all the way to the Missouri River and back to Arkansas.

Shell Knob, Missouri—Shell Knob is a thriving resort community located on Table Rock Lake in eastern Barry County. It was established in the 1830s but was never more than a small village of perhaps a hundred people or fewer until the lake was built in the 1950s.

Shepherd of the Hills—*Shepherd of the Hills* is a novel by Harold Bell Wright that was published in 1907 and is often credited with helping popularize Branson, Missouri, and its environs as a resort area. Based on the time Wright spent living on land owned by John Ross of Mutton Hollow, Taney County, the novel tells the story of Dad Howitt, a reclusive old man called the shepherd of the hills, and his relationship with "Old Matt" Matthews and his family. Shepherd of the Hills Homestead, featuring Old Matt's cabin, is a tourist attraction on Highway 76 between Branson and Silver Dollar City. For over fifty years until it discontinued in 2013, a play based on the novel was presented during summer evenings in an outdoor theater at the site.

Shepherd of the Hills Fish Hatchery—Located near Table Rock Dam in Taney County, Missouri, the Shepherd of the Hills Fish Hatchery is the Missouri Department of Conservation's largest trout-rearing hatchery.

Shepherd Mountain—Located near Ironton, Missouri, Shepherd Mountain has long been popular for hiking, and a new hiking trail was opened there in 2013.

Sheppard, Henry—Henry Sheppard was a colonel of Enrolled Missouri Militia who played an important role in the defense of Springfield during the Battle of Springfield in January 1863.

Sherman, Harold Morrow—Harold Morrow Sherman was a nationally known author and lecturer in the fields of self-help and extrasensory perception (ESP) during the mid-1900s. He also was active in community development in Stone County, Arkansas, where he lived for many years prior to his death in 1987.

Sherman, Jory—Jory Sherman was a Pulitzer Prize-nominated author of historical, western, and mystery novels. He lived a number of years in Branson, Missouri, and wrote extensively about the Ozarks. He died in 2014.

Sherwood, Missouri—Sherwood was a town in western Jasper County prior to and during the Civil War. On May 19, 1863, it was burned to the ground by Federal troops from Baxter Springs, Kansas, in retaliation for the killing of about eighteen black soldiers near Sherwood the previous day by Confederate guerrillas under Thomas Livingston.

Shiloh Museum of Ozark History—The Shiloh Museum of Ozark History is a regional history museum focusing on northwest Arkansas. In addition to numerous artifacts and exhibits, the museum also houses a research library with many books, periodicals, files, and photographs on the Ozarks. Located in Springdale, the museum is a department of the City of Springdale but is run in part by volunteers and supported partly by membership fees and contributions.

Shirley, Arkansas—Shirley is a town of about 225 people in northeastern Van Buren County. A nearby community called

Settlement predated Shirley, but Shirley was not established until 1911 when the Missouri and North Arkansas Railroad came through the area. The town is home to the Shirley Public Schools.

Shirley, Myra Maybelle--see Belle Starr

Shoal Creek—Shoal Creek is a tributary of Spring River in southwest Missouri. It forms in northern Barry County and flows through Newton and Jasper counties before entering Kansas and emptying into Spring River near Riverton.

Short, Dewey Jackson—Dewey Short was college professor, a Methodist pastor, and a politician from southwest Missouri. Born in Galena, he served twelve terms in the U.S. House of Representatives between 1929 and 1957.

Sidney, Arkansas—Sidney is a town of about 180 people in southwestern Sharp County. Although the area was settled prior to the Civil War, the community got its first post office in 1878 and was named Sidney at that time, reportedly in honor of Confederate general Albert Sidney Johnston.

Sigel, Franz—Franz Sigel was a Union officer during the Civil War who played prominent roles in several battles that occurred in the Ozarks. As a colonel, he led the Union forces at the Battle of Carthage. He was promoted to brigadier general shortly before the Battle of Wilson's Creek, where he served under General Nathaniel Lyon. General Sigel commanded two divisions at the Battle of Pea Ridge and was promoted to major general shortly afterwards.

Siloam Springs, Arkansas—Siloam Springs is a town of about 15,000 people in southwestern Benton County near the Oklahoma border. Hico, a predecessor of Siloam Springs, was established nearby in 1855. In 1880, Siloam Springs was established as a mineral-water resort just south of Hico on Sager Creek, which was named after the first white settler in the area, Simon Sager. In 1882, a post office was established at Siloam Springs, and the Hico post office closed. Although it later reopened, the town of Hico was eventually engulfed by Siloam Springs. Siloam Springs boomed as a mineral-water resort after a railroad reached the town in 1893. Today, the town is home to John Brown University, the Siloam Springs School District, the Siloam Springs Museum, and Allens, Inc. (aka the Allen Canning Company).

Siloam Springs, Missouri—Siloam Springs is an unincorporated community in west-central Howell County. The area was known for its curative springs for many years before Dr. Jonathan Brown established a health resort at the location about 1866. The resort was known at first as Brown Springs, but Brown's daughter suggested the name Siloam Springs after the healing pool mentioned in the Bible. D.F. Martin took over the place and laid out a town he called Martinsville, but the post office remained Siloam Springs. Siloam Springs thrived during the 1880s and 1890s, when it had a population of about 600, but little remains today to suggest its previous prosperity.

Silver Dollar City—Silver Dollar City is a theme park in Stone County, Missouri, west of Branson on Highway 76. It was established in 1960 as a replica of an 1880s Ozarks village and centered around Marvel Cave, but it has since expanded to include many rides and attractions and has become one of the largest tourist destinations in the Ozarks. It hosts several popular festivals each year, such as the National Harvest and Cowboy Festival, featuring traditional crafts, and World-Fest, celebrating music from around the world.

Silver Mines Recreation Area—Located along the St. Francis River west of Fredericktown, Missouri, Silver Mines Recreation Area offers

St. Francis River at Silver Mines Recreation Area. *Courtesy Wikimedia*

camping facilities and outdoor activities. A silver mine thrived at the site for about three years in the late 1870s, and a community called Silver Mountain sprang up on the nearby ridge.

Simmons Iron Mountain—Simmons Iron Mountain was a ninety-foot-high hill about a mile southwest of Salem, Missouri, with a base of about thirty acres and a high concentration of iron ore, which was mined extensively during the late 1800s. Among Missouri's iron-laden mountains, it was second in size only to Iron Mountain in St. Francois County.

Sims, Leonard H.—Leonard H. Sims was a U.S. representative from Springfield, Missouri, from 1845 to 1847. He is remembered mainly for a famous speech he gave on the "Oregon Question," in which he advocated a hard line in the U.S.'s boundary dispute with Great Britain over a contested section of the Oregon Territory.

Sinking Creek Natural Bridge—Also called the Sinks, the Sinking Creek Natural Bridge is a natural rock bridge spanning Sinking Creek, a tributary of the Current River, near the community of Sinking in Shannon County, Missouri. The tunnel below the bridge is sometimes large enough to float through in a boat. See *The Ozarks Mountaineer*, March-April 2012.

Sisco, Marideth—Marideth Sisco is a writer, storyteller, folksinger, and the host of public radio's "These Ozarks Hills."

Sleeper, Missouri—Sleeper is an unincorporated community in Laclede County northeast of Lebanon. Established in the early 1870s as a station along the Atlantic and Pacific Railroad, it was named for a construction gang foreman who helped build the road and was originally called Sleeper's Switch because of a spur at the site where trains could switch cars.

Slickers—The Slickers was a vigilante group in Benton and Polk counties, Missouri, during the 1840s that grew out of the Turk-Jones feud. The vigilante Turks whipped or "slicked" those who supposedly had committed crimes, but the victims were targeted primarily for siding with the Jones faction. The Slicker movement spread to other parts of Missouri, but it remains most identified with the Turk-Jones feud, which ended only after the principals on both sides had been either killed or run out of the region.

Smallin Cave (aka Smallin Civil War Cave)—Smallin Cave is a commercial cave in Christian County, Missouri, about five miles northeast of Ozark. Henry Rowe Schoolcraft mentioned the cave prominently in the journal he kept during his exploration of the Ozarks in 1818, and it is, therefore, considered the first cave in the Ozarks to be discovered by white men. The cave was thought to have been used for military purposes during the Civil War, and over the years it has also been explored and used by private groups and individuals. It opened for tours in 2010.

Exploring Smallin Cave. *Courtesy Smallin Civil War Cave archives 2015.*

Sligo, Missouri—Sligo is a small community in northeast Dent County. It was established during the 1880s after the Sligo Furnace Company built an iron ore furnace at the site. The town was named Sligo after the company. Hundreds of people flocked to the town in search of work. At the furnace's peak of operation, Sligo had a population of about 1,000 people. The iron furnace closed in 1923, and today little remains in Sligo to suggest its earlier prominence.

Sligo and Eastern Railroad—The Sligo and Eastern Railroad was a short-line railroad during the first third of the twentieth century that ran from Sligo east to Dillard, eleven miles away, primarily serving the iron works at Sligo.

Smirnoff, Yakov—Yakov Smirnoff is a Ukrainian-American comedian who gained fame in the United States in the 1980s and has been performing regularly in Branson since the 1990s.

Smith, Gerald Lyman Kenneth—Gerald Lyman Kenneth Smith was an American minister and political organizer. He was a leader in Louisiana governor Huey Long's Share Our Wealth program during the Depression and later founded the anti-Semitic Christian Nationalist Crusade. He ran for president as the candidate of the isolationist America First Party in 1944 and also belonged to the pro-Nazi Silver Shirts organization about the same time. Smith retired to Arkansas and is best known in the Ozarks for building and promoting the Christ of the Ozarks statue at Eureka Springs.

Smith, Jason—Jason Smith is an attorney and politician from Salem, Missouri, who was elected to the U.S. House of Representatives in 2013.

Smith, Obadiah—During the Civil War, Obadiah Smith was a Missouri state representative from Cedar County. A strong Union man, he was killed by guerrillas under William Quantrill during their raid through the county in the spring of 1863.

Smith, Sarah Jane—Sarah Jane Smith was a young woman from Washington County, Arkansas, who was arrested by Union authorities in 1864 for destroying telegraph wires along the Wire Road between Rolla and Springfield. Tried and convicted, she was sentenced to hang, but her sentence was later commuted after she became seriously ill while in prison at St. Louis.

Smithville, Arkansas—Smithville is a town of about 75 people in eastern Lawrence County. It was the seat of Lawrence County from 1837 until 1868. Two Civil War skirmishes occurred near Smithville, one on June 7, 1862, and another on April 13, 1864. Smithville is also known as the town nearest the site of the infamous shootout between law officers and tax fugitive Gordon Kahl on June 2, 1983, that left Kahl and Lawrence County sheriff Gene Matthews dead.

Snowball, Arkansas—Located in western Searcy County, Snowball was once a thriving little town, but little remains of it today.

Snowdale State Park—See Lake Hudson.

Snowstorms—The biggest snowstorm ever recorded at the Springfield, Missouri, weather station occurred on February 21-22, 1912, when 24.1 inches of snow were recorded. The November 5-6, 1951 snowstorm, when 19.5 inches were recorded, and the March 16-17, 1970 snowstorm, when 23.9 inches were recorded, are also particularly noteworthy because they occurred near the beginning and near the end respectively of the winter season. During the March 1970 storm, Neosho recorded 27 inches, which is a Missouri record for a single snowstorm. On February 9, 2011, Siloam Springs recorded 24.5 inches of snow, just a half inch below the Arkansas record for a 24-hour period. The Ozarks have also seen several historic ice storms, notably the storm of January 2007, when an estimated three-fourths of Springfield residents lost electricity due to downed power lines.

November 1951 snowstorm in the Ozarks. *Author's collection.*

Southeast Missouri State University—Located at Cape Girardeau, Southeast Missouri State University (aka SEMO) is a public institution of higher learning offering undergraduate and graduate degrees. It was established in 1873 as Southeast Missouri Normal School and had three other names before it adopted its present name in 1973. It has a student body of about 12,000.

Southern Memorial Association of Washington County—See Confederate Cemetery

South Fork, Missouri—South Fork is an unincorporated community in Howell County west of West Plains on U.S. Highway 160. It is named for its location on the South Fork of Spring River, and it was formerly known as Cross Roads.

South Greenfield, Missouri—South Greenfield is a community of about 90 people three miles south of Greenfield in Dade County. In 1881, when a railroad bypassed Greenfield to the south, many citizens and businessmen of Greenfield moved to a point on the railroad, hoping the rest of the town, county seat and all, would follow. However, a branch road was built to Greenfield, and with its completion, South Greenfield's hopes of becoming the seat of and the most prominent town in Dade County soon faded, although it did attain a population as high as 600 before declining.

South Lead Hill, Arkansas—South Lead Hill is a town of about 100 people located in Boone County a couple of miles south of Lead Hill on Highway 7. It came into being about 1950 when Bull Shoals Lake was being created and Lead Hill had to be moved to higher ground. Instead of staying with the original town, some people chose instead to move to the new town of South Lead Hill.

Southwest Baptist University—Southwest Baptist University is a private institution of higher education affiliated with the Missouri Baptist Convention. Its main campus is located at Bolivar, Missouri, with branch campuses at Mountain View, Salem, and Springfield. Originally established at Lebanon in 1878, the school moved to Bolivar the next year. The college offers associate, bachelor, and advanced degrees, and student enrollment is approximately 3,600.

Southwest City, Missouri—Southwest City is town of about 940 people in McDonald County in the extreme southwest corner of the state. A post office at the site was originally named Honey Creek, but after the town was laid out in 1870, the name was changed to Southwest City because of its location. Bill Doolin's outlaw gang held up a bank at Southwest City in 1894, killing a prominent citizen in the process. The town formerly had a high school but now has only a grade school, which is part of the McDonald County School District.

Southwest Missouri Electric Railway—The Southwest Missouri Electric Railway was an electric streetcar service established at Webb City, Missouri, in 1893. With about ninety-four miles of track, it served the Tri-State mining district of Missouri, Kansas, and Oklahoma during the late 1800s and early 1900s.

Southwest Trail—Originally an Indian trace, the Southwest Trail was a nineteenth century trail, running from St. Louis to the Red River on the southern border of Arkansas, that settlers going to Texas used.

It generally followed the eastern edge of the Ozarks as it passed through southern Missouri and northern Arkansas. During the nineteenth century, it was often called by other names, including the Arkansas Road and the National Road.

Sparta, Missouri—Sparta is a town of about 1,755 people in Christian County. It was laid out in 1885 and reportedly named after Sparta, Tennessee, where the mother of founder J.J. Bruton was from. Sparta is home to the Sparta R-3 Schools.

Spavinaw, Oklahoma—Spavinaw is a town of about 435 people in eastern Mayes County. The first white settler came to the vicinity in 1829, but the Cherokee Indians later took over the area. Spavinaw is known as the birthplace of Mickey Mantle, and it is home to the Spavinaw Public Schools.

Spavinaw Lake—Spavinaw Lake is a 1,584-acre lake on the east side of Spavinaw, Oklahoma.

Spavinaw State Park—Spavinaw State Park is an Oklahoma state park located at the edge of Spavinaw Lake.

Splitlog, Missouri—Splitlog is a small community in northwest McDonald County, Missouri. It was established by Mathias Splitlog, the so-called "Millionaire Indian," in the late 1880s when he moved across the border from his home at Cayuga, Indian Territory. He soon built a railroad called the Splitlog Line that connected his new town to Neosho and Joplin, but the town's growth sputtered after Splitlog was duped and lost money in a fake gold mining scheme. (See Cayuga, Oklahoma)

Spokane, Missouri—Spokane (pronounced with a long "a") is a community of about 200 people on U.S. Highway 160 in southern Christian County. It was established as a post office on the old Wilderness Road in 1892. Spokane is home to the Spokane R-7 Schools.

Spook Light of Joplin—The Joplin Spook Light (aka the Hornet Spook Light or Quapaw Spook Light) is an eerie light that appears at night in a remote area near the Missouri-Oklahoma border about ten miles southwest of Joplin, Missouri. It has been attracting the curious to the spot since at least the 1930s. Many theories have been offered for its existence, from supernatural tales about ghosts carrying lanterns to scientific explanations about distant car headlights.

Spook Light of Joplin. *Photo by the author.*

Springdale, Arkansas—Springdale is a city of about 73,000 people located mainly in northern Washington County but spilling over into Benton County. It was established prior to the Civil War as Shiloh and incorporated in 1878 as Springdale. Home to Tyson Foods, it is known as "The Poultry Capital of the World." Springdale is the birthplace of several major trucking firms. The former home of Springdale College, the town is currently home to a branch of Northwest Arkansas Community College, to the Northwest Technical Institute, and to the Springdale Public School District, which includes two high schools. The Ozark Regional Arts and Crafts Show, held at Springdale in both the spring and fall, is one of the largest craft fairs in the region and the largest indoor craft fair in Arkansas.

Springfield, Battle of—Part of Brigadier General John S. Marmaduke's first invasion of Missouri, the Battle of Springfield was a Civil War battle fought at Springfield, Missouri, on January 8, 1863, between Confederate forces under Marmaduke and Union forces under Brigadier General Egbert B. Brown. The action was a Union victory, since Marmaduke was unable to take the town.

Springfield, Missouri—Springfield is a city of about 160,000 people and the seat of Greene County. It was laid out in 1835 as the seat of the county, which had been formed two years earlier. The largest town in the Ozarks, Springfield is sometimes called the "Queen City of the Ozarks." Springfield is home to the Dickerson Park Zoo, Battlefield Mall, the Springfield-Greene County Botanical Center, the Springfield Art Museum, the History Museum on the Square, the Missouri Sports Hall of Fame, the Springfield-Branson National Airport, and the Springfield R-12 School District, which includes five high schools. Among the popular annual festivals held in Springfield is Firefall, a Fourth of July music extravaganza and patriotic celebration. Among the well-known people who either were born or grew up in Springfield are Olympic speed skater Emily Scott, NBA basketball player Anthony Tolliver, and former MLB baseball player Steve Rogers.

Springfield Cardinals—The Springfield Cardinals, based in Springfield, Missouri, are a double-A Minor League affiliate baseball team of the St. Louis Cardinals. They play their home games at John Q. Hammons Field.

Springfield Easter Lynchings—A notorious triple lynching occurred on the public square in Springfield, Missouri, during Easter weekend of 1906. Two black men who were suspected of assaulting a white woman were dragged from the county jail and hanged, despite the fact that evidence existed to suggest their innocence. Then a third black man, incarcerated on an unrelated charge, was dragged from the jail and made to suffer a like fate.

Springfield News-Leader—The *Springfield News-Leader* is the predominant newspaper for the city of Springfield, Missouri, and its coverage spans much of the entire Ozarks. It traces its roots to the *Springfield Leader*, which began publication in 1867.

Springfield Normal School—The Springfield Normal School was a forerunner of the Fourth District State Normal School, which evolved into what is known today as Missouri State University. Founded in 1894, the Springfield Normal School was located at the corner of Cherry and Pickwick.

Springfield Plateau—See Ozark Mountains.

Springfield Road—See Wire Road.

Springfield Three, The—The Springfield Three is an unsolved missing person case that began shortly after Suzie Streeter and Stacy McCall graduated from Kickapoo High School on June 6, 1992. After attending a graduation party, Streeter and McCall returned to the home of Sherrill Levitt, Streeter's mother, in the early morning hours of June 7, and neither the girls nor Levitt were ever heard from again. The whereabouts or remains of the three women have never been discovered.

Spring Garden, Missouri—Spring Garden is a small community in northern Miller County near the Cole county line. In the late 1800s, it was a thriving place and was home to the Miller County Academy (later the Miller County Institute).

Spring River—There are two Spring rivers in the Ozarks. One has its headwaters near Verona, Missouri, and flows in a generally westward direction into the southeast corner of Kansas. The other forms in Howell County, Missouri, as an underground river and flows southward into Arkansas, where it rises to the surface just below the state line at Mammoth Spring. The Spring River then continues into Arkansas in a southeasterly direction and empties into the Black River.

Spurlock, Pearl—Pearl Spurlock was a famed promoter of Branson and a tour guide for the area during the 1920s.

Squires, Missouri—Squires is an unincorporated community in southern Douglas County on State Highway 5. It was named in 1888 when John Squire's petition for a post office in his store was granted. Squires thrived for a while during the late 1800s and early 1900s, and several businesses and homes are still located there.

Staffelbach, Nancy "Old Lady"—Nancy Staffelbach was the notorious madam of a brothel in Galena, Kansas, who, along with her common-law husband and two of her sons, was convicted of murdering a man who called at the bordello late one night in 1897.

Stafford, Jim—Jim Stafford is a singer and comedian who gained famed in the 1970s for songs such as "Spiders and Snakes" and who has been performing regularly in Branson since 1990.

Stanford, Frank—Frank Stanford was a prolific American poet known especially for his epic poem *The Battlefield Where the Moon Says I Love You.* Stanford grew up partly in Mountain Home, attended the University of Arkansas, and lived briefly in Eureka Springs. He killed himself in 1978 when he was just shy of his thirtieth birthday.

Stanton, Missouri—Known mainly as the home of Meramec Caverns, Stanton is a small community in Franklin County along I-44.

Stark City, Missouri—Stark City is a village of about 140 people in eastern Newton County, Missouri. It was named for William P. Stark, who established a large nursery there in 1907.

Starke, Pauline—Pauline Starke was an actress born in Joplin, Missouri, in 1901, who starred in silent films during the 1920s.

Starr, Belle—Belle Starr (nee Myra Maybelle Shirley) was an infamous outlaw during the post-Civil War era. Born near Carthage, Missouri, in 1848, she spent most of her adult life in Indian Territory (now Oklahoma), and she is sometimes called the "Queen of the Oklahoma Outlaws."

Belle Starr's childhood home, now located at Red Oak II near Carthage, Mo.. *Photo by the author.*

Starr, Emmett—From Adair County, Oklahoma, Emmett Starr was a historian of the Cherokee people. He was noted especially for his *History of the Cherokee Indians and Their Legends and Folklore*, published in 1922.

Fred Starr—An educator and author from northwest Arkansas, Fred Starr was known for his writings about the Ozarks during the mid-1900s, including his newspaper essays called "Plain Tales from the Ozarks" and his book entitled *Of These Hills and Us.*

Starr, Henry—Henry Starr was a notorious outlaw whose "career" spanned the Old West era of the late 1800s and the gangster era of the 1920s. Born near Nowata in Indian Territory, Starr is most infamous in the Ozarks for a bank robbery in 1893 at Bentonville, Arkansas, and another one in 1921 at Harrison during which he was killed.

Starr, Tom—Tom Starr was a grandfather of Henry Starr and father-in-law of Belle Starr. He was involved on the side of the Treaty Party in a feud between factions of the Cherokee Indian tribe prior to the Civil War and became known as an outlaw, at least by the Anti-Treaty Party. (See Cherokee Indians)

Steele, Phillip—Phillip Steele was an author from Springdale, Arkansas, noted particularly for his books about notorious characters like Belle Starr. He died in 2007.

Steelville, Missouri—Steelville is a town of about 1,645 people and the seat of Crawford County. It was laid out in 1835 by James Steel and named in his honor. In 1898, Steelville suffered a devastating flood that claimed the lives of thirteen people and destroyed much property. The town is home to the Steelville R-3 School District.

Stewart, Payne—Payne Stewart was a professional golfer from Springfield, Missouri. Winner of eleven PGA Tour events, including three majors, he died in an airplane accident in 1999. A section of I-44 that passes through Springfield is named in his honor.

Stiles, Jackie—During her basketball career at Missouri State University in Springfield from 1998 to 2001, Jackie Stiles became the all-time leading scorer in NCAA Division I women's basketball. She was named Rookie of the Year in the WNBA in 2001 before her professional career was cut short by injuries. She is currently an assistant coach at MSU.

Stilwell, Oklahoma—Stilwell is a town of about 4,000 people and the seat of Adair County. It was established in 1896 when the Kansas City Southern Railroad was built through the area and named for Arthur Stilwell, founder of the railroad. Stilwell became the county seat in 1910 after vying several years with Westville, which had previously been the seat. Strawberries were a major crop in Adair County during the Depression and World War II years, and the Oklahoma governor and legislature proclaimed Stilwell the "Strawberry Capital of the World" in 1949. Today, Stilwell still holds a strawberry festival each year, and it is home to the Indian Capital Technology Center and the Stilwell Public Schools.

Stockard, Sallie Walker—Sallie Walker Stockard was the author of a book in the early 1900s about the history of Lawrence, Jackson,

Independence, and Stone counties, Arkansas. It is often called simply *The Arkansas Book.*

Stockton, Missouri—Stockton is a town of about 1,820 people and the seat of Cedar County. It was established as the county seat in 1846 under the name of Lancaster. The next year the name was changed to Fremont, and in 1856 it was changed to Stockton after Commodore Robert Stockton of Mexican War fame. The courthouse at Stockton was burned by Confederates during Colonel Shelby's 1863 invasion of Missouri. Stockton is home to the Stockton R-1 School District and the Hammonds black walnut processing company.

Stockton Lake—Stockton Lake is a manmade reservoir near Stockton, Missouri, in Cedar County. Created in 1969 by the damming of the Sac River, it covers thirty-nine square miles and has 298 miles of shoreline. The 2,716-acre Stockton State Park is located on the lakeshore.

Stockton State Park—See Stockton Lake.

Stone County, Arkansas—Located in the north central part of the state, Stone County was formed in 1873 from parts of Independence, Izard, Searcy, and Van Buren counties, and Mountain View was named the county seat the same year.

Stone County, Missouri—Located in southwest Missouri bordering Arkansas, Stone County was organized in 1851 out of territory taken from Taney County and named for Taney County judge William Stone. Galena was laid out as the county seat the following year.

Stone, Edward Durell—Edward Durell Stone was an influential twentieth century architect and early proponent of modern architecture in America. Born and reared in Fayetteville, Arkansas, he is known for his design, in association with Philip Goodwin, of New York City's Museum of Modern Art, among other works.

Stony Battery, Skirmish at—The Skirmish at Stony Battery was a Civil War action that occurred on April 20, 1863, near Patterson, Missouri. Pursued by several thousand men under Confederate general John S. Marmaduke, the Third Missouri State Militia under Colonel Edwin Smart burned Patterson before abandoning it and retreating toward Pilot Knob. Two companies of the Union regiment made a stand at Stony Battery, a gorge near the Wayne-Iron county line through which the road passed. About thirty Union soldiers were killed in the action, but the hard fighting and entrenched Federal position helped deter a further pursuit by the Confederates, despite their vastly superior numbers.

Stotts City, Missouri—Stotts City is a town of about 220 people in western Lawrence County. It was founded in the 1880s as a lead mining community and named for Greene Casey Stotts, a resident of the area and a former Union army officer. Stotts City boomed in the late 1800s and early 1900s, reaching a peak population of about 900 in 1910. World War I hero and Congressional Medal of Honor recipient Charles Denver Barger grew up in Stotts City.

Stout Creek Shut-In—See Johnson Shut-Ins State Park

Stoutland, Missouri—Stoutland is a village of about 190 people straddling the Camden-Laclede county line. It was founded in 1869 as a stop on the Atlantic & Pacific Railroad and named after Captain Stout, an official with the railroad. Stoutland is home to the Stoutland R-2 Schools. The 1910 murder of Jasper Francis, chronicled in the 2007 book *Murder on Rouse Hill*, occurred near Stoutland.

Stover, Missouri—Stover is town of about 1,100 people in western Morgan County. It was founded at its present location in 1903 when a railroad came through the area, and the original town of Stover slightly to the southwest came to be known as Old Stover. Stover was named after John H. Stover, a U.S. congressman from the area. The town is home to the Morgan County R-1 Schools.

Stover, John Hubler—John Hubler Stover was an attorney from Morgan County, Missouri, who served as a U.S. representative from 1868 to 1869.

Strafford, Missouri—Strafford is a town of about 2,360 people in eastern Greene County along I-44. It was established as a railroad town in 1870 and reportedly named for Strafford, Connecticut. Strafford hosts an annual Route 66 Days festival, and it is home to the Strafford R-6 Schools.

Strang, Oklahoma—Strang is a community of about 100 people in northeast Mayes County. Although post offices by other names existed in the same area as early as 1902, the Strang post office was not established until 1913 when a railroad was being built in the area.

Strawberry Industry—The Strawberry industry was important to the Ozarks' economy from about the 1880s until approximately the 1940s. It was centered in the southern part of the Arkansas Ozarks near the Arkansas River valley but was scattered throughout other parts of the region as well. Strawberry growing was especially prevalent, for instance, in the area of Sarcoxie, Missouri, which billed itself as the "Strawberry Capital of the World."

Strawberry River—The Strawberry River is a tributary of the Black River that winds through northern Arkansas for about eighty miles. It forms in Fulton County and flows generally southeasterly through Izard, Sharp, and Lawrence counties, joining the Black in northeast Independence County.

Street, Gabby—Gabby Street was a Major League Baseball player, manager, and broadcaster during the early 1900s. He lived much of his adult life in Joplin, Missouri, where a street was named after him.

Sturgis, Samuel D.—Samuel D. Sturgis was Union officer who succeeded to the command of the Union forces at the Battle of Wilson's Creek after the death of General Nathaniel Lyon.

Success, Missouri—Success is an unincorporated community at the junction of Highway 17 and Highway 32 in northwest Texas County. Settled about 1880, it was first called Hastings but became Success when a post office was established in 1883. The original town was located about a mile north of its current site, and that location is now called Old Success. During the 1930s, the town was moved to the intersection of the two highways and briefly called Wye City to suggest the shape of the town, but the name soon reverted to Success.

Sugar Loaf Mountain—See Greers Ferry Lake

Sullivan, Missouri—Sullivan is a town of about 7,100 people along I-44 on the Franklin-Crawford county line. Stephen Sullivan laid out the town. In 1859 when a railroad was being built through the area, he donated land and a building for the depot, and the railroad named the town after him. The Mt. Helicon Post Office, which had been established in the same area in 1856, was then discontinued. Sullivan is home to the Sullivan Public Schools, and the rural school districts of Spring Bluff and Strain-Japan are just outside Sullivan.

Sulphur Springs, Arkansas—Sulphur Springs is a town of about 500 people in the northwest corner of Benton County near the Missouri and Oklahoma borders. A post office was established at the site in 1878. The town, named for its nearby springs, was laid out as a mineral water resort in 1885, and it prospered after a railroad arrived in 1891. In 1924 evangelist John E. Brown opened John Brown University in Sulphur Springs but soon consolidated the school with his operations in Siloam Springs. The Sulphur Springs Public Schools consolidated with nearby Gravette in 1965.

Sulphur Rock, Arkansas—Sulphur Rock is a town of about 450 people in Independence County about six miles east of Batesville. Located along the Old Military Road, the place had a post office as early as 1834. The town took its name from the presence of two large sulphur springs in the area that supposedly had medicinal properties. From 1872 to 1906, the town was home to the Sulphur Rock Male and Female Academy. Sulphur Rock had a mule-drawn streetcar that was in existence until 1926, and it was the last mule-powered car to operate in the U.S. The Sulphur Rock Public Schools consolidated with Batesville in 2005.

Summersville, Missouri—Summersville is a town of about 500 people located mainly in southeastern Texas County on the Shannon County line. A post office was established there in 1874, and the community was named for Jesse and Thomas Summer. The town is home to the Summersville R-2 Schools.

Summit, Arkansas—Summit is a town of about 600 people in Marion County. It was established in 1904 when a railroad came through the area and a depot was built a couple of miles north of Yellville on higher ground. Today, the two towns are separated by Division Street, and Summit has sometimes been called North Yellville because of its proximity to its better known neighbor.

Sundown Towns—See Racial Cleansing

Sunklands Natural Area—Part of the larger Sunklands Conservation Area of the Missouri Department of Conservation, the Sunklands Natural Area preserves the longest sinkhole valley in Missouri. It is located northwest of Eminence in Shannon County.

Sunrise Beach, Missouri—Sunrise Beach is a village of about 435 people on the Camden-Morgan county line.

Sutton, Eddie—Eddie Sutton is a retired basketball coach who led four teams, including the University of Arkansas, to the Final Four.

Swan Creek—Swan Creek is a twenty-one-mile tributary of the White River. It forms in Christian County, Missouri, and flows generally south to join the White near Forsyth in Taney County.

Swedeborg, Missouri—Swedeborg is an unincorporated community in northwest Pulaski County. It was established about 1880 along the railroad between Crocker and Richland and was settled mainly by

Swedish immigrants. It no longer has a post office but is still home to the Swedeborg R-3 School District, an elementary-only district.

Sweeny, Thomas W.—Thomas W. Sweeny was a Union general during the Civil War. In the Ozarks, he is remembered for leading an expedition from Springfield to Forsyth in July 1861 and for his participation in the Battle of Wilson's Creek the following month.

Sylamore, Arkansas—Sylamore is an unincorporated community in Stone County. It was originally on the west side of the White River. However, the east side took the name Sylamore after a rail station was located there in 1902, and the west side became known as Allison.

Sylamore, Skirmish at—The Skirmish at Sylamore (aka the Skirmish at Kickapoo Bottom) was a Civil War action that occurred on May 29, 1862, about three miles north of Sylamore, Arkansas, between Confederate and Union cavalry. Casualties were few on both sides, and the outcome was considered a stalemate. Sylamore was also the site of skirmishing on January 23 and January 26 of 1864.

Syllamo Mountain Bike Trail—The Syllamo Mountain Bike Trail is a popular motor biking trail near Mountain View, Arkansas, consisting of about fifty miles of interconnecting loops.

Syracuse, Missouri—Syracuse is a town of about 175 people in northern Morgan County.

T

Table Rock Lake—Table Rock Lake is a reservoir in southwest Missouri created by the construction of Table Rock Dam on the White River. Located near Branson, the dam was built between 1954 and 1958. The lake has over 800 miles of shoreline and covers about 43,100 acres, mostly in Stone and Barry counties. The 350-acre Table Rock State Park is located on the east side of the lake near the dam.

Tabuchi, Shoji—Shoji Tabuchi is a Japanese-American singer and fiddle player who has performed in Branson since the early 1980s.

Tahlequah, Oklahoma—Located at the western edge of the Ozarks, Tahlequah is a city of about 15,800 people and the seat of Cherokee County. It was founded in 1839 as the capital of the Cherokee people after many members of the tribe were forced west along the Trail of Tears. It is home to Northeastern State University and the Tahlequah

Public Schools, and it is still the headquarters of the Cherokee tribe. Tahlequah is featured in the well-known novel *Where the Red Fern Grows* by Wilson Rawls.

Tahlequah welcoming sign. *From www.city-data.com.*

Talking Rocks Cavern—Formerly known as Fairy Cave, Talking Rocks Cavern is a tour cave in Stone County, Missouri, just west of Silver Dollar City. Explored in 1896, it was first opened to the public in 1907.

Tall Timber Trio—Consisting of Slim Wilson, his nephew Speedy Haworth, and Bob White, the Tall Timber Trio was a country music group popular in the Ozarks during the mid-twentieth century.

Taney County, Missouri—Taney County, bordering Arkansas in southwest Missouri, was established in 1837 from territory taken from Greene County and named after Justice Roger B. Taney of the U.S. Supreme Court. Forsyth, which had been laid out the previous year, was named the county seat.

Taneyville, Missouri—Taneyville is a village of about 400 people in northern Taney County. Dating from before the Civil War, it was originally called Taney City, but it became Taneyville about 1894. It is the home of the Taneyville R-2 Schools, a K-8 district.

Tan-Tar-A—Located near Osage Beach, Missouri, on the Lake of the Ozarks, Tan-Tar-A is a one of the largest and best-known resorts in the region.

Taos, Missouri—Taos is a town of about 880 people in eastern Cole County.

Taum Sauk Hydroelectric Power Station—Taum Sauk Hydro-electric Power Station, an electric power plant of the AmerenUE Electric Company, is located at Profitt Mountain near Lesterville, Reynolds County, Missouri. The electrical generators are powered by water flowing from a reservoir at the top of the mountain through a 7,000-foot tunnel bored through the mountain to a lower reservoir. Visitors could formerly drive to the top of the mountain to view the operation before a breach in the upper reservoir in 2005.

Taum Sauk Mountain—Taum Sauk Mountain is the highest natural elevation in Missouri. It is located in Iron County and is part of the St. Francois Mountains. Geologists believe that Taum Sauk and its neighbors may be among the few areas in the United States that were never submerged by ancient seas. Mina Sauk Falls, the highest waterfall in Missouri, is located on Taum Sauk Mountain.

Taum Sauk Mountain State Park—Taum Sauk Mountain State Park was established at the site of Taum Sauk Mountain in 1991. It covers about 7,450 acres and is popular for camping and hiking. It and the contiguous Johnson Shut-Ins State Park in adjoining Reynolds County are under common jurisdiction, and together they make up the second-largest state park in the state at almost 16,000 acres. The Taum Sauk Trail, featuring the Devil's Tollgate, a canyon-like formation created by huge boulders on either side of the trail, goes through the state park.

Tavern Creek—Tavern Creek is an approximately forty-mile tributary of the Osage River, which forms in northern Pulaski County, Missouri, and winds generally northward through Miller County to the Osage.

Taylor, Gene—Gene Taylor was a Republican politician from Southwest Missouri who served eight terms in the U. S. Congress from 1973 to 1989. He was born near Sarcoxie and served as mayor of the town during the 1950s while starting a local automobile dealership, which he continued to run until after he was elected to Congress.

Taylor, Theodore T.—Theodore T. Taylor was a colonel in the Missouri State Guard and later a captain in the Confederate army. A resident of Springfield at the outbreak of the Civil War, he briefly commanded the Southern forces there during the late summer of 1861 after Sterling Price marched north to the Missouri River following the Confederate victory at Wilson's Creek.

Temperature Extremes—All the temperature extremes in the Ozarks have occurred in the region's fringe areas. The coldest temperature ever recorded is -40 degrees Fahrenheit on February 13, 1905, at Warsaw, Missouri, at the northwest edge of the region. Warsaw is also tied with Union, Missouri, for the hottest temperature ever recorded in Missouri with 118 degrees on July 14, 1954, while Ozark, Arkansas, lying on the southern outskirts of the Ozarks, recorded 120 degrees on August 10, 1936.

Tenkiller, Oklahoma—Tenkiller is community of about 550 people in Cherokee County, located on the banks of Tenkiller Ferry Lake at the western edge of the Ozarks.

Teresita, Missouri—Established in 1904, Teresita is an unincorporated community in western Shannon County. The infamous Welton murder happened near Teresita in 1919.

Texas County, Missouri—Located in south central Missouri, Texas County is the largest county in the state. It was originally called Ashley County when it was formed in 1843, but the name was changed to Texas in 1845 in honor of the Republic of Texas. Houston was laid out and named the county seat the following year in honor of Sam Houston.

Texas Road—The Texas Road was a road running generally north and south through Indian Territory in the western Ozarks that white settlers often used when traveling to Texas prior to the Civil War. The Military Road and the Shawnee Trail approximated the Texas Road, and the three terms were sometimes used almost interchangeably.

Thayer, Missouri—Thayer is a town of about 2,250 people in Oregon County near the Arkansas border. Laid out in 1882 as a railroad town, it was originally named Augusta, but the name was changed to Thayer in honor of Nathaniel Thayer, a wealthy stockholder in the railroad. Thayer is home to the Thayer R-2 School District.

Theodosia, Missouri—Theodosia is a village of about 250 people located in southwest Ozark County on Bull Shoals Lake. The post office was established in 1887, and the place was named for the first postmaster's wife.

Tiemann Shut-Ins—See Millstream Gardens Conservation Area.

Thomas, Andy—Andy Thomas is an artist from Carthage, Missouri, known especially for his Civil War and western paintings.

Thomas, David Yancey—David Yancey Thomas was chairman of the Department of History at the University of Arkansas at Fayetteville for twenty-eight years, and he was instrumental in establishing the Arkansas Historical Association in 1941. He was the author of several books about Arkansas and its people.

Thomasville, Missouri—Thomasville is a small community in northwest Oregon County. Originally called Rich Woods, it is the oldest community in the county, having been settled in the 1810s. The town of Thomasville was laid out in 1846 as the first county seat. The county seat was moved to Alton in 1851 when Howell County was carved out of Oregon County. A good portion of Thomasville was burned during the Civil War, but the town rebuilt and thrived after the war until, during the twentieth century, time began to pass it by.

Thorncrown Chapel—Thorncrown Chapel is a chapel located in Eureka Springs, Arkansas, that has won numerous awards for its architecture. Designed by architect E. Fay Jones, it was financed and built on land owned by Jim Reed, and it opened in 1980.

Thorncrown Chapel at Eureka Springs. *Courtesy Wikimedia.*

Thornton, Joe—Joe Thornton was a notorious character who mortally wounded a Joplin policeman in the summer of 1885 and was lynched by the townspeople before the officer died.

Three Brothers, Arkansas—Three Brothers is an unincorporated community located on U.S. Highway 5 in Baxter County a few miles south of the Missouri line.

Three Rivers Community College—Three Rivers Community College is a junior college at Poplar Bluff, Missouri. Opened in 1967, it has a student population of almost 5,000, and it has several other centers throughout southeast Missouri in addition to the main campus at Poplar Bluff.

Tiff City, Missouri—Tiff City is an unincorporated community in western McDonald County near the Oklahoma line. It was platted in 1881 and named for the barite ore, also called tiff, which was found nearby. Barite has been more extensively mined in other parts of the Ozarks, notably the Tiff District of Washington County, Missouri.

Tillman, John N.—Born near Springfield, Missouri, John N. Tillman graduated from the University of Arkansas, practiced law in Fayetteville, and served as president of the university from 1905 to 1912. He represented northwest Arkansas in the U.S. House of Representatives from 1915 to 1929.

Timbo, Arkansas—Timbo is an unincorporated community in Stone County. It is known for its tradition of old-time music. Singer and songwriter Jimmy Driftwood lived at Timbo, and folklorist and music producer Alan Lomax recorded folk music there.

Tin Mountain—Tin Mountain is located about nine miles southwest of Fredericktown, Missouri. In 1870, after Iron Mountain had become famous for the purity of its iron ore, an elaborate mining operation was begun at Tin Mountain under the belief that the mountain contained tin, but the operation collapsed as quickly as it began when almost no tin was found.

Tipton, Missouri—Tipton is a town in east-central Moniteau County. It was established in 1858 as the western terminus of the Pacific Railroad and grew rapidly. Later the same year, it also became the eastern terminus of the Butterfield Overland Stage. Gene Clark, musician for the New Christy Minstrels and the Byrds, was born in Tipton and is buried there. Tipton has a population of slightly over 3,000, and it is home to the Tipton R-6 School District. Although many residents of Tipton do not consider themselves part of the Ozarks, by most geographic definitions the town is at least on the edge of the Ozarks.

Tipton Ford Train Wreck—On August 5, 1914, a passenger train of the Missouri and North Arkansas Railroad collided head-on with a Kansas City Southern freight train at Tipton Ford in Newton County, Missouri, killing approximately fifty people. Many of the victims were black residents of Neosho returning home from an Emancipation Day celebration at Joplin. A mural at the First United Methodist Church of Neosho commemorates the spirit of unity between black and white citizens of Neosho that followed the tragic event.

Tomato Industry—The growing and canning of tomatoes was very important to the economy of the Ozarks from the 1890s to approximately the 1950s, with the industry's peak years being the 1920s and 1930s. Most of the canneries were small, family-owned operations, and almost every small town in the region had a cannery. In Missouri, Webster County alone had an estimated 100 canneries during the early 1900s. Many Ozarkians supplemented their income not only by growing tomatoes but also by working in the canneries, and tomatoes were sometimes called the "red gold of the Ozarks." The tomato industry waned after World War II, as small family farms gave way to specialized farming.

Tontitown, Arkansas—Tontitown is a town in Washington County of about 2,500 people. It was established in 1898 by Catholic priest Pietro Bandini as a colony for Italian immigrants. The town still retains a distinctive Italian character, and it hosts an annual grape festival celebrating its Italian heritage

Totten, James—James Totten was a Union general during the Civil War. He commanded the District of Southwest Missouri during the summer and fall of 1862 and later in the war commanded the District of Central Missouri.

Tracey, John P.—John P. Tracey was a Civil War solider, a newspaperman, and a politician from Springfield, Missouri. He served as a U.S. congressman from southwest Missouri from 1895 to 1897.

Trail of Tears—The Trail of Tears is a name given to the several routes followed by Native Americans, mostly Cherokee, when they were forcefully removed by the U.S. government from the Southeast and relocated to lands in Indian Territory (present-day Oklahoma) during the 1830s. The term, which derives from the immense suffering that the tribes endured along the way, may also refer to the removal itself. Most of the several different routes utilized during the removal passed through or skirted the Ozarks. The National Park Service delineates the Trail of Tears with historic markers and maintains various sites along the way as the Trail of Tears National Historic Trail.

Trail of Tears Drama—*The Trail of Tears* drama is an outdoor play that has been performed since 1969 in the Tsa-La-Gi amphitheater near Tahlequah, Oklahoma. It depicts the removal of the Cherokee from their ancestral homeland during the early 1800s.

Trimble, James William—James William Trimble was a lawyer and politician from Berryville, Arkansas, who represented northwest Arkansas in the U.S. House of Representatives from 1945 to 1967.

Tripoli Mining—The mining of tripoli, a microcrystalline form of quartz used in grinding and polishing, began in southwest Missouri in 1871 when Thomas L. Luscombe discovered large deposits of the mineral, sometimes called "cotton rock," in western Newton County and began mining and shipping it. Tripoli is still mined in Seneca, Missouri, today. It was also mined in Benton County, Arkansas, from approximately 1929 to 1949.

Tri-State Mining District—The Tri-State Mining District is a term used to indicate the northeast tip of Oklahoma, the southeast corner of Kansas, and the southwest part of Missouri, where lead and zinc were mined in large quantities during the late 1800s and early 1900s.

Tri-State Tornado of 1925—Claiming 695 lives, the Tri State Tornado of March 18, 1925, was the deadliest tornado in U.S. history. It first sat down near Ellington in the eastern Missouri Ozarks and then crossed Illinois into Indiana, leaving a 219-mile track of destruction in its wake.

Trout Fishing in America—Trout Fishing in America is a folk-rock musical duo best known for its family and children's songs. The four-time Grammy nominated duo is based in northwest Arkansas near Prairie Grove.

Truitt's Cave—Truitt's Cave is a former show cave in Lanagan, Missouri, that was famous for its underground restaurant. The cave closed about ten years ago. Named for John A. Truitt, the so-called

"Caveman of the Ozarks," it was one of several show caves developed by Truitt in the area during the early twentieth century.

Truman, Harry S—Born on the fringes of the Ozarks at Lamar, Missouri, in 1884, Harry S Truman was the 33rd president of the United States, serving from 1945 to 1953.

Truman Reservoir—Originally called the Kaysinger Bluff Reservoir, the Truman Reservoir (aka Truman Lake) is the largest manmade lake in Missouri. It was formed by the damming of the Osage River west of Warsaw. Construction began in 1964 and was completed in 1979, and during the interval the name was changed to Truman Reservoir in honor of former President Truman. Much of the lake, which covers about 55,600 acres, is located in Benton County, where the dam is, but the waters also spill into several surrounding counties.

Tumbling Shoals, Arkansas—Tumbling Shoals is a community of about 1,000 people in central Cleburne County near Heber Springs.

Tunas, Missouri—Tunas is an unincorporated community on State Highway 73 in northern Dallas County. During the early to mid-1900s, Tunas had a high school and several businesses, but little remains of the once-thriving village.

Tunnel Bluff—Tunnel Bluff is a natural tunnel in a bluff about fifty feet above the channel of the Current River near the Carter-Ripley county line in southeast Missouri.

Turnbo, Silas C.--Silas C. Turnbo was a farmer and "scribbler," as he called himself, who collected hundreds of stories and reminiscences about life during the 1800s along the White River Valley of northwest Arkansas and southwest Missouri. Two volumes of his stories were published during the early 1900s as *Fireside Stories of the Early Days in the Ozarks*, but many were never published. The Turnbo Collection, including his original manuscripts, is held at the Springfield-Greene County Library.

Turpentine Creek Wildlife Refuge—Turpentine Creek Wildlife Refuge is a sanctuary for big cats and other endangered wildlife located near Eureka Springs, Arkansas.

Tuscumbia, Missouri—Tuscumbia is a village of about 200 people and the county seat of Miller County. It was surveyed and named the county seat shortly after county formation in 1837. It is thought that the town was named after Tuscumbia, Alabama. Tuscumbia is home to the Miller County R-3 Schools and the Miller County Museum.

Tutt-Everett War—The Tutt-Everett War was a violent struggle over political power in Marion County, Arkansas, during the 1840s that mainly involved the Tutt and Everett families, who were allied with the Whig and Democratic parties respectively. It spanned about six years and claimed the lives of up to fourteen victims. The feud began at a political gathering in Yellville in 1844 and, after a period of rising tensions and minor confrontations, it reached a climax with a shootout in Yellville on October 9, 1848, that claimed the life of Simmons "Sim" Everett, a leader of the Everett faction. The Everetts retaliated two days later by killing several members of the King family, who had participated in the shootout on the side of the Tutts. The Arkansas governor called out the militia to restore order, but it was disbanded six weeks later. The final act of the "war" was the murder in 1850 of Hansford "Hamp" Tutt, a senior member of the Tutt family.

Twelve Corners—Twelve Corners is a historic community in Benton County, Arkansas, near Pea Ridge. It is the site of one of the oldest churches in the county. During the Civil War, Confederates camped at Twelve Corners at the time of the Battle of Pea Ridge.

Twin Bridges State Park—Twin Bridges State Park is an Oklahoma state park in Ottawa County on the north side of Grand Lake. Named for two bridges that carry traffic across arms of the lake along U.S. Highway 60, it is known for its quiet atmosphere and good fishing.

Twin Falls—See Ozark National Forest.

Twin Oaks, Oklahoma—Twin Oaks is a community of about 190 people in southern Delaware County.

Tyrone, Missouri—Tyrone, a small community in Texas County, was the site of a mass murder on February 26, 2015, when Joseph Jesse Aldridge killed seven people and then took his own life.

Tyson Foods—Tyson Foods is a corporation based in Springdale, Arkansas. It is the second largest producer and marketer of chicken, beef, and pork in the world. The company was founded in 1935 by John W. Tyson.

U

Ulman, Missouri—Ulman is an unincorporated community in Miller County about six miles south of Tuscumbia. Originally called

Ulman's Ridge, the place was named for a Mr. Ulman who settled in the area well before the Civil War, but the town was not established until the late 1800s.

Underhill, Wilbur—Wilbur Underhill was a notorious gangster during the 1920s and early 1930s who operated in the Tri-State area of Missouri, Kansas, and Oklahoma, earning the nickname the Tri-State Terror. He was the most wanted man in the region by the time he was mortally wounded by law officers in Oklahoma in late 1933. He died in early 1934 and was brought back to his hometown of Joplin, Missouri, for burial.

Union, Missouri—Union is the county seat of Franklin County at the northeast edge of the Ozarks. It has a population of about 10,000 people and is the home to the Union R-11 School District and to East Central College, a community college with four other branches throughout central Missouri.

Union City, Missouri—Union City is a small community in northern Stone County. Previously called School, it was a booming little town in the early 1900s with four general stores and several other businesses, but scarcely anything remains to suggest its former prosperity. Joplin was also briefly called Union City during its early history.

Union Pacific Railroad—Dating from 1861, the Union Pacific Railroad has grown through acquisition of other railroads like the Missouri Pacific and is now the largest system in the United States and is BNSF's chief competitor. The Union Pacific's lines in the Ozarks are primarily in the fringe areas of the region

Uniontown, Arkansas—Uniontown is a small community in Crawford County near the Oklahoma border. It is the site of the Slack-Comstock-Marshall Farm, which is on the National Register of Historic Places.

United Keetoowah Band—The United Keetoowah Band is a Cherokee Indian tribe headquartered in Tahlequah, Oklahoma. Most of the members of the tribe are descendants of the "Old Settlers," who migrated to Arkansas and Oklahoma about 1817. On the other hand, members of the much larger Cherokee Nation, which also is headquartered at Tahlequah, mostly descend from the Cherokee who were forcibly relocated in the late 1830s.

University of Arkansas-Fayetteville—The University of Arkansas-Fayetteville is a public, land-grant institution of higher learning located at Fayetteville, Arkansas, offering four-year undergraduate and graduate degrees in a wide variety of fields. Begun in 1871 as Arkansas Industrial University, it is the main campus of the University of Arkansas System and is considered a research university with a high level of research activity. It has a student population of almost 25,000.

University of the Ozarks—The University of the Ozarks is a four-year private institution of higher learning in Clarksville, Arkansas. Situated in the Arkansas River Valley, it is, despite its name, not technically in the Ozarks.

Upton, Lucille Morris—Lucille Morris Upton was a newspaper reporter and columnist best known for her "Over the Ozarks" and "Good Old Days" columns in Springfield, Missouri, newspapers during the 1940s, 1950s, and 1960s. She also authored a book about the Bald Knobbers.

Urbana, Missouri—Urbana is a town of about 420 people in northwest Dallas County. A post office named Andersonville existed nearby or at the same site prior to the Civil War, but the name was changed to Urbana in the late 1800s. Urbana is home to the Skyline Hickory County R-1 Schools.

V

Valles Mines, Missouri—Valles Mines is an unincorporated community in southern Jefferson County. It was founded by Francois Valle as a lead mining camp during the late 1700s.

Valley Springs, Arkansas—Valley Springs is a town of about 175 population in southeast Boone County. Settled in the mid-1800s, it was originally called Twin Springs because two underground springs surfaced at the site. Valley Springs is home to the Valley Springs School District.

Van Buren, Arkansas—Van Buren, the county seat of Crawford County, is a town of about 23,000 people. Located on the Arkansas River, it is not, strictly speaking, part of the Ozarks, but it is often considered to be at the edge of the region.

Van Buren, Missouri—Van Buren is the county seat of Carter County. The town was formed in 1833 as the county seat of Ripley County and named for then Vice-President Martin Van Buren. When a portion of Ripley County that included Van Buren became part of Carter County in 1859, Van Buren was named the seat of the new county. About the same time, the site of the town was moved from the west side of the Current River to its present location on the east side, and the original site became known as Old Van Buren. Van Buren has a population of about 820 people, and it is home to the Van Buren R-1 Schools. There was also a Van Buren about five miles southeast of Linn, Missouri, that was laid out about 1841 to be the seat of Osage County, but it quickly died when it did not achieve that aim.

Van Dorn, Earl—Earl Van Dorn was a Confederate general during the Civil War known in the Ozarks primarily for his defeat at the Battle of Pea Ridge.

Vaughan, Joseph Floyd "Arky"—Joseph Floyd "Arky" Vaughan was a Major League Baseball player for the Pittsburgh Pirates and Brooklyn Dodgers, primarily a shortstop, during the 1930s and 1940s. Born in Clifty, Arkansas, he got his nickname because of his Arkansas drawl. He was elected to the Hall of Fame in 1985.

Vera Cruz, Missouri—Vera Cruz is a small community in eastern Douglas County. Originally called Red Bud, it served as the first county seat of Douglas County. A dispute over the location of the county seat resulted in its being moved to Arno in 1869 and finally to Ava in 1871.

Vernon County, Missouri—Vernon County is located in southwest Missouri bordering Kansas. The southeast corner of the county is at the edge of the Ozarks.

Verona, Missouri—Verona is a town of about 700 people located in southern Lawrence County. It was settled by Swedish families in the early 1870s. In 1875 a colony of Waldensians arrived in the community from Italy by way of South America and ultimately settled in Barry County just south of Monett. Verona is home to the Verona R-VII School District.

Versailles, Missouri—Founded in 1835, Versailles is the county seat of Morgan County. It was named after Versailles, France, but the Missouri town is pronounced Ver-Sayles. Versailles survived two disastrous fires in the 1880s. Today, it has a population of about 2,700 people and is home to the Morgan County R-2 Schools and the Morgan County Historical Museum. Joseph Franklin Rutherford, founder of the Jehovah's Witnesses, was born at Versailles, and Bud Walton, co-founder of Wal-Mart, opened his first store in Versailles.

Viburnum, Missouri—Viburnum is a town of about 800 in northwest Iron County. It started as a small settlement along the railroad during the iron and lead smelting boom in the area during the late 1800s and was named for the viburnum honeysuckle. After virtually dying out, the town revived in the 1950s when lead mining once again flourished in the region. Today, a mining facility of the Doe Run Company, one of the largest lead mining companies in the world, is located near Viburnum, and the town is home to the Iron County C-4 School District.

Vichy, Missouri—Vichy is an unincorporated village in southern Maries County on U. S. Highway 63 about ten miles north of Rolla. It sprang up during the early 1880s as a mineral-water resort and was named for the French city of Vichy. It is the site of the Vichy Campground Church of God, and the Rolla National Airport is located nearby.

Vienna, Missouri—Vienna is the county seat of Maries County. It was founded in 1855 and reportedly named after Vienna, Austria, as a compromise after a county judge wanted to name it Vie Anna in memory of a relative. It has a population of slightly over 600 people and is home to the Maries R-1 School District.

Villa Ridge, Missouri—Villa Ridge is a community of about 2,420 people in northeast Franklin County.

Vining, Peggy—Peggy Vining is the Poet Laureate of Arkansas. She has been active in several regional writers' organizations, including the Eureka Springs-based Ozark Creative Writers, which she directed for over ten years.

Viola, Arkansas—Viola is a town of about 380 people in Fulton County. It is home to the Viola Public Schools.

Virdon, Bill—Bill Virdon was a Major League Baseball player and manager who grew up in West Plains and attended Drury College in Springfield. He was an outstanding defensive centerfielder for the St. Louis Cardinals and Pittsburgh Pirates during the 1950s and 1960s, and he managed the Pirates, the New York Yankees, the Houston Astros, and the Montreal Expos during the 1970s and 1980s.

W

Waco, Missouri—Waco is a town of about 90 people in western Jasper County near the Kansas border. It was laid off in 1878, and it is thought that it was named for Waco, Texas.

Waddill, James R.—James R. Waddill was a U.S. congressman who lived at Springfield, Missouri, and represented the old Sixth District in the southwest part of the state from 1879 to 1881.

Wade, William H.—William H. Wade was a U.S. congressman from Greene County, Missouri, from 1885 to 1891. He died in 1911 and is buried at Maple Park Cemetery in Springfield.

Wagoner, Porter—Porter Wagoner was a county music singer who achieved his greatest fame during the 1960s and early 1970s when his weekly syndicated television show was at its peak of popularity. Waggoner was born and grew up in West Plains, Missouri, and he appeared regularly on the Ozark Jubilee in Springfield during the mid-1950s. He died in 2007. A street in West Plains is named for him.

Walker, David—David Walker was a prominent citizen of early-day Fayetteville and a member of the convention that drafted Arkansas's first constitution. He was a lawyer and a leading Whig politician prior to the Civil War and after the war served as a justice on the state supreme court.

Walker, James David—James David Walker was a colonel in the Confederate army during the Civil War and a U. S. senator from Arkansas from 1879 to 1885. He lived most of his life in Fayetteville and died there in 1906.

Walker, Tandy—Tandy Walker was a Confederate officer who led the First Regiment Choctaw and Chickasaw Mounted Rifles at the First Battle of Newtonia in September 1862.

Waller, Charles, hanging of—Charles Waller was hanged at Marshfield, Missouri, on May 17, 1872, in the only legal execution in Webster County history, for the triple murder of William Newland, his wife, and their eighteen-month-old son. A reported 5,000 to 7,000 people attended the hanging.

Wal-Mart Stores—Wal-Mart Stores, branded as Walmart, is a large corporation that runs a worldwide chain of discount and warehouse stores. Started in 1962 by Sam Walton in Rogers, Arkansas, and now headquartered in Bentonville, Walmart is the largest employer in the United States and the world's most profitable retail outlet.

Walnut Grove, Missouri—Walnut Grove is a town of about 670 people located in northwest Greene County. The area was settled before the Civil War and named for a grove of timber at the site that was composed mostly of walnut trees. The town was often called Possum Trot during its early days, and the community now hosts a festival each September called Possum Trot Days. Former major league baseball player Ken Gables was born and died in Walnut Grove. The town is home to the Walnut Grove R-5 Schools.

Walnut Ridge, Arkansas—Walnut Ridge is a town of about 5,000 people and the county seat of Lawrence County. The town was established in 1875 when a railroad came through the area. A community by the same name that had already existed nearby for a few years became known as Old Walnut Ridge, and most residents moved to the new town. Walnut Ridge became a dual county seat with Powhatan in 1870 and became the sole county seat in 1963. The town was the site of an infamous race war in 1912, home to the Walnut Ridge Army Flying School during World War II, and the site of the Beatles' stopover in 1964. Today, it is home to the Walnut Ridge Schools, which are part of the Lawrence County School District.

Walton Arts Center—The Walton Arts Center is a visual and performing arts center in Fayetteville on the campus of the University of Arkansas.

Walton, Sam—Sam Walton was the founder of Wal-Mart and Sam's Club. He opened Walton's Five and Dime in Bentonville, Arkansas, in 1950 and soon owned a chain of Ben Franklin stores. In 1962, he opened the first Wal-Mart in Rogers.

War Eagle Arts and Crafts Fair—The War Eagle Arts and Crafts Fair (aka Ozark Arts and Crafts Fair) is a four-day event held each October at the War Eagle Mill near the small community of War Eagle in eastern Benton County, Arkansas. Begun in 1954, it is perhaps the largest arts and crafts festival in the Ozarks, drawing an estimated 130,000 visitors annually. The historic War Eagle Mill is a working mill that was built in 1973 on the same foundation as its predecessor, which was built shortly after the Civil War on the same site as two earlier mills.

War Eagle Cavern—War Eagle Cavern is a commercial cave on Beaver Lake about fifteen miles east of Rogers, Arkansas. Opened to the public in 1978, it offers walking tours.

Ward, Essie Ann Treat—Essie Ann Treat Ward was an artist whose paintings depicting farm animals and rural life are considered excellent examples of primitive art, a style of folk painting. Treat was born and grew up in Searcy County, Arkansas, and she is sometimes called the Grandma Moses of the Ozarks. Her paintings are displayed throughout the world, but probably the largest collection is owned by the Shiloh Museum at Springdale.

Ward, Leo—Leo Ward was the creator of the Arkansas Blue Bird of Happiness, a little bird-shaped figurine made of blue glass. Since their introduction in 1982, almost ten million bluebirds have been sold worldwide. Although Ward is retired, the bluebirds are still produced at Terra Studios, which he founded in the 1970s near Durham, Arkansas.

Wardsville, Missouri—Wardsville is a village of about 1,500 people in Cole County approximately eight miles due south of Jefferson City. It is home to the Blair Oaks R-2 School District.

Warsaw, Missouri—Warsaw is a town of about 2,125 people and the seat of Benton County. It was laid out as the county seat in 1838 and was reportedly named after Warsaw, Poland, in honor of Polish patriot Tadeusz Koscuiszko. The town was burned during the Civil War and was the site of several skirmishes. Former Major League Baseball player Jerry Lumpe grew up at Warsaw. The town is home to the Warsaw R-9 Schools.

Washburn, Missouri—Washburn is a town of about 435 people in southwest Barry County. It was settled before the Civil War and named Keetsville. It was destroyed during the war. Rebuilt after the war, it was renamed Washburn in 1868 and incorporated in 1880. Washburn is home to the Southwest R-5 School District.

Washington, Missouri—Washington is a town of about 14,000 on the Missouri River in northern Franklin County. It is home to the Washington R-12 Schools.

Washington County, Arkansas—Washington County, located in the northwest part of the state, was created in 1828 when Lovely County, which contained the territory of present-day Washington, was abolished. The town of Washington Courthouse, located near the center of the new county, became the county seat, but its name was changed to Fayetteville the following year.

Washington County, Missouri—Washington County is located in the eastern Ozarks in the east central part of Missouri. Mining in the area and scattered settlement began in the late 1700s, and the county was established in 1813 from territory taken from Ste. Genevieve County. Potosi was named the county seat in 1814.

Washington State Park—Washington State Park is an 1,800-acre Missouri state park northeast of Potosi on the Washington-Jefferson county line. The picnic shelters and other structures at the park were built by African-American stonemasons of the Civilian Conservation Corps during the Depression.

Watie, Stand—Stand Watie (Cherokee for "stand firm") was a Cherokee Indian leader and Confederate brigadier general during the Civil War. After other Treaty Party leaders were killed in 1839 by Anti-Treaty Party members, Stand Watie emerged as the main leader of the

Cherokee chief and Confederate general Stand Watie. *Stand Watie #31455 in the collection of Wilson's Creek National Battlefield, Courtesy of the National Park Service.*

Treaty faction. When the Civil War began, most Cherokees joined the Confederacy, and Stand Watie rose to the rank of brigadier general. Most of his activities during the war were confined to Indian Territory (e.g. the two battles of Cabin Creek), but his forces also played an important role at the Battle of Pea Ridge. Stand Waite is buried at Polson Cemetery in Delaware County, Oklahoma, just across the state line from Southwest City, Missouri. (See Cherokee Indians)

Watson, Patrick Samuel Gideon—Considered the father of Baptist history in Arkansas, Patrick Samuel Gideon Watson was an itinerant preacher who established several Baptist churches in northern Arkansas prior to the Civil War.

Watts, Oklahoma—Watts is a town of about 325 people in northeast Adair County near the Arkansas state line. Watts is home to the Watts Public School.

Waugh's Farm, Skirmish at—The Skirmish at Waugh's Farm was a Civil War action that occurred about twelve miles west of Batesville, Arkansas, on February 18, 1864. A body of Confederate cavalry under Captain George Rutherford attacked a Union wagon train under Captain William Castle, killing four men, wounding ten, and capturing 32, with only one reported Confederate casualty.

Wayne County, Missouri--Located in southeastern Missouri at the edge of the Ozarks, Wayne County was created in 1818. At the time, it encompassed almost all of the southern part of Missouri Territory and was sometimes referred to as the State of Wayne. Greenville was laid off as the county seat in 1819.

Waynesville, Missouri—Waynesville is a town of about 5,000 people in central Missouri and the seat of Pulaski County. It was laid off in 1834 as the county seat shortly after the county was formed and was supposedly named for Revolutionary War general Anthony Wayne. Waynesville is home to the Waynesville R-6 Schools.

Weaver, Dennis—Dennis Weaver was a television and film actor best known for his TV roles in *Gunsmoke, Gentle Ben,* and *McCloud.* He grew up in Joplin, Missouri, where a street is named for him.

Weaver, Emily—Emily Weaver was a young woman from Batesville, Arkansas, who was arrested in 1864 in St. Louis by Union authorities and sentenced to hang as a spy, but her case was eventually dropped for lack of evidence.

Weaver Brothers and Elviry—Originally from Christian County, Missouri, the Weaver Brothers and Elviry (Leon and Frank Weaver, known as Abner and Cicero; and Leon's wife, June Petrie Weaver, known as Elviry) was a popular country music and comedy touring act during the 1920s. It combined hillbilly humor and various musical performances similar to the TV show "Hee Haw" decades later.

Weaubleau, Missouri—Weaubleau is a town of about 420 people located in southwestern Hickory County. It was surveyed in 1880, having grown up around Weaubleau Christian Institute, a male and female academy that had been started on the prairie about ten years earlier by the Christian denomination. The town was originally called Haren or Haran but soon became known as Weaubleau. The Weaubleau Institute lasted until well into the 1900s. Today, the town is home to the Weaubleau R-3 Schools.

Weaubleau-Osceola Structure—The Weaubleau-Osceola structure is a crater nineteen kilometers wide in St. Clair County, Missouri, centered near the community of Vista. It is believed to have been caused by a meteor impact millions of years ago. Surrounding the impact area are spherical rock formations of varying size, called the Missouri rock balls, which probably formed at the time of the impact. Similar geologic features in the Missouri Ozarks include the Decaturville dome in Camden County, the Hazelgreen volcanics near the Laclede-Pulaski County line, the Crooked Creek structure in southern Crawford County, the Furnace Creek volcanics in Washington County, and the Avon structure in Ste. Genevieve County. Because all of these features occur linearly along the same latitude, some scientists have postulated that they were created at the same time by a series of meteor impacts, but others have disputed this hypothesis, claiming that at least some of them are volcanic in origin.

Webb City, Missouri—Webb City is a town of about 11,000 in Jasper County. It was founded as a lead mining community in 1875 and was a booming mining town until after World War I. Today, Webb City is known, among other reasons, as the home of the Praying Hands statue. It is also known for its high school football teams, which have won numerous state champion-ships and produced many outstanding players, like former NFL defensive end Grant Wistrom. Former NBC correspondent Lisa Myers also graduated from Webb City High. The town is home to the Webb City R-7 School District.

Kneeling Miner statue at Webb City, Mo. *Photo by the author.*

Webster County, Missouri—Webster County was formed in 1855 from territory taken from Greene and Wright counties. Because Marshfield was the largest town in the new county and its soon-to-be-named county seat, the county was named for U.S. senator Daniel Webster from Marshfield, Massachusetts.

Weer, William—William Weer was a Union colonel during the Civil War. He led the so-called Indian Expedition into Indian Territory in 1861 and played important roles in the Battle of Newtonia in September of 1862 and the Battle of Prairie Grove in December of 1862.

Welch Spring—Located on the Current River in Shannon County, Welch Spring is the fifth-largest spring in the state of Missouri. In the early twentieth century, Dr. C.H. Diehl, believing the waters had healing powers, built a hospital and healing resort at the site, but it never attracted many people and was sold by the county at a tax sale in 1933.

Welling, Oklahoma—Welling is a community of about 670 people in Cherokee County.

Welton Murder Case—The Welton murder case was a notorious crime that occurred in Shannon County, Missouri, in January of 1919. Frank Welton deserted his common-law wife, Carrie Hofland, and Carrie tracked him down and killed his new wife, Pearl Welton, on a farm near Teresita. Both Hofland and Welton were convicted of murder, although Welton's conviction was overturned.

Wenrich, Percy—Percy Wenrich was composer of ragtime music during the early 1900s. His popular songs included "When You Wore a Tulip and I Wore a Big Red Rose." He was born in Joplin, Missouri, in 1887 and lived there until he was a teenager.

Wentworth, Missouri—Wentworth is a village of about 150 people in northeast Newton County. It was established as a mining town in the 1880s.

West, Kincheon "Kinch"—Kincheon "Kinch" West was a Confederate-allied guerrilla during the Civil War. He was from Dade County, Missouri, and is best known for his raid on Melville (now Dadeville) in that county on June 14, 1864.

West Aurora, Missouri—West Aurora is a small village in Miller County that sprang up about a mile southwest of Aurora Springs when a Missouri Pacific Railroad station was located there in the early 1880s.

West Eminence, Missouri—West Eminence is a small village about a mile and a half west of Eminence in Shannon County. It sprang up in the early 1900s after the Missouri Mining and Lumber Company located a sawmill in the vicinity, and it quickly grew to a reported population of several thousand people. The lumber boom lasted only about twenty years, and today little remains of West Eminence's glory days.

Western Grove, Arkansas—Western Grove is a town of about 385 people located on U.S. Highway 65 in northeast Newton County. It is home to Western Grove High School, which is part of the Ozark Mountain School District.

West Fork, Arkansas—West Fork is a town of about 2,320 people in Washington County about ten miles south of Fayetteville along U.S. 71/I-540. It was established in 1885 with the coming of a railroad through the area, but it grew slowly until recent decades, when its growth accelerated as the town became a bedroom community for Fayetteville. It is home to the West Fork Public Schools.

West Fork, Missouri—West Fork is a small community in northwest Reynolds County. It was established near the turn of the twentieth century and named for its location on the West Fork of the Black River. It is the home of the West Fork Mine.

Westphalia, Missouri—Westphalia is town of about 400 people in Osage County. It was settled during the mid-1830s by a Catholic colony from the Westphalia region of Germany. Although most people of Westphalia would probably not consider themselves residents of the Ozarks, the town is, by generally accepted geographic definitions, at least on the edge of the Ozarks. Westphalia is home to the Fatima School District.

West Plains, Missouri—West Plains is a town of 12,000 people and the seat of Howell County. It was founded about 1849 and given its name because of its location on the plains west of Thomasville, the nearest town. It was selected the county seat soon after Howell County was formed in 1857. The town was destroyed during the Civil War but quickly rebuilt afterward. Notable people who were born or lived at West Plains include actor Dick Van Dyke, country singers Porter Wagoner and Jan Howard, baseball players Preacher Roe and Bill Virdon, Civil War general Egbert B. Brown, and novelist Daniel Woodrell. The town is home to the West Plains R-7 Schools.

West Plains Campus-Missouri State University—MSU West Plains is a branch of Missouri State University. The satellite campus at West Plains offers two-year degrees, and more advanced degrees are available through the outreach program of the main campus, which is located at Springfield.

West Plains Dance Hall Explosion—On April 13, 1928, an explosion in a West Plains building where a Friday night dance was being held ignited a fire that engulfed the building and killed 39 people, mostly young people attending the dance. See *West Plains Dance Hall Explosion* by Lin Waterhouse.

West Siloam Springs, Oklahoma—West Siloam Springs is a town in southeast Delaware County on the Arkansas line. It was established in the 1960s when the population of Siloam Springs, Arkansas, spilled across the state line in sufficient numbers to warrant an Oklahoma-based city government.

Westville, Oklahoma—Westville is a town of about 1,640 people in eastern Adair County near the Arkansas state line. When Adair County was formed in 1907, Westville was selected as the county seat partly because of its location at the intersection of two important railroads, but the seat was moved to Stilwell in 1910. Westville is the home of the Westville Public School.

Wheatland, Missouri—Wheatland is a town in western Hickory County with a population of about 370. It was established after the Civil War in the late 1860s. It is home to the Wheatland R- 2 Schools.

Wheaton, Missouri—Wheaton is a town of about 700 people in western Barry County. It was platted in 1907 as a stop along the Missouri and North Arkansas Railroad, which was under construction at the time. Wheaton is home to the Wheaton R-3 School District.

Whitaker Point (aka Hawksbill Crag)—Whitaker Point is a rocky outcropping along Whitaker Point Trail in the Ozark National Forest about eleven miles southwest of Ponca, Arkansas. It is a popular spot for nature photographers.

White County, Arkansas—Located in central Arkansas, White County was formed in 1835 from parts of Independence, Jackson, and Pulaski counties, and Searcy was named the county seat. Only the northeast and north central parts of White County are in the Ozarks.

White Church, Missouri—White Church is a small community north of West Plains in Howell County. It got its name because a Cumberland Presbyterian church was built there during the Civil War era, plastered, and painted white. Other later churches were also painted white.

White River—The White River is an approximately 720-mile long tributary of the Mississippi River that flows through Arkansas and Missouri. It forms in northeast Arkansas in the Boston Mountains southeast of Fayetteville, loops northward into Missouri, and then flows in a generally southeast direction back into Arkansas and to its confluence with the Mississippi. It is impounded by eight dams along its course.

White-tailed deer—White-tailed deer were plentiful in the Ozarks until the late 1800s, when destruction of habitat and over-hunting began drastically to reduce their numbers. In the 1920s and 1930s, when perhaps 1,000 or fewer remained, Arkansas, Missouri, and Oklahoma began enforcing laws limiting the hunting of deer and also began bringing in deer from other states. The population of deer in the Ozarks has rebounded to over a million, and fall deer hunting season is a time that many hunters eagerly look forward to each year. In 1993, Arkansas named the white-tailed deer its official state mammal.

Whitewater, Missouri—Settled in 1866, Whitewater is a village of about 125 people in southwest Cape Girardeau County.

Whitewater Scandal—The Whitewater Scandal was a series of investigations leading to the impeachment of President Bill Clinton. It began as an inquiry into land transactions involving Clinton and his wife, Hillary Rodham Clinton, in 1978 when he was attorney general of Arkansas. The term "Whitewater" derived from the Whitewater Development Corporation, which the Clintons formed with James and Susan McDougal to develop a 230-acre tract of land on the White River in Marion County.

Wilburn Brothers—The Wilburn Brothers was a popular country music duo consisting of brothers Doyle and Teddy Wilburn. Born and reared in Hardy, Arkansas, the brothers were discovered as child performers and brought to the Grand Ole Opry in 1940 as the Wilburn Children. From the 1950s to the 1970s, they enjoyed success as the Wilburn Brothers.

Wild Animal Safari—Dating to 1971 when it opened as Exotic Animal Paradise, Wild Animal Safari is a 300-acre commercial animal park and tourist attraction just east of Strafford, Missouri, on I-44.

Wildcat Glades Conservation and Audubon Center—Wildcat Glades Conservation and Audubon Center is a park and conservation area at the south edge of Joplin, Missouri, that preserves some of the last remaining chert glades. There are only about 60 acres of chert glades in the world, and almost half of them are located here.

Wilder, Laura Ingalls—Laura Ingalls Wilder was an American author famous for her Little House series of children's books. In 1894, she and her husband moved to their Rocky Ridge Farm near Mansfield, Missouri, where, beginning in the early 1930s, she wrote her books. She lived there until her death in 1957. Based on her childhood experiences on the Great Plains, the Little House books inspired the 1970s and 1980s TV series *Little House on the Prairie*.

Laura Ingalls Wilder home at Mansfield, Mo. *Courtesy Wikipedia.*

Wilderness, Missouri—Wilderness is an unincorporated community in northeast Oregon County established about 1881. The name derives from the Irish Settlement, a community established near the Ripley-Oregon county line for poor Irish families by missionary-minded Catholic priests in the late 1850s. By the spring of 1859, about forty families had settled on the land. However, the community was devastated during the Civil War, leaving the area in ruins, and it became known as the Irish Wilderness. The area is now designated and protected as a wilderness by the U.S. government.

Wilderness Road of the Ozarks—Built shortly after the Civil War, the Wilderness Road of the Ozarks ran from Berryville, Arkansas, to Springfield, Missouri.

Wildlife Management Areas—The Arkansas Game and Fish Commission oversees more than 100 wildlife management areas, which are places for public hunting at little or no cost to participants. The areas are also used for picnicking, camping, and other outdoor activities. The largest WMA in the state is the Ozark National Forest Wildlife Management Area, which encompasses nearly 680,000 acres in north-central Arkansas. Missouri also has wildlife management areas, although they are usually called by other names such as conservation areas.

Willard, Missouri—Willard is a town of about 5,300 population in Greene County. It was laid out as a railroad town in 1884 by Dr. E. T. Robberson, and it was initially named after him. The name was changed when the first storeowner applied for a post office and was told there was already a post office in Missouri named Robberson or Robertson. Willard is home to the Willard R-2 Schools. Two Olympic athletes, Jason Pyrah and Lori Endicott, graduated from Willard High School, as did professional boxer B.J. Flores.

Williams, Clyde—Clyde Williams was a politician from Desoto, Missouri, who served in the U.S. House of Representatives from 1927 to 1929 and from 1931 to 1943.

Williams, George H.—George H. Williams was born at California, Missouri, attended Drury College in Springfield, and was a U.S. senator from Missouri from 1925 to 1926.

Williams, James M.--James M. Williams was a Union colonel during the Civil War. He commanded the First Kansas Colored Infantry at the battles of Cabin Creek and Honey Spring in Indian Territory in July of 1863.

Williams, Jeff—During the Civil War, Jeff Williams was a "mountain Unionist" or Union guerrilla from northern Conway County, Arkansas, where he lived on a farm. In the spring of 1862, his band joined the regular Union army, but after the term of their enlistment expired, they soon returned home and waged guerrilla warfare against irregular Confederate forces in the area until Williams was killed in February of 1865.

Williams, Miller—Miller Williams was an acclaimed poet and a professor of literature and creative writing at the University of Arkansas, where he served for many years as director of the university press. He died in 2015. Famous singer Lucinda Williams is his daughter.

Williams Baptist College—Williams Baptist College is a private, four-year, coeducational institution of higher learning located at Walnut Ridge, Arkansas. Founded at Jonesboro in 1941 as a two-year school called Southern Baptist College, it moved to Walnut Ridge in 1947, became a four-year college in 1984, and changed its name in 1991 to honor its founder, H.E. Williams.

Williamsville, Missouri—Williamsville is a town of about 350 people in Wayne County. It was laid out in 1872 along the line of the St. Louis, Iron Mountain and Southern Railroad, and it grew to a population of 100 within two years. Today, the town is home to the Williamsville Elementary School, which is part of the Greenville R-2 School District.

Williford, Arkansas—Williford is a town of about 75 people in northern Sharp County. It was established in the 1870s and named for Ambrose Williford, who helped organize the town. It is home to the Williford Public Schools.

Williford, C.C.—C.C. Williford was a colorful and legendary weatherman for Springfield, Missouri, radio station KWTO during the 1930s, 1940s, and early 1950s.

Willow Springs, Missouri—Willow Springs is a town of about 2,200 people in northern Howell County. It was named for a post office that was established several miles east of town at a spring surrounded by willow trees. The post office was moved to the town's current location in 1869. Willow Springs is home to the Willow Springs R-4 School District.

Wilson's Cave, Legend of—Wilson's Cave is located in Miller County, Missouri, near Iberia on the Barren Fork of Big Tavern Creek. According to legend, John Wilson and his family lived in the cave for a couple of years when they first arrived in the area about 1810 as very early white settlers, and by his request, Wilson was buried in the cave when he died over forty years later.

Wilson Creek—Wilson Creek is a tributary of the James River. It forms at Springfield and runs about fifteen miles southwest to the James. The creek gave its name to an important Civil War Battle that was fought near the stream.

Wilson, Charles Banks—Charles Banks Wilson was an American artist who was born in Springdale, Arkansas, and grew up in Miami, Oklahoma. Known especially for his western paintings, he died in 2013.

Wilson, Charles Morrow—Charles Morrow Wilson was a nationally known author and native of Fayetteville, Arkansas, whose books included several on Ozarks folkways, including *The Bodacious Ozarks*, published in 1959.

Wilson, Slim—Clyde Carol "Slim" Wilson was a singer, songwriter, and radio and TV personality who was well known in country music circles in the Ozarks for over fifty years, both as an individual performer and as a member of the Goodwill Family and the Tall Timber Trio. Nationally, he was perhaps best known as a regular performer in the late 1950s on ABC-TV's *Ozark Jubilee*, which was broadcast from Springfield, Missouri, and he later hosted his own show on local television in Springfield.

Wilson's Creek, Battle of—The Battle of Wilson's Creek was a Civil War battle fought about ten miles southwest of Springfield, Missouri, on August 10, 1861. The first major battle of the war west of the Mississippi, it resulted in a Union defeat and gave Southern forces temporary control of southwest Missouri. Confederate casualties totaled about 1,200 in killed, wounded, and missing, while the Union forces had about 1,300 casualties, including their leader, General Nathaniel Lyon, who was killed.

Wilson's Creek National Battlefield—Wilson's Creek National Battlefield is a national park near Republic, Missouri, which preserves the history of the Battle of Wilson's Creek.

Windsor, Missouri—Windsor is a town of about 2,900 people in Henry County on the northwest fringe of the Ozarks.

Windyville, Missouri—Windyville is an unincorporated community in eastern Dallas County. At one time, it was a thriving village with several businesses and a high school. The town is now virtually deserted, and since its demise, a legend has arisen suggesting that the town's buildings and cemeteries are haunted.

Wine Industry—German immigrants brought winemaking to the Hermann area in Gasconade County on the northern fringes of the Ozarks in the 1840s. After the Civil War German-Swiss immigrants introduced winemaking to the Altus area of Arkansas, and about the same time Hermann Jaeger brought grape-growing and winemaking to Newton County, Missouri. Around 1900, Italian immigrants introduced winemaking to the Tontitown, Arkansas, and Phelps County, Missouri, areas. Wine is still made in most of these areas today.

Winona, Missouri—Winona is a town of about 1,335 people in southeastern Shannon County. It got its start as a lumber town in 1889. Winona is a female Sioux name and a character in Longfellow's

"Hiawatha," but the town was reportedly named by Minnesota lumbermen after their hometown. Winona is home to the Winona R-3 Schools.

Winrod, Gordon—Gordon Winrod is an anti-Jewish minister who served over ten years in prison for abducting six of his grandchildren and holding them on his compound near Gainesville, Missouri, in 1994 and 1995.

Winslow, Arkansas—Winslow is a town of about 400 people in southern Washington County. The site was a stage stop called Summit House when a post office was established there in 1876. It was renamed after Edward F. Winslow, president of the Frisco Railroad, when the railroad reached the community in the early 1880s. Winslow was a popular summer resort during the late 1800s and early 1900s. Old West gunfighter John Joshua Webb died at Winslow in 1882, and western fiction writer Douglas C. Jones was born there in 1924. During the early 1900s, Winslow was home of the Helen Dunlap Memorial School for Mountain Girls. The Winslow Public Schools were consolidated with Greenland in 2005.

Wire Road—The Wire Road, often called the Old Wire Road today, was a road running from St. Louis to Fort Smith that got its name during the Civil War era when telegraph wires were strung along its path. Built during the 1830s as the Springfield Road or the St. Louis to Springfield Road, it generally followed an even earlier Indian trace known as the Osage Trail.

Wirth, Arkansas—Wirth is a small community in northern Sharp County. The area was sparsely settled until the 1880s when an influx of German immigrants moved there, and the town of Wirth, named for one of the German settlers, was established. Wirth was a prosperous little town during the early years of the twentieth century, but little remains of it today.

Withrow Springs State Park—Withrow Springs State Park is located in Madison County, Arkansas, about five miles north of Huntsville. The main feature of the park, Withrow Spring, was named after Richard Withrow, an early settler in the area. The park opened in 1965, and it offers camping, hiking, and other outdoor activities.

WMBH—WMBH is a radio station in Joplin, Missouri. Begun in 1926, it is sometimes cited as the first radio station in Joplin, although another short-lived station actually predated it.

Wolf, John Quincy, Jr.—Born and reared in Batesville, Arkansas, John Quincy Wolf, Jr. was a college English professor but is best remembered as a collector of Ozarks folklore and folk music, mostly from around the Batesville area. Among his "discoveries" was folksinger Jimmy Driftwood, who credited Wolf with convincing him to audition for the Nashville producers who eventually signed him to a record contract. The John Quincy Wolf, Jr. Folklore Collection is held at Lyon College in Batesville.

Wolf, Jacob—see Jacob Wolf House

Womack, Steve—A former mayor of Rogers, Arkansas, Steve Womack has represented the northwest part of the state in the U.S. House of Representatives since 2011.

Women's Community Club Band Shell—The Women's Community Club Band Shell is a landmark in Spring Park at Heber Springs, Arkansas, that is on the National Register of Historic Places. Built during the Depression as a New Deal public works project, it is still used for concerts and other performances.

Wonderland Cave—Wonderland Cave is a commercial cave and tourist site at Bella Vista, Arkansas. Its history as a well-known attraction dates at least to the 1930s, when it was home to an underground nightclub that hosted dances and other entertainment. It was placed on the National Register of Historic Places in 1988.

Wood, Forrest Lee—Forrest Lee Wood is considered the father of the modern bass boat. Born and reared in Flippin, Arkansas, he began his outdoor career as a fishing guide in the area and started Ranger Boats in 1968.

Wood, Reuben T.—Reuben T. Wood was a labor leader and a politician from Springfield, Missouri. He was a U.S. congressman representing southwest Missouri from 1933 to 1941 and was president of the Missouri Federation of Labor before and after his congressional term.

Woodrell, Daniel—Daniel Woodrell is an American novelist, perhaps best known for his 2006 novel *Winter's Bone*, an adaptation of which was made into a popular movie. Woodrell was born in Springfield, Missouri, and most of his stories are set in the Missouri Ozarks.

Woodson K. Woods Memorial Conservation Area—Located southeast of St. James, Missouri, the Woodson K. Woods Memorial

Conservation Area preserves 5,658 acres of land in Crawford and Phelps counties.

Wright, Harold Bell—Harold Bell Wright was a best-selling American author whose novel *The Shepherd of the Hills*, which is set in the Ozarks, is often credited with helping to popularize the Branson area as a tourist destination. Prior to gaining fame as a novelist, Wright was a minister, and he pastored churches at Pierce City, Missouri, and Lebanon, Missouri, among other places.

Harold Bell Wright Museum housed in church pastored by Wright at Pierce City. *Photo by author.*

Wright County, Missouri—Located in south central Missouri, Wright County was formed in 1841 from Pulaski County and named for Silas Wright, a U.S. senator from New York.

Writers Hall of Fame—The Writers Hall of Fame is an organization established in Springfield, Missouri, in 1994 to honor accomplished writers. Many but not all of its honorees have a tie to the Ozarks.

Wyandotte, Oklahoma—Wyandotte is a town of about 335 people located in eastern Ottawa County near the Missouri border. It is the tribal headquarters of the Wyandotte Nation. The Wyandotte Indians were moved to the area in 1867, and the tribe gives the town its name. Wyandotte is home to the Wyandotte Public Schools and three casinos.

Wyandotte Nation's tribal headquarters at Wyandotte, Oklahoma. *Photo by the author.*

Y

Yell, Archibald—Archibald Yell was a circuit judge during the territorial days of Arkansas and became the state's first representative to the U.S. House. He was the state's second governor and later returned to the House of Representatives. As colonel of an Arkansas regiment during the Mexican War, he died leading a heroic charge at the Battle of Buena Vista. He is buried at Fayetteville, where he made his home.

Yellowhammer—Part of the back-to-the-land movement of the 1970s, Yellowhammer was a women's communal living farm in Madison County, Arkansas, during the mid to late seventies.

Yellville, Arkansas—Yellville is the county seat of Marion County. Originally called Shawneetown because of the Shawnee Indians who lived in the area during early frontier days, the community changed its name to Yellville in 1836 when Marion became a county and the town was named the county seat. The new name was selected in honor of Archibald Yell, Arkansas's first representative to the U.S. House. Yellville has a population of about 1,200 people, and it is home to the Yellville-Summit School District.

Yocum, Arkansas—Yocum was a once thriving little town in northeast Carroll County, but little remains of it today. A Civil War skirmish occurred on nearby Yocum Creek on November 15, 1862.

Yocum Silver Dollar—The legend of the Yocum Silver Mine and the Yocum Silver Dollar is one of numerous legends about lost treasure in the Ozarks. A family named Yocum or Yoakum were among the first white settlers in present-day Stone County, Missouri, and they were friendly with the area's Delaware Indians, who supposedly worked a silver mine near the James River. The Yocums traded horses and blankets to the Indians in exchange for the mine and started minting their own silver dollars, and the coins became a common medium of exchange in the Ozarks during the 1820s and 1830s. That Yocum dollars existed is a fairly well established fact, but, instead of coming from a silver mine, they probably came from Federal specie the Yocums got through illegal trade with the Indians and then recast to hide their illegal activities. (See Lynn Morrow, "The Yocum Silver Dollar," in *White River Valley Historical Quarterly*, Spring 1985.)

Young Brothers—Brothers Harry and Jennings Young, two small-time crooks, became infamous for a January 2, 1932, shootout with law officers at the Young farm just west of Springfield, Missouri, near Brookline that left six lawmen dead. The so-called Young Brothers Massacre still stands as the deadliest shootout in history for U.S. law enforcement. The Young brothers were themselves killed by Houston, Texas, police a few days later.

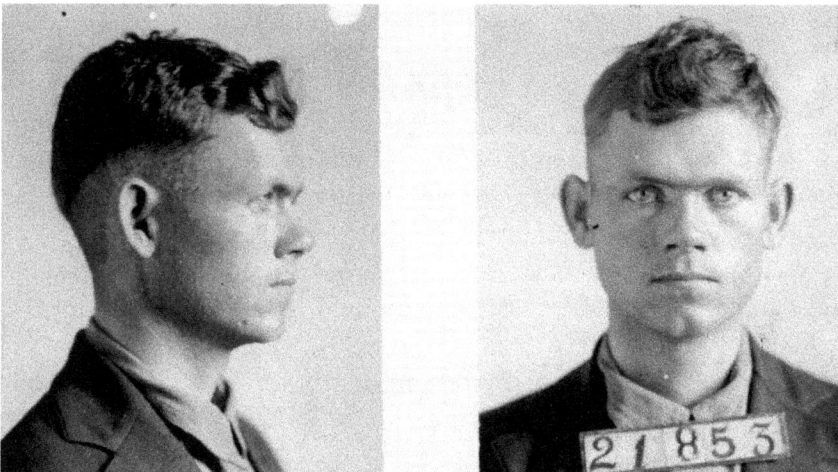

Mug shots of Jennings Young. *Author's collection.*

Young, Richard and Judy Dockery—Richard and Judy Dockery Young are well-known storytellers from Stone County, Missouri, whose audiobooks include *Ozark Ghost Stories* and *Ozark Tall Tales*

Younger Brothers—Brothers Cole, Jim, John, and Bob Younger were part of the notorious James-Younger outlaw gang during the late 1800s. Perhaps the gang's two most notable exploits in the Ozarks were the train robbery at Gad's Hill in Wayne County, Missouri, in January of 1874 and the shootout with Pinkerton agents near Osceola in St. Clair County later the same year.

Z

Zagonyi's Charge—After the Battle of Wilson's Creek in August of 1861, Confederate-allied forces took possession of Springfield. In the fall of the same year, General John C. Fremont marched on Springfield with a large force of Union soldiers with plans to take back the town. After a forced march that started north of Bolivar and covered fifty miles, Fremont's body guard, led by Major Charles Zagonyi, reached Springfield on the late afternoon of October 25. The undisciplined Missouri State Guard troops that had been left to defend the town formed a line of battle about a mile west of Springfield on the Mount Vernon Road, but they broke and ran when Zagonyi, despite being outnumbered, led a daring charge against them. The State Guard vacated Springfield, and Union forces took control of the town, although they would stay only a few days.

Zanoni, Missouri—Zanoni is an unincorporated community in Ozark County and the site of a historic mill.

Zena, Oklahoma—Zena is a small community in Delaware County about ten miles southwest of Grove or northwest of Jay. It was established in what was then Indian Territory during the 1890s and named for Asenith Wood, the wife of the first postmaster .

Zinc, Arkansas—Zinc is a town of about 100 people in eastern Boone County. It was a center for zinc and lead mining during the early 1900s.

Zion, Arkansas—Zion is a small community in Izard County about nine miles east of Melbourne. It was hit by a devastating tornado in 2008.

Selected Bibliography

Encyclopedia of Arkansas History and Culture. Online at http://www.encyclopediaofarkansas.net/.

Oklahoma Encyclopedia of History and Culture. Online at http://digital.library.okstate.edu/encyclopedia/.

Conard, Howard L. ed. *Encyclopedia of the History of Missouri, a Compendium of History and Biography for Ready Reference,* 6 vols. New York: The Southern History Company, 1901.

Christensen, Lawrence O., et. al., eds. *Dictionary of Missouri Biography.* Columbia: University of Missouri Press, 1999.

Pfister, Fred. *Insiders' Guide to Branson and the Ozark Mountains,* Seventh Edition. Guilford, CT: Globe Pequot Press, 2009.

Rafferty, Milton D. *The Ozarks: Land and Life.* Fayetteville: University of Arkansas Press, 2001.

Rafferty, Milton D. *The Ozarks Outdoors: A Guide for Fishermen, Hunters, and Tourists.* Norman: University of Oklahoma Press, 1985.

Moser, Arthur Paul *Directory of Towns, Villages and Hamlets Past and Present of Missouri.* http://thelibrary.org/lochist/moser/.

OzarksWatch Video Magazine. Online at http://video.optv.org/program/ozarkswatch-video-magazine/.

Stevens, Walter B. *Centennial History of Missouri (The Center State),* 4 vols. St. Louis: S.J. Clarke Publishing Company, 1921.

About the Author: Larry Wood has been writing about the Ozarks for over forty years. His magazine, journal, and newspaper articles have appeared in a wide variety of publications, including *Gateway Heritage*, *Missouri Life*, *Missouri Historical Review*, *The Ozarks Mountaineer*, and *Wild West Magazine*. He is also the author of fourteen books, most of them pertaining to the history of the Ozarks and surrounding regions. Wood is currently a staff writer for *Show Me the Ozarks Magazine*, and he maintains a blog on Ozarks history at www.ozarks-history.blogspot.com.

www.ingramcontent.com/pod-product-compliance
Lightning Source LLC
Chambersburg PA
CBHW051941090426
42741CB00008B/1223